ENGLISH MILITARY NEWS PAMPHLETS, 1513-1637

MEDIEVAL AND RENAISSANCE
TEXTS AND STUDIES
VOLUME 379

ENGLISH MILITARY NEWS PAMPHLETS, 1513-1637

DAVID RANDALL

ACMRS
(Arizona Center for Medieval and Renaissance Studies)
Tempe, Arizona
2011

Published by ACMRS (Arizona Center for Medieval and Renaissance Studies)
Tempe, Arizona
© 2011 Arizona Board of Regents for Arizona State University.
All Rights Reserved.

Library of Congress Cataloging-in-Publication Data

Randall, David, 1972-
  English military news pamphlets, 1513-1637 / David Randall.
      p. cm. -- (Medieval and Renaissance texts and studies ; v. 379)
  Based on the author's thesis (doctoral)---Rutgers University, 2005.
  Includes bibliographical references.
  ISBN 978-0-86698-427-0 (alk. paper)
  1. Europe--History, Military--1492-1648--Sources. 2. Military history,
Modern--16th century--Sources. 3. Military history, Modern--17th
century--Sources. 4. Great Britain--History, Military--1485-1603--Sources.
5. Pamphlets--Great Britain--History. I. Arizona Center for Medieval and
Renaissance Studies. II. Title.
  D214.R36 2011
  355.00942'09031--dc22

                                                                    2011007175

∞
This book is made to last. It is set in Adobe Caslon Pro,
smyth-sewn and printed on acid-free paper to library specifications.
Printed in the United States of America

TABLE OF CONTENTS

INTRODUCTION

This edition of military news pamphlets is intended for a broad range of students and scholars.[1] In the first place, it is meant to aid students of military history. The pamphlets I have transcribed collectively provide a good source-book both for the conduct of military campaigns and for the different aspects of military life in Renaissance Europe;[2] I believe they will be useful to the generally interested reader, to the undergraduate student, and to the professional scholar. For the last, this is stated with the obvious understanding that a command of the manuscript source material is the *sine qua non* for a proper understanding of Renaissance military history. That said, I do not think print sources are valueless—particularly as regards the everyday life of Renaissance soldiery. I believe military historians are a little inclined to dismiss the value of news pamphlets such as these; this edition is meant in part to remind military historians of their existence, and to champion their value.[3]

---

[1] This Introduction adapts material that appears in David Randall, *Credibility in Elizabethan and Early Stuart Military News* (London: Pickering and Chatto, 2008); and idem, "Epistolary Rhetoric, the Newspaper, and the Public Sphere," *Past and Present* 198 (2008): 3–32.

[2] "Renaissance," "Renaissance Europe," and "Renaissance England," here and throughout, refer generally to the two centuries between 1450 and 1650.

[3] For an introduction to the very large scholarly literature on Renaissance European land warfare, and its social and cultural effects, see Geoffrey Parker, *The Military Revolution: Military Innovation and the Rise of the West, 1500–1800* (Cambridge: Cambridge University Press, 1996); Clifford J. Rogers, ed., *The Military Revolution Debate: Readings on the Military Transformation of Early Modern Europe* (Boulder, CO: Westview Press, 1995); Bert S. Hall, *Weapons and Warfare in Renaissance Europe: Gunpowder, Technology, and Tactics* (Baltimore: Johns Hopkins University Press, 2002); J. R. Hale, *War and Society in Renaissance Europe, 1450–1620* (Baltimore: Johns Hopkins University Press, 1986); and Michael Murrin, *History and Warfare in Renaissance Epic* (Chicago: University of Chicago Press, 1997). For an introduction to Renaissance English land warfare in particular, see Mark Charles Fissel, *English Warfare, 1511–1642* (London and New York: Routledge, 2001); Paul E. J. Hammer, *Elizabeth's Wars: War, Government and Society in Tudor England, 1544–1604* (Houndmills: Palgrave Macmillan, 2003); John McGurk, *The Elizabethan Conquest of Ireland: The 1590s Crisis* (Manchester: Manchester University Press, 1997); John S. Nolan, *Sir John Norreys and the Elizabethan Military World* (Exeter: University of Exeter Press, 1997); R. B. Wernham, *After the Armada: Elizabethan*

These news pamphlets are also intended to be of value to what are variously called news historians, print culture historians, and historians of the book. Military news pamphlets were a considerable proportion of the entire corpus of news pamphlets in the sixteenth and seventeenth centuries, and integral in the evolution of the modern news. This edition is meant to provide these scholars with a sense of the basic form and varying possibilities of the genre, to give them a sense of the genre in itself, and to allow them to compare it with the other specific genres of news and print culture in this time period. It has also been presented in hopes that other scholars, with different areas of expertise, will assemble parallel editions, whether of military news pamphlets in other languages, or of different genres of news in English.[4] Furthermore, these pamphlets should be of interest to scholars of Renaissance literature and rhetoric. They form a significant genre of non-fiction Renaissance English prose, and include contributions by literary men such as George Gascoigne, Thomas Churchyard, Anthony Nixon, and Hugh Peters. Highly rhetorical in structure, they also demonstrate the link between medieval and Renaissance rhetorical practice and early modern and modern journalistic style.

Finally, these pamphlets are fun to read. They are funny, vivid, insightful, and appalling. Not universally so—the lists of burned towns or dead officers defy literary polish. But they are generally marked by a high level of readability, and often with gripping style. I hope that any reader will enjoy them as much as I have.

The Renaissance English military news pamphlet emerged as a genre from multiple sources. A major source appears to have been the unselfconscious report of recent events, haphazardly recorded as newsletter or chronicle, and with undigested newsletters incorporated into chronicles as blithely as undigested newsletters would later be incorporated into corantos (early newspapers; see below). In medieval England, military news appeared in such newsletters and chronicles from the twelfth century on, growing in frequency until they were quite common

---

England and the Struggle for Western Europe, 1588–1595 (Oxford: Clarendon Press, 1984); and idem, *The Return of the Armadas: The Last Years of the Elizabethan War against Spain, 1595–1603* (Oxford: Oxford University Press, 1994).

[4] For an introduction to Renaissance English news and pamphlets, see Sandra Clark, *The Elizabethan Pamphleteers: Popular Moralistic Pamphlets 1580–1640* (Rutherford, NJ: Fairleigh Dickinson University Press, 1983); D. C. Collins, *A Handlist of News Pamphlets, 1590–1610* (London: The Guardian Press, 1943); Brendan Dooley and Sabrina A. Baron, eds., *The Politics of Information in Early Modern Europe* (London and New York: Routledge, 2001), chaps. 1–4; Adam Fox, *Oral and Literate Culture in England 1500–1700* (Oxford: Oxford University Press, 2000), 335–405; Alexandra Halasz, *The Marketplace of Print: Pamphlets and the Public Sphere in Early Modern England* (Cambridge: Cambridge University Press, 1997); Joad Raymond, *Pamphlets and Pamphleteering in Early Modern Britain* (Cambridge: Cambridge University Press, 2003); and Paul Voss, *Elizabethan News Pamphlets: Shakespeare, Spenser, Marlowe and the Birth of Journalism* (Pittsburgh: Duquesne University Press, 2001).

during the Hundred Years War, and switching in language from Latin and French to English.[5] The writers of these newsletters were likely to have been the ancestors of the sorts of English gentlemen who wrote newsletters in early modern England, but their general anonymity makes any such statement highly speculative.[6] By the mid-fourteenth century, such newsletters had a number of standard characteristics, such as "the details of battle casualties, the expression of sorrow for the slain, and of satisfaction, or gratitude, for a small death-roll on one's own side. Knowledge is often shown of details not likely to be remembered except by an eye-witness."[7] In the substance of military news, there would be great continuity between these medieval newsletters and Renaissance military news pamphlets.

But if the unselfconscious medieval newsletter was the ancestor for the substance of the Renaissance English military news pamphlet, it was the English private news letter that was the ancestor of its form and intellectual assumptions. These letters, drawing ultimately upon the medieval tradition of dictaminal rhetoric — the epistolary rhetoric used in the *ars dictaminis,* the medieval art of letter writing — emerged most directly from the late medieval and Renaissance English practice of modeling familiar letters upon official letters.[8] The

---

[5] For the indistinct boundary between chronicle and news in medieval England, see D. R. Woolf, "Genre into Artifact: The Decline of the English Chronicle in the Sixteenth Century," *Sixteenth Century Journal* 19 (1988): 321–54; idem, *Reading History in Early Modern England* (Cambridge: Cambridge University Press, 2000), 26–28. For the presence of newsletters in medieval England and their intermixture with and incorporation into chronicles, see D. W. Burton, "1264: Some New Documents," *Historical Research* 66 (1993): 317–28; H. W. C. Davis, "A Contemporary Account of the Battle of Tinchebrai," *English Historical Review* 24 (1909): 728–32; James Gairdner, ed., *Three Fifteenth-Century Chronicles* (London, Camden Society, 2nd ser., 28, 1880), 156, 158–59; V. H. Galbraith, ed., *The Anonimalle Chronicle, 1333 to 1381* (New York: Barnes & Noble and Manchester University Press, 1970), xxvi–xxvii, 160, 162, 164, 171–72; J. R. Maddicott, "The Mise of Lewes, 1264," *English Historical Review* 98 (1983): 588–603, here 592–95; M. C. Prestwich, "The English Campaign in Scotland in 1296 and the Surrender of John Balliol: Some Supporting Evidence," *Bulletin of the Institute of Historical Research* 49 (1976): 135–38; E. L. G. Stones, "English Chroniclers and the Affairs of Scotland, 1286–1296," in *The Writing of History in the Middle Ages: Essays Presented to Richard William Southern,* ed. R. H. C. Davis and J. M. Wallace-Hadrill (Oxford: Oxford University Press, 1981), 323–48; idem and Margaret N. Blount, "The Surrender of King John of Scotland to Edward I in 1296: Some New Evidence," *Bulletin of the Institute of Historical Research* 48 (1975): 94–106, esp. 103.

[6] Stones, "English Chroniclers," 338.

[7] Stones, "English Chroniclers," 339.

[8] David Randall, "Sovereign Intelligence and Sovereign Intelligencers: Transforming Standards of Credibility in English Military News from ca. 1570 to 1637" (Ph.D. diss., Rutgers University, 2005), 95–103.

internal communications of the state, the letters written from one state official to another, provided the content and the form for the private news letter; parallel to the letter of news they sent to other state officials, government agents also began to write familiar letters of news to their friends and their kin. As Zaret puts it, "transmission of news by private letters evolved as a literary practice as an extension of scribal practices animated by narrowly strategic purposes: diplomatic dispatches, military intelligence, official record keeping, and business communications."[9]

As Englishmen came to write of news in their vernacular private letters, humanist epistolary rhetoric superimposed itself upon dictaminal structure to provide the English news letter its particular configuration, diction, and persuasive arguments. Italian humanist epistolary rhetoric of the fifteenth century, communicated and reinforced by intermediaries such as Desiderius Erasmus and Juan Luis Vives,[10] became pervasive in England by the mid-sixteenth century;[11] mid-Tudor English treatises of rhetoric generally followed humanist strictures.[12] Significantly, the letters cited as models to be imitated by the English letter manuals of the era recapitulate the intellectual lineage between fifteenth-century Italy, the Erasmian humanists of early sixteenth-century northern Europe, and mid-Tudor England: in addition to the usual exemplars of antiquity (Cicero, Pliny, et al.), the second part of William Fulwood's *The Enimie of Idlenesse* (1568) reproduced the letters of fifteenth-century Italian humanists, while Abraham Flemming's *A Panoplie of Epistles* (1576) reproduced the letters of sixteenth-century

---

[9] David Zaret, *Origins of Democratic Culture: Printing, Petitions, and the Public Sphere in Early-Modern England* (Princeton: Princeton University Press, 2000), 118–19.

[10] See particularly their treatises on letter-writing: Desiderius Erasmus, *Opus de conscribendis epistolis* (Basel, 1522); and Juan Luis Vives, *De conscribendis epistolis* (Antwerp, 1534).

[11] Charles Fantazzi, "General Introduction," in Juan Luis Vives, *De Conscribendis Epistolis*, ed. and trans. idem (Leiden and New York: E. J. Brill, 1989), 9–17; Walter J. Ong, "Tudor Writings on Rhetoric, Poetic, and Literary Theory," in idem, *Rhetoric, Romance, and Technology* (Ithaca and London: Cornell University Press, 1971), 48–103, here 71–74. For the pervading influence of ethical, rhetorical humanism on Renaissance England, which provided the essential background for the English fusion of humanism and epistolary rhetoric discussed in this study, see Quentin Skinner, *Reason and Rhetoric in the Philosophy of Hobbes* (Cambridge: Cambridge University Press, 1996), 19–211.

[12] E.g., Leonard Cox, *The art or crafte of rhetoryke* (London, 1532, STC 5947); Richard Sherry, *A Treatise of Schemes and Tropes* (London, 1550, STC 22428); Thomas Wilson, *Arte of Rhetorique* (London, 1553, STC 25799); Richard Rainolde, *A Booke called the Foundacion of Rhetorike* (London, 1563, 20925a.5). Sloane speaks of a brief period of dominance of humanist rhetoric in England, between 1553, when Thomas Wilson's *Arte of Rhetorique* appeared, and the 1580s, when the logic and rhetoric of Ramus began to challenge the humanist conception of rhetoric: Thomas O. Sloane, *Donne, Milton, and the End of Humanist Rhetoric* (Berkeley and Los Angeles: University of California Press, 1985), 130–44, esp. 130.

humanists, both Italian and non-Italian.[13] Thus, when Englishmen came to consider the news letter, they placed it within the traditional categories of epistolary rhetoric.[14] In Renaissance English letter-writing manuals, themselves remote descendants of the *ars dictaminis* letter-writing manuals, model news letters were included among their various categories.[15] Significantly, Angel Day in his *The English Secretorie* (1592) categorized these news letters both as narrative letters and as familiar letters:

> Touching now our *Familiar Letters*, they also are to be drawn under their several titles, as *Narratory* and *Nunciatory*, somewhat falling into the demonstrative kind before remembered, wherein we express and declare to those far from us, the matters or news presently in hand amongst us.[16]

Furthermore, Day wrote in the 1586 edition of *The English Secretorie* that a letter could cover "all occurrences whatsoever, [which] are thereby as faithfully advertised, pursued, and debated, as firmly might fall out in any personal presence or otherwise to be remembered." More particularly, Day explicitly added that in Epistles Nunciatory, "we advertise the news of any public or private matters unto our friends."[17] Day's editions of *The English Secretorie* explicitly confirm that humanist epistolary rhetoric continued to provide the form of Renaissance English news letters.[18]

---

[13] William Fulwood, *The Enimie of Idlenesse: Teaching the Maner and Stile How to Endite, Compose and Write All Sorts of Epistles and Letters* (London, 1568, STC 11476), 91v–104v; Abraham Flemming, *A Panoplie of Epistles: or, A Looking Glasse for the Unlearnd. Conteyning a Perfecte Plattforme of Inditing Letters of All Sorts, to Persons of Al Estates and Degrees* (London, 1576, STC 11049), 314–412.

[14] For Spanish parallels, see Pedro Cátedra, "En los orígenes de las *epístolas de relación*," in María Cruz García de Enterría *et al.*, *Las relaciones de sucesos en España (1500–1750)* (Alcalá: Servicio de Publicaciones de la Universidad de Alcalá, 1996), 33–64; Carmen Espejo Cala, "El orígen epistolar de las relaciones de sucesos de la edad moderna," in *La Correspondencia en la Historia: Modelos y prácticas de escritura epistolar*, ed. Carlos Sáez and Antonio Castillo Gómez (Madrid: Calambur, 2002), 157–67, here 162–63.

[15] Angel Day, *The English Secretorie* (London, 1592 edn, STC 6402), 8–21, second pagination [*The Second Part of the English Secretory*], 66–67; Thomas Gainsford, *The Secretaries Studie: Containing New Familiar Epistles, or Directions, for the Formall, Orderly, and Iudicious Inditing of Letters* (London, 1616, STC 11523), title page, 104–24. Also see Jean Robertson, *The Art of Letter Writing: An Essay on the Handbooks Published in England During the Sixteenth and Seventeenth Centuries* (London: University Press of Liverpool and Hodder & Stoughton Ltd., 1942), esp. 9–24.

[16] Day, *The English Secretorie* (1592), 24.

[17] Angel Day, *The English Secretorie* (London, 1586, STC 6401), 1, 42.

[18] Howell identifies the English rhetorical schools of the late sixteenth century as "neo-Ciceronian" and Ramusian, and emphasizes that Day's work is neo-Ciceronian in

The shift in medium of English military news from these written letters to the printed pamphlet happened slowly. As early as 1482 a translation of Guillaume Caoursin's *The Siege of Rhodes* had been printed in English. A trickle of printed military news pamphlets followed over the next eighty years: those which survive include *Hereafter ensue the trewe encountre* (1513), *The tryumphant vyctory of the imperyall mageste agaynst the turkes* (1532), Alfonso Avalos Vasto's *A joyfull new tidynges of the goodly victory that was sent to the Emperour* (1543), *The late expedicion in Scotlande* (1544), *Certayn and tru good nues, from the syege of the isle Malta* (1565), *A copie of the last advertisement that came from Malta* (1565), and *Newes from Vienna* (1566). But these, to my knowledge, are all the surviving printed military news pamphlets in English dating up to 1566.[19] We may presume that more were printed, but the first generations of military news pamphlets in England have made a light impress on the historical record.[20]

Only with the wars in France and the Netherlands from the 1560s onward did the number of printed military news pamphlets begin to rise to an appreciable number; only with the entrance of England into the war with Spain in 1585 did these pamphlets begin to appear in mass. Streckfuss's tabulation of the number of extant English news pamphlets shows a decided increase in these decades: 1561–1570, 55; 1571–1580, 68; 1581–1590, 161; 1591–1600, 165. This

---

character, not Ramusian: Wilbur Samuel Howell, *Logic and Rhetoric in England, 1500–1700* (Princeton: Princeton University Press, 1956), 329–30. While Ciceronian rhetoric was then and is now often contrasted with humanist rhetoric, Henderson reminds us that in the sixteenth century the terms were used (and creatively misused) to refer to a significantly overlapping body of rhetorical theory and practice: Judith Rice Henderson, "Erasmian Ciceronians: Reformation Teachers of Letter-writing," *Rhetorica* 10 (1992): 273–302. As regards the classifications used in this work, Day's work should be taken as essentially an example of humanist rhetoric.

[19] *The tryumphant vyctory of the imperyall mageste agaynst the turkes* ([London,] 1532, STC 5018) is analyzed and transcribed in Mary Carpenter Erler, "Süleyman's 1532 Vienna Campaign: An English News Dispatch," *The Slavonic and East European Review* 65 (1987): 101–12. Jacques de Bourbon, *The begynnynge and foundacyon of the holy hospytall, & of the ordre of the knyghtes hospytallers of saynt Johan baptyst of Jerusalem* ([London,] 1524, STC 15050) consists largely of an account of the entirety of the 1522 Turkish siege of Rhodes, on the borderline between history and news, titled "The Syege Cruell Oppugnacyon and Lamentable Takynge of the Cyte of Rodes."

[20] For the existence of a "print revolution" in early modern Europe, see Elizabeth L. Eisenstein, *The Printing Revolution in Early Modern Europe* (Cambridge: Cambridge University Press, 1983). For the print revolution's slow, complex unfolding, and an interpretation that emphasizes social and cultural transformation over technological transformation, see Adrian Johns, *The Nature of the Book: Print and Knowledge in the Making* (Chicago and London: University of Chicago Press, 1998). For a general history of the English press before Elizabeth, see D. M. Loades, "The Press under the Early Tudors," *Transactions of the Cambridge Bibliographical Society* 4 (1964): 29–50.

rise correlates remarkably with the onset of war, and much of it was accounted for by the rise in number of pamphlets of military news and/or other military-related subjects.[21] Bennett notes that news from France in the year 1590 alone included four news reports about the battle of Ivry, and ten pamphlets (including one published in mid-January 1591) summarizing the (largely military) news from June to December.[22]

The genre of the military news pamphlet began to decline with the rise of the newspaper. Between 1618 and 1621 corantos, the first form of newspapers, appeared in the Netherlands, were translated for the English market, and began to be published by Englishmen themselves. Military news pamphlets became less common thereafter, although they, and semi-annual intelligencers, provided a somewhat greater proportion of military news between 1632 and 1638, when corantos were banned.[23] Thereafter, with the breakdown of royal censorship during the British Civil Wars, newspapers flourished, and finally brought an end to the heyday of the military news pamphlet.[24]

The pamphlet was a form of cheap print — an ephemeral publication, largely destined for the trash heap rather than the library or the archive.[25] Elizabethan and early Stuart military news pamphlets were relatively plentiful, as compared to their early- and mid-Tudor predecessors (see above), but no more than one or two copies survive of most news pamphlets of the era. Very often, all that is left is the title entered into the *Stationers' Register*.[26]

The military news pamphlet, despite the usual haziness of genre boundaries,[27] possessed a distinct subject matter and form. Its subject matter can perhaps best

---

[21] Richard Streckfuss, "News before Newspapers," *Journalism & Mass Communication Quarterly* 75 (1998): 84–97, here 87.

[22] H. S. Bennett, *English Books and Readers 1558 to 1603* (Cambridge: Cambridge University Press, 1965), 236.

[23] Dahl does not include these semi-annuals in his bibliography: Folke Dahl, *A Bibliography of English Corantos and Periodical Newsbooks 1620–1642* (London: The Bibliographical Society, 1952), 221–22.

[24] Raymond, *Pamphlets and Pamphleteering in Early Modern Britain*, 151–60.

[25] For cheap, ephemeral print in early modern England, see Fox, *Oral and Literate Culture in England*, 335–405; Raymond, *Pamphlets and Pamphleteering in Early Modern Britain*, 4–26; Margaret Spufford, *Small Books and Pleasant Histories: Popular Fiction and its Readership in Seventeenth-century England* (London: Methuen, 1981); Tessa Watt, *Cheap Print and Popular Piety 1550–1640* (Cambridge: Cambridge University Press, 1991).

[26] Voss, *Elizabethan News Pamphlets*, 19–21. Some titles, however, may have been entered in anticipation of publishing a pamphlet that never actually made it to the press: Voss, *Elizabethan News Pamphlets*, 21.

[27] For a classification and discussion of the main pamphlet genres, see Clark, *The Elizabethan Pamphleteers*; Raymond, *Pamphlets and Pamphleteering in Early Modern Britain*, 101–22.

be discerned by contemporaneous perceptions of it. John Taylor wrote of an English audience with a clear idea of, and desire for, military news:

> And as for newes of battailes, or of War . . .
> At Ordinaries, and at Barbers-shoppes,
> There tydings vented are, as thick as hoppes,
> How many thousands such a day were slaine,
> What men of note were in the battell ta'ne,
> When, where, and how the bloody fight begun,
> And how such sconces, and such townes were won,
> How so and so the Armies bravely met,
> And which side glorious victory did get:
> The month, the weeke, the day, the very houre,
> *And time, they did oppose each others power.* [28]

A 1630 coranto wrote simply that "most mens desire is to heare of [military] action."[29] Contemporaries also had a fair idea of what was a battle, what a skirmish, and what was peace (or at least the absence of open conflict). Thomas Gainsford certainly knew what battles were, defining "set Battails" as "one dayes tryall by equall agreement of both parties," and carefully distinguishing between such set battles and the more usual sallies and skirmishes engaged in by the Turks and the Poles.[30]

The form of the military news pamphlet was also reasonably standard. In pamphlet after pamphlet, a campaign, a siege, or a battle happened at such a place and such a time. So many of the enemy were killed and so many were taken prisoner. Such and such notable incidents occurred. There were significant variations of emphasis, but military news pamphlets throughout the Renaissance bore a distinct family resemblance, and habitually fashioned themselves from these basic building blocks. These were the standards of the genre from which individual examples would deviate.

Military news pamphlets were remarkably cosmopolitan, both in their subject matter and in their provenance. Christian-Muslim conflict excited continuing interest, despite the remoteness of England from the front lines of religious war, and Englishmen's intra-Christian hostility to the Catholic protagonists of these reports. A steady trickle of military news pamphlets came throughout this period from the bloody Christian-Muslim frontiers of Europe—Malta, Cyprus, Croatia, Vienna, Hungary, and Poland (e.g. *Certayn and tru good nues, from the*

---

[28] John Taylor, *Taylor his Trauels* (London, 1621, STC 23802.5), sig. A4r.

[29] *The Continuation of the most remarkable occurrences of Newes* (16 July 1630, Numb. 9, STC 18507.205), 14.

[30] *The Strangling and Death of the Great Turke, and his two sonnes* (London, 1622, STC 18507.62), 10.

syege of the isle Malta [1565], *Newes from Vienna* [1566]).[31] Dramatic battles at any distance were likely to engage some English interest, and a sporadic supply of reports of battles came from Geneva or Sweden or Russia (e.g. Anthony Nixon, *Swethland and Poland Warres* [1610]).[32] News of interest to England's foreign suppliers of news was also overrepresented in England's news circuits: for a notable example, given the great influence of Dutch printers on English news, a very great number of Dutch exploits were either printed in England or printed in English in the Netherlands. *A True Report of all the proceedings of Grave Mauris before the Towne of Bercke* (1601), printed in London from a Dutch translation, and other reports of Dutch feats in the Low Countries and nearer Germany probably also appealed to a genuine English interest, but Hendrik Cornelis Loncq's *A true relation of the vanquishing of the towne of Olinda* (1630), printed in Amsterdam, about the Dutch capture of Pernambuco in Brazil, can hardly have been a subject of great concern to England. Availability of copy rather than intense demand probably best explains its publication in English.

But the strongest factor affecting the geographic distribution of these reports was English interest in and participation in wars abroad.[33] The wars Englishmen cared about and the wars Englishmen fought in—largely overlapping categories—were heavily overrepresented in the military news pamphlets. Partly this was a function of demand; partly it was a question of supply. A large portion of these pamphlets drew upon accounts provided by English participants writing home. So, when England was slipping towards, or engaged in, open hostilities with Spain, a very large number of the pamphlets concerned the wars in the Netherlands (broadly, 1566 to 1609, though with the heaviest interest from 1585 to 1604) and the civil wars in France (especially from 1589 to 1593). England was less directly engaged in the Thirty Years War, but concern about the fortunes of the Protestant cause, and some participation by English and Scottish soldiers, maintained a significant level of interest. A significant number of pamphlets come from Englishmen serving in the Netherlands (1622–1637), and from Scots serving in the Swedish armies (especially 1629 to 1634).

Very few pamphlets came from Ireland. That Irish news was technically domestic news, not foreign, and therefore subject to the censorship of the crown, was probably one factor that reduced, if it did not eliminate, reports from

---

[31] Also see Nestore Martinengo, *The true Report of all the successe of Famagosta* (London, 1572, STC 17520) [Cyprus], *A true discourse wherin is set downe the wonderfull mercy of God* (London, 1593, STC 5202) [Croatia], *A True Relation of taking of Alba-Regalis* (London, 1601, STC 256.5) [Hungary], and *Newes from Poland* (London, 1621, STC 20083).

[32] Also see *The troubles of Geneua* (London, 1591, STC 11727); Anthony Nixon, *The warres of Swethland* (London, 1609, STC 18594); Henry Brereton, *Newes of the present miseries of Rushia* (London, 1614, STC, 21462).

[33] Matthias A. Shaaber, *Some Forerunners of the Newspaper in England, 1476–1622* (Philadelphia: University of Pennsylvania Press, 1929), 123–26.

Ireland.[34] Perhaps more to the point was that battles in Ireland were normally inglorious and indecisive,[35] and sometimes consisted of humiliating defeats that the English (see below) were reluctant to see publicized.[36] Even notable English victories, such as Kinsale, were not much reported in print. Were the English embarassed to have to fight the Irish at such great length? Was rebellion unmentionable? Was it simply that Irish campaigns were weary and dull? It is difficult to explain absence, but one must note Ireland's diminished presence in the military news pamphlets.[37]

The provenance of the military news pamphlets was also remarkably cosmopolitan. Englishmen preferred to read news written by Englishmen, and the monolingual majority perforce read their military news in English. As a community of news writers and readers, their material was in English. Yet they were not isolated from news in foreign languages—although the act of translation was an essential bridge to bring it into the community. London printers arranged to have a large number of foreign news letters and news pamphlets translated into

---

[34] Domestic news was not banned, but was subject to prosecution if it overstepped the (hazy) bounds of governmental sensitivity: see Sheila Lambert, "State Control of the Press in Theory and Practice: The Role of the Stationers' Company before 1640," in *Censorship and the Control of Print in England and France 1600–1910*, ed. Robin Myers and Michael Harris (Winchester: St Paul's Bibliographies, 1992), 1–32, here 1–3, 9–10.

[35] J. Payne Collier, ed., *Trevelyan Papers*, Part 2, Camden Society, 1st Ser., 84 (London: Camden Society, 1863), 94; Agnes Latham and Joyce Youings, eds., *The Letters of Sir Walter Ralegh* (Exeter: University of Exeter Press, 1999), 3; Norman Egbert McClure, ed., *The Letters and Epigrams of Sir John Harington: Together with The Prayse of Private Life* (Philadelphia: University of Pennsylvania Press, 1930), 69–70; Sarah Williams, ed., *Letters Written by John Chamberlain during the reign of Queen Elizabeth*, Camden Society, 1st Ser., 79 (Westminster: Camden Society, 1861), 21; Huntington Library, Stowe Collection, Nugent Papers, Military Affairs, Box 41, filed in Personal Box 1(4), fol. 1r.

[36] Williams, ed., *Letters Written by John Chamberlain*, 17.

[37] There were no printed news pamphlets about the English conquest of Cadiz in 1596 owing to an unusual factional deadlock. Essex had performed valiantly at Cadiz, but any publicizing of his military prowess would have tilted the English political balance too far in his direction, so Elizabeth and the Privy Council ordered a ban on printing any account of Cadiz. See Paul E. J. Hammer, "Myth-making: Politics, Propaganda and the Capture of Cadiz in 1596," *Historical Journal* 40 (1997): 621–42, here 631–35. A generation later, in 1627, Buckingham promoted his political position against a broader, more inchoate opposition by arranging for publication of upbeat relations from Ré—until the final disastrous retreat, at which point his pet printer Thomas Walkley adopted a most discreet silence. See Thomas Cogswell, "The Politics of Propaganda: Charles I and the People in the 1620s," *Journal of British Studies* 29 (1990): 187–215, here 202–3; idem, "The People's Love: The Duke of Buckingham and Popularity," in *Politics, Religion and Popularity in Early Stuart Britain: Essays in Honour of Conrad Russell*, ed. idem, Richard Cust, and Peter Lake (Cambridge: Cambridge University Press, 2002), 224–31.

English, usually rendering the translations' source anonymous in the process.[38] The act of translation, recorded in dozens of military news pamphlets, was an acknowledged, essential part of the constitution of the genre. English military news was inseparable from its European sources—Englishmen probably read more military news written by continental Europeans than military news written by Scotsmen, Welshmen, or Irishmen. So the shadow of translation gave English military news pamphlets an essential element of the genre's character.

Naturally enough, questions of credibility and truthfulness were of great importance for the genre—as the very repetition of the word "true" in so many pamphlets' title pages bore witness (e.g., *The True Reporte of the Service in Britanie* [1591], Philip Vincent, *A True Relation of the Late Battel fought in New England* [1637]).[39] Military news pamphlets, in consequence, possessed a number of distinctive genre characteristics. The first of these was plain style, which had also been characteristic of medieval epistolary rhetoric, the genre ancestor of the news pamphlet.[40] From the sixteenth century on, however, plain language, unstylish but informative, was also coming to be perceived as an indicator of truth.[41] This

---

[38] Technically, the act of acquiring the text was done by what we would now call the publisher, but who was then generically referred to as the printer. The publisher could be the printer, the bookseller, both, or neither. See Peter W. M. Blayney, "The Publication of Playbooks" in *A New History of Early English Drama*, ed. John D. Cox and David Scott Kastan (New York: Columbia University Press, 1997), 383–422, here 391–92; Raymond, *Pamphlets and Pamphleteering in Early Modern Britain*, 55–56.

[39] David Randall, "Joseph Mead, Novellante: News, Sociability, and Credibility in Early Stuart England," *Journal of British Studies* 45 (2006): 293–312; Raymond, *Pamphlets and Pamphleteering in Early Modern Britain*, 105–6; Voss, *Elizabethan News Pamphlets*, 54–66. Cf. G. K. Hunter, "Truth and Art in History Plays," in *Shakespeare Survey: An Annual Survey of Shakespeare Studies and Production* 42 (Cambridge, 1989), 15–24, here 16–17.

[40] Ronald G. Witt, "Medieval Italian Culture and the Origins of Humanism as a Stylistic Ideal," in idem, *Italian Humanism and Medieval Rhetoric* (Aldershot: Ashgate, 2001), no. I, here 44.

[41] Barbara J. Shapiro, *Probability and Certainty in Seventeenth-Century England: A Study of the Relationships between Natural Science, Religion, History, Law, and Literature* (Princeton: Princeton University Press, 1983), 227–66; eadem, *A Culture of Fact: England, 1550–1720* (Ithaca and London: Cornell University Press, 2000), 58–59, 72, 94–95, 160–65. For the general shift towards the plain style in in early modern English prose, see Robert Adolph, *The Rise of Modern Prose Style* (Cambridge, MA and London: MIT Press, 1968), esp. 132, 135, 141–241. For the links between the epistemological and aesthetic shift towards facticity and the rise of the plain style, and the related incorporation of the (plain and factual) genres of news and history into the novel genre, see Lennard J. Davis, *Factual Fictions: The Origins of the English Novel* (New York: Columbia University Press, 1983), 42–84; J. Paul Hunter, *Before Novels: The Cultural Contexts of Eighteenth-Century English Fiction* (New York and London: W. W. Norton & Company, 1990), 167–224; Robert Mayer, *History and the Early English Novel: Matters of Fact from Bacon to*

plain style soon became the standard for journalism in general, and military news in particular.[42] Unlike deliberately literary style, which implied the leisure to write exquisitely, and hence distance in time and place from the events described, plain style gave the impression of unmediated, immediate description of events, and the pressure of military life. Plain style also fit the canons of soldierly honor and style—a soldier was plain-spoken, bluff, unlike the courtier who knew how to shape his words with deliberate effect. In 1591 G. B., citing Roman figures iconically associated with plain style, wrote that *"nothing (saith* Quintilian*) so much commendeth the person of the writer, as the truth of the subject, he proposeth to write: And certes nothing advanced so highly* Julius Caesars *historie, as truth polished with Eloquence discreetly."*[43] In 1631 Hugh Peters called himself "a stranger to the Language" who would "shew truth in her nakednesse."[44] Indeed, literary polish became a whipping boy for pamphleteers boasting of their crude truthfulness. As the author of a 1626 account boasted, *"Expectest thou from hence a matter beautified with Learned phrayses, or adorned with Schollerlike tearmes, thy expectation is frustrated: grapes may not be had from a thorny hedge."*[45]

The second genre characteristic of the military news pamphlets was committed partiality. While impartiality had been a source of credibility as far back as the ancient historians, and had never disappeared as a source of credibility in the Western tradition,[46] it was distinctly a minor register in these military news pamphlets. Partly this was the result of censorship and self-censorship: the English state kept an eye on printed news throughout this period, and its punitive

---

Defoe (Cambridge: Cambridge University Press, 1997); Michael McKeon, *The Origins of the English Novel 1600–1740* (Baltimore: Johns Hopkins University Press, 1987), 45–128; Ian Watt, *The Rise of the Novel: Studies in Defoe, Richardson and Fielding* (Berkeley and Los Angeles: University of California Press, 1957), 9–34.

[42] Shaaber, *Some Forerunners of the Newspaper in England, 1476–1622*, 218–21; Joad Raymond, *The Invention of the Newspaper: English Newsbooks 1641–1649* (Oxford: Clarendon Press, 1996), 129. For explicit Taciteanism in military news, see *The great and famous battel of Lutzen* ([London,] 1633, STC 12534), sig. A4v. Also see Clark, *The Elizabethan Pamphleteers*, 224–79.

[43] G. B., *Newes out of France for the Gentlemen of England* (London, 1591, STC 1030.7), sig. A4r.

[44] Hugh Peters, *Digitus Dei: or, Good Newes from Holland* (Rotterdam, 1631, STC 19798.3), 2.

[45] I. B., *A Plaine and true relation, of the going forth of a Holland fleete* (Rotterdam [actually London?], 1626, STC 1043), *iii*.

[46] John Marincola, *Authority and Tradition in Ancient Historiography* (Cambridge: Cambridge University Press, 1997), 158–74; Shapiro, *Probability and Certainty in Seventeenth-Century England*, 147–49, 190–92; Shapiro, *A Culture of Fact: England, 1550–1720*, 26–30, 56–58, 93–94.

powers encouraged a positive and supportive outlook in the press. [47] Clearly, the more dismal manuscript news letters were hardly ever allowed near a printing press; what is less clear (lacking most manuscript originals) is how much censorship altered such letters as did emerge in print. The manuscript originals of two pamphlets about the Irish wars, however, do provide us some insight. A. M.'s *The True Reporte of the prosperous successe which God gave unto our English Souldiours* (1581) paraphrased from, and drew very largely upon, the letter from Arthur Grey de Wilton to Elizabeth that described Grey's 1580 victory at Smerwick. The pamphlet varied from the letter in small, but telling, details: for example, the letter described the massacre of the Catholic prisoners in terms of the English soldiery getting out of hand, while the pamphlet implied the massacre was a deliberate act by Grey. This revision seems to have been meant to be complimentary: Grey apparently preferred to be seen as in command of his troops, even if that also made him into a butcher. [48] Similarly, *A Letter from a Souldier of good place in Ireland* (1602) was allowed to appear in print at all precisely because it was the positive, quasi-official account of the victory. Yet the pamphlet cannot be said to be particularly censored or propagandistic as compared to its manuscript original, the English campaign journal. It displayed, rather, more subtle editing, which magnified the role of Lord Mountjoy and minimized the role of his colleagues—the pamphlet may have been written by Mountjoy's secretary, Fynes Moryson. [49] Censorship played a role in deciding which manuscripts were chosen

---

[47] For the regulation of print in Elizabethan and early Stuart England, particularly the operations of the Stationers' Company, see Fredrick Seaton Siebert, *Freedom of the Press in England 1476–1776: The Rise and Decline of Government Control* (Urbana: University of Illinois Press, 1965), 64–87, 127–46. For arguments of the effectiveness of censorship and self-censorship in pre-Civil War England, see Christopher Hill, "Censorship and English Literature," in *The Collected Essays of Christopher Hill*, vol. 1: *Writing and Revolution in 17ᵗʰ Century England* (Amherst, MA: University of Massachusetts Press, 1985), 32–71; and Annabel Patterson, *Censorship and Interpretation: The Conditions of Writing and Reading in Early Modern England* (Madison: University of Wisconsin Press, 1985), esp. 3–23, 44–119. For contrary arguments, see Cyndia Susan Clegg, *Press Censorship in Jacobean England* (Cambridge: Cambridge University Press, 2001), 161–96; Lambert, "State Control," 1–32; Edwin Haviland Miller, *The Professional Writer in Elizabethan England: A Study of Nondramatic Literature* (Cambridge, MA: Harvard University Press, 1959), 171–202; and Raymond, *Pamphlets and Pamphleteering in Early Modern Britain*, 70. Also see Michael Colin Frearson, "The English Corantos of the 1620s" (Ph.D. diss., Cambridge University, 1993), 238–40, 245–70.

[48] Vincent P. Carey, "Atrocity and History: Grey, Spenser and the Slaughter at Smerwick (1580)," in *Age of Atrocity: Violence and political conflict in early modern Ireland*, ed. David Edwards, Padraig Lenihan, and Clodagh Tait (Dublin: Four Courts Press, 2007), 79–94.

[49] Hiram Morgan, "The Victor's Version" in *The Battle of Kinsale*, ed. idem (Bray, Co. Wicklow: Wordwell, 2004), 379–90, here 379–81.

for the press at all; after that initial selection, the transition from manuscript to print was marked more by subtle shifts to emphasize the role of particular individuals.

Avowedly friendly news, however, could also function as not-so-hidden critique of the government. Military news of the 1620s and 1630s that reported Protestant military victories in Germany (*A Journall or Daily Register of all those warlike Atchievements which happened in the Siege of Berghen-up-Zoome* [1622], Hugh Peters, *Digitus Dei, or Good Newes from Holland* [1631]) implicitly functioned as Puritan pressure on the English government to join the Protestant military alliance fighting in Germany, and (by comparison with Protestant soldier-heroes such as Gustavus Adolphus) criticized the peaceful policies of James and Charles.[50] Royal censorship of the news—and, ultimately, Charles's ban of corantos from 1632 to 1638—was also rooted in a desire to rid the monarchy of their all-too-helpful friends in the press.

But partiality also reflected the genuine urge by newswriters to keep up the morale of the political nation as a whole. Furthermore, partiality also sustained the claim that news pamphlets provided a form of good counsel for the policy-makers of the nation, given in a spirit of *amicitia*.[51] This aspiration in the news pamphlets toward a spirit of *amicitia* was crucial: friends were supposed not merely to supply the news, but to wish well of their friends as they told the news, and to believe the best of their friends. Impartiality, objectivity, was *unfriendly*. While these military news pamphlets were not supposed to lie, or distort the truth too woefully, they were supposed to put the best possible construction on events.

So victories were reported far more often than defeats. There are a large number of military news pamphlets with encouraging titles: a partial list includes *Discourse and true recitall of everie particular of the victorie obtained by the French King* (1590), *True discourse of the overthrowe given to the common enemy at Turnhaut* (1597), *True Reporte of the Great overthrowe lately given unto the Spaniards in their resolute assault of BERGEN OP ZOAM* (1605), *More Newes of the Good Successe of the Duke of Brunswicke* (1623), and Hendrik Cornelis Loncq's *A true relation of the vanquishing of the towne of Olinda* (1630). The unwillingness to speak of defeat in these military news reports also registered the great importance of partiality. S. W.'s *The Appollogie of the Illustrious Prince Ernestus, Earle of Mansfield* (1622) explained that the defeat at Zablati came only after Mansfield's forces "spent all their bullets, as also the buttons of their dublets, and their powder, and being

---

[50] Thomas Cogswell, *The Blessed Revolution: English Politics and the Coming of War, 1621–1624* (Cambridge: Cambridge University Press, 1989), 21; D. M. Loades, "Illicit Presses and Clandestine Printing in England, 1520–1590," in *Too Mighty to be Free*, ed. A. C. Duke and C. A. Tamse (Zutphen: Walburg Press, 1987), 9–27, here 24.

[51] John Guy, "The Rhetoric of Counsel in Early Modern England," in *Tudor Political Culture*, ed. Dale Hoak (Cambridge: Cambridge University Press, 1995), 292–310, here 294.

out of all hope of reliefe, they yeelded upon condition."[52] Where defeats were mentioned—such as an English mine blowing up friendly soldiers by accident at s' Hertogenbosch in 1629—they were usually within the context of an eventual victory that drew the sting from what now became merely a tactical setback.[53]

Swethland and Poland Warres (1610) did relate a defeat, in excruciating detail, but there are a number of reasons for this. To begin with, this report of an English regiment's misfortunes in Swedish service—shipwrecked in Denmark and almost massacred by the Danish peasantry, marched from Finland into Russia in the heart of winter, abandoned by their Russian allies when the Poles attacked them, and utterly defeated by the Poles—was an admonitory piece, clearly meant in part (despite the protest that "farre are my thoughts (God beares record of them) from any such disswasion") to "terrifie those that never bare Armes; nor followed the fortunes of a Souldier, from ever going into *Sweden* and to serve in those warres."[54] In a piece which spent more than half its length on the difficulties the shipwrecked soldiers had escaping with their lives from murderous Danish peasants, the emphasis was clearly on the sufferings of the soldiers, not on the outcome of the war. Furthermore, this was a relatively low-stakes war for the English readership: not fought directly by the English state, or even by neighboring Calvinists such as the Dutch or the Huguenots, nor against England's traditional Spanish or French antagonists. A defeat could be admitted with relative ease in a contest between Lutheran Swedes and Catholic Poles in the heart of distant Russia. But such examples were few and far between in an overwhelming report of victories.

For similar reasons, it was unacceptable to acknowledge in printed news that friendly soldiers were weak and miserable. Save for rare and genre-bound anomalies like *Swethland and Poland Warres* (1610),[55] there was silence in print about the parts of a soldier's life that would inspire pity—and contempt. These were reserved for letters—as often as not letters within the government, where such information was vital. Throughout this period, descriptions of friendly soldiers' weakness and misery remained too unfriendly to let into the military news pamphlets.

A related aspect of these military news pamphlets' partiality was their staunch reiteration of Protestant, anti-Catholic sympathies. This was the age of religious war—civil and foreign, across all western and central Europe, reaching its peaks in northwestern Europe's late sixteenth-century wars with Spain and in the Thirty Years War, and thus coinciding exactly with and prompting the peak production of military news pamphlets. Not all wars were religious, of

---

[52] S.W., *The Appollogie of the Illustrious Prince Ernestus, Earle of Mansfield* (Heidelberg [i.e., London], 1622, STC 24915), 13.

[53] Henry Hexham, *A Historicall Relation of the Famous Siege of the Busse* (Delft, 1630, STC 13262), 19.

[54] Anthony Nixon, *Swethland and Poland Warres* (London, 1610, STC 18596), sig. B2r.

[55] For example, Nixon, *Swethland and Poland Warres* (1610), sig. D3r.

course, and not all military news was about religious wars. *A true discourse of the occurrences in the warres of Savoy* (1601) reported on Catholic France's invasion of Catholic Savoy; and Henri de Schomberg's *A relation sent to the French king by the Marshall de Schomberg* (1632) narrated a civil war among Catholic French factions. The usual complications acknowledged, the members of these faiths conceived of themselves as bitter enemies, and as bitter enemies Protestant and Catholic were engaged in what Shapin refers to as "the ultimate incivility[, which] is the public withdrawal of trust in another's access to the world and in another's moral commitment to speaking truth about it."[56] The great civility, after all, was with the highest truth, God himself; to be out of communion with that truth was to make all lesser truths impossible.[57] At the very least, Catholics, even gentle Catholics, could not be trusted to tell the truth "in any matter impinging upon their faith."[58] News of Protestant-Catholic battles clearly fell into this category. To be credible, reports of these battles had to express partiality with the Protestant cause, and deny all credibility to Catholic reports. There is an obvious sectarian application to the claim that "I will by Gods grace speake nothing but the Truth."[59] The corollary was that those without God's grace—Catholics—could only speak lies. As Barnabe Riche put it,

> Have they [Catholics] not made sundry profers to stirre up seditious tumultes, nay what doo they leave unattempted, to disturbe this happye governement: But would you have some speciall markes howe you may knowe them, then listen, and by these meanes you may easely smell them out: You shall have them inquiring of newes, spreading of rumours, lying, forging, counterfeiting and dissembling, what action hath there beene so honourably performed, sithe that noble Earle of *Leicester* undertooke these lowe country servies, whych hath not beene defaced (heere at home) by our slaundering Papistes.

---

[56] Steven Shapin, *A Social History of Truth: Civility and Science in Seventeenth-Century England* (Chicago and London: University of Chicago Press, 1994), 36.

[57] The intense providentialism in these news reports, and unwillingness to note punishing providences, are also the result of this partiality. The trustworthy informant by definition deserved to be providentially blessed; to lack providence's blessings was to be untrustworthy. Friends were the beneficiaries of providence, and they could suffer no hostile providential judgements; to say otherwise was to breach the norms, and trust, of civility. For providentialism in military news, and the evidentiary basis on which the above analysis has been made, see David Randall, "Providence, Fortune, and the Experience of Combat: English Printed Battlefield Reports, circa 1570–1637," *Sixteenth Century Journal* 35 (2004): 1053–77.

[58] Shapin, *A Social History of Truth*, 96.

[59] Doctor Welles, *A True and Ample Relation of all such occurrences as have happened in the Palatinate* (London, 1622, STC 25233), 3.

> What good news hath there come over which they have not paraphrased, what enterprise so justly attempted, wheich they have not eclipsed, or what exployt so bravely accomplished; which they have not metamorphised: Such is the devotion of our religious Catholiques, that they straine no curtesie to forge lyes, to practise treasons, to commit murthers, to stirre uppe rebellions, nay what outrage is there so mischeevous, which they wil not enter into to doo their holy father service.[60]

To report a Catholic victory opened the suspicion that you yourself were a Catholic or a Catholic sympathizer; to report news of Protestant victories abroad was to declare one's Protestant identity and sympathies. Some writers could be coolly secular in their tone, and occasionally even critical of Puritan fervor,[61] but by and large any sentiment, or explanatory religious framework, was fervently anti-Catholic in tone.[62]

The result was that very few military news pamphlets written by Catholics (whether English or foreign) were read in England. This was unlikely to have been caused by any difference other than religion. Catholic news pamphlets were probably rather similar in form and content to English news pamphlets; Spanish military news reports in the 1620s and 1630s certainly seem very similar to their English counterparts.[63] But Catholic military newswriters are most notable for their absence. The great majority of translated military news pamphlets came from Protestant Dutchmen, Frenchmen, and Germans, writing avowedly, and often stridently, as (usually Reformed) Protestants. After the publication of Álvaro de Bazan's *Relation of the expongnable attempt and conquest of the yland of Tercera* (1583), a Spanish pamphlet describing the conquest of the Azores from Portuguese and French troops, the eruption of open war with Spain meant that virtually no military news pamphlets of Catholic origin appeared in England for two generations. To listen to enemies, to repeat their lies, could only undermine the credibility of the news. When it did appear, it had to be explicitly labeled a lie. A translation of a Spanish report of a battle in the Caribbean between

---

[60] Barnabe Riche, *A Path-way to Military practise* (London, 1587, STC 20995), sig. C3v.

[61] William Lithgow, *A True and Experimentall Discourse, upon the beginning, proceeding, and Victorious event of this last siege of Breda* (London, 1637, STC 15717), 34–35.

[62] E.g., *A Discourse more at large of the late overthrowe given to the King of Spaines armie at Turnehaut* (London, 1597, STC 22993), 5, 7; Hexham, *A Historicall Relation of the Famous Siege of the Busse* (1630), 45. "Anti-Catholic" here follows Lake's definition, and means the spectrum of Protestants, including but not limited to the intensely godly, who could be mobilized by anti-popery sentiments. See Peter Lake, "Anti-Popery: The Structure of a Prejudice," in *Conflict in Early Stuart England: Studies in Religion and Politics, 1603-1642*, ed. Richard Cust and Ann Hughes (London and New York: Longman, 1989), 72–106.

[63] See the collection of Spanish printed news reports in British Library, 593.h.17.

English and Spanish ships only appeared under the marvelously declarative title *A Libell of Spanish Lies* (1596). When a report from the siege of s' Hertogenbosch in 1629 included the sermon given by the town's Catholic bishop to enhearten the townsmen to endure the Protestant siege a while longer, the newswriter had to counter the speech with a poem at the end of the news report: *"You friendly Reader heare, / how that this foolish Prelate, / Poore peoples eyes would bleare / with fabl's he doth relate, / In stead of giving glory / to God, and Christ our hope, / To trust in his false story, / and Pardons of the Pope."*[64]

The exceptions to this rule of Protestant partiality were English translations of Catholic reports of battles against Muslim enemies. These were printed in England throughout this period: For example, *Certayn and tru good nues, from the syege of the isle Malta* (1565), *Newes from Vienna* (1566), *The true Report of all the successe of Famagosta* (1572), *True Newes of a notable victorie obtayned against the Turkes* (1598), *A True Relation of taking of Alba-Regalis* (1601), *Good newes from Florence* (1614), and *Newes from Poland* (1621). In these circumstances, a common Christian identity apparently overcame the reluctance to use Catholic sources. A similar chain of logic probably explains the publication of *A true Reporte of the taking of the great towne and castell of Polotzko* (1579), which narrated a Catholic Polish triumph over Orthodox Muscovite enemies. But these reports were few and far between. By and large, the Catholic was the enemy to English newsreaders, and they did not take him as a source of news.

That said, Catholic news could be read when it testified against the Catholic interest. This was not the voluntarily given news of a friend, but news captured, so to speak, from an informant and extorted against his will—and therefore acceptable. The proof that such information was credible was that it spoke badly of Catholics. An informant who reported against his own interest must be presumed to be reporting reluctantly, under the coercion of the truth and his captors, and therefore with some credibility. A Protestant reader could take as credible Catholic testimony of Catholic defeats. So Thomas Digges in *A Briefe Report of the Militarie Services done in the Low Countries, by the Erle of Leicester* (1587) based his account "of the enimies doings" in part upon the enemy's own "intercepted letters."[65] The wish for the enemy to have witnessed victory sometimes made the very absence of such witness notable: *A Jornall of Certaine principall passages* (1629) remarked that the Protestant thanksgiving for the victory at Wesel celebrated at the siege of s' Hertogenbosch was not witnessed by the commander of the Spanish garrison, "because hee had the gout."[66] *A Description of S'Hertogenbosh . . . Together with the principall points and passages concerning the last Siege* (1629) included what purported to be an entire Spanish journal of the

---

[64] *A Iornall of Certaine principall passages* (London, 1629, STC 13248.4), 12–18.
[65] Thomas Digges, *A Briefe Report of the Militarie Services done in the Low Countries, by the Erle of Leicester* (London, 1587, STC 7285), 2.
[66] *A Iornall of Certaine principall passages* (1629), 7.

entire victorious Dutch siege of s' Hertogenbosch.[67] It is difficult to tell whether it is real or not: it is somewhat more dour and downcast than the Protestant siege-journals that appear in the printed news, but comparable to manuscript journals of the disastrous expedition to Ré. Whether true or not, its appearance in an English military news pamphlet testified to the genre's limited capacity to use Catholic sources to verify accounts of Protestant victory.

The third characteristic of the genre, related both to partiality and to plain style, is their rhetorical purpose. The genre was rooted in medieval epistolary rhetoric's twinned desire to inform and to persuade, and propaganda of one sort or another governed what was said, what was omitted, and the manner of presentation. The aspiration toward credibility was inseparable from the aspiration toward persuasion. Partiality and reports of victories were one aspect of this rhetoric; so too was the promotion of individual military commanders (often by writers who were their junior officers), and the denigration of the skill and virtue of rivals and enemies. Particular political projects also slip into the narratives: *Discourse of such things as are happened in the armie of my lordes the princes of Navarre, and of Condey* (1569) mixes Huguenot military victory with justification of the Huguenot revolt;[68] *A Letter from a Souldier of good place in Ireland* (1602) spends as much time explaining Lord Deputy Mountjoy's willingness to accept Don Juan del Aguila's surrender of Kinsale on generous terms as it does describing his previous military victories; and *A True Relation of the Late Battel fought in New England* (1637) is in many ways a real-estate prospectus for New England settlement disguised as a military news pamphlet. These pamphlets must be read with a wary eye—but when their rhetorical nature is recognized, they may also be admired for their rhetorical artistry.

It must also be stated plainly that we will never have more than a hazy idea of who read military news pamphlets.[69] By its very nature, reading leaves less of

---

[67] The Spanish Day-register is in *A Description of S'Hertogenbosh . . . Together with the principall points and passages concerning the last Siege* (London, 1629, STC 19555), 34–52.

[68] A great quantity of Huguenot propaganda and political thought slipped into England via the dozens of military news pamphlets concerning the French Civil Wars: Lisa Ferraro Parmelee, *Good newes from Fraunce: French Anti-League Propaganda in Late Elizabethan England* (Rochester: University of Rochester Press, 1996).

[69] Albeit some clues as to the social characteristics of the intended audience for popular print can be deduced from cost, typography, paper size, and paper quality. See Blayney, "The Publication of Playbooks," 414–15; Charles C. Mish, "Black Letter as a Social Discriminant in the Seventeenth Century," *PMLA* 68 (1953): 627–30; Raymond, *Pamphlets and Pamphleteering in Early Modern Britain*, 5, 72–73; Keith Thomas, "The Meaning of Literacy in Early Modern England," in *The Written Word: Literacy in Transition*, ed. Gerd Baumann (Oxford: Clarendon Press, 1986), 97–131, here 99; Voss, *Elizabethan News Pamphlets*, 78–81.

an impress on the historical record than does writing.[70] Military news pamphlets were not expensive, and were perceived at the time as appealing to a broad, vulgar audience: Therefore we may reasonably believe that it included a relatively broad readership (in social terms). On the other hand, this perception should not be taken too far. Military news pamphlets explicitly addressed themselves to an audience of gentlemen. *Good newes for the King of Bohemia?* (1622) addressed itself to the *"Gentle Reader,"* in a phrase that has come down to modern times.[71] This address was doubtless aspirational, as well as complimentary to an audience probably less gentle in fact.[72] After all, *A Trumpet to call souldiers on to noble actions* (1627) addressed itself to "Noble Souldiers, wishing you all no worse fortune in

---

[70] Levy notes that there are no booksellers' inventories from the late 1580s to the early 1600s, and the surviving library inventories provide fragmentary information at best: Fritz Levy, "The Decorum of News," in *News, Newspapers, and Society in Early Modern Britain*, ed. Joad Raymond (London: Frank Cass, 1999), 12–38, here 25. Heroic efforts have begun to give us something of a history of reading in early modern England, but these are most effective as microstudies of individual readers who happen to have left behind an unusually rich trove of evidence. See Lisa Jardine and Anthony Grafton, "'Studied for Action': How Gabriel Harvey Read his Livy," *Past and Present* 129 (1990): 30–78; John S. Morrill, "William Davenport and the 'silent majority' of Early Stuart England," *Journal of the Chester Archaeological Society* 58 (1975): 115–29; Kevin Sharpe, *Reading Revolutions: The Politics of Reading in Early Modern England* (New Haven and London: Yale University Press, 2000); William H. Sherman, *John Dee: The Politics of Reading and Writing in the English Renaissance* (Amherst, MA: University of Massachusetts Press, 1995). For more general studies of the history of reading in early modern England, see *Books and Readers in Early Modern England: Material Studies*, ed. Jennifer Anderson and Elizabeth Sauer (Philadelphia: University of Pennsylvania Press, 2002); David Cressy, *Literacy and the Social Order: Reading and Writing in Tudor and Stuart England* (Cambridge: Cambridge University Press, 1980); Eugene R. Kintgen, *Reading in Tudor England* (Pittsburgh: University of Pittsburgh Press, 1996); Kevin Sharpe and Steven N. Zwicker, *Reading, Society, and Politics in Early Modern England* (Cambridge: Cambridge University Press, 2003); D. R. Woolf, *Reading History in Early Modern England* (Cambridge: Cambridge University Press, 2000).

[71] *Good newes for the King of Bohemia?* ([London, 1622,] STC 18507.40), 1. The address to the "Gentle Reader" was also used in *A true declaration of the streight siedge laide to the Cytty of Steenwich* (London, 1592, STC 23241), sig. A3r; *A true relation of such battailes* ([London, 1622,] STC 18507.37A), 1; *The affaires of Italy* ([London,] November 20, 1623, Numb. 4, STC 18507.133), 1; and *The newes and affaires of Europe* (London, January 15, 1624, Numb. 10, STC 18507.139), 1. *Coppies of letters sent from personages of Accompt* (1622) addressed itself to the "Courteous Reader": *Coppies of letters sent from personages of Accompt* ([London, 1622,] STC 18507.56a), sig. A2r.

[72] The gentle reader was also supposed to be a friendly reader; the address to and invocation of the gentle reader reinforced the ideals of partiality. See Heidi Brayman Hackel, *Reading Material in Early Modern England: Print, Gender, and Literacy* (Cambridge: Cambridge University Press, 2005), 116–25.

your Battailes, no no lesse fame, than here the Sweves have atchieved, I leave you to reade that which may serve as a patterne and president for all heroicall spirits to follow."[73] The "Noble Souldiers" of comfortable England doubtless thrilled to think of themselves as martial; but this is addressed to the ideal self-image of the audience, not in actuality. The same is very likely true of addresses to gentlemen. Still, we should not assume that the disjuncture of aspiration and reality was total: could it have been an effective selling ploy if there were no actual gentle readers of military news pamphlets? We may believe that the genre remained moderately exclusive and was not read universally—perhaps not even by a majority of Englishmen.

That noted, their readership probably still included a remarkably broad section of Englishmen. In general, we believe that men and women of all classes and places inquired after the latest word from travelers of all sorts.[74] By at least the 1620s literate Englishmen not only read the news themselves but also read the news out loud to their illiterate companions.[75] While the direct evidence we have of news reading is largely from the gentry classes, with occasional pieces of evidence from the merchant and artisan classes,[76] indirect evidence suggests (if it does not prove) a far wider readership of news pamphlets.[77] The evidentiary basis is unpleasantly thin: still, it suggests we would be wiser to err in overestimating news readership than in underestimating it.

The following pamphlets were selected to provide a sense of the genre's range. They include examples fairly evenly distributed in time between 1513 and 1637; accounts of battles in Scotland and Ireland, the Netherlands and France, Malta and Hungary, Russia and New England; pamphlets drawn from letters written by Englishmen, and pamphlets drawn from letters or pamphlets written by a variety of continental Europeans, both Protestant and Catholic; accounts of battles, sieges, and extended campaigns. They include pamphlets by the four most famous literary contributors to the genre, George Gascoigne, Thomas Churchyard, Anthony Nixon, and Hugh Peters, and they include reports of

---

[73] *A Trumpet to call souldiers on to noble actions* (London, 1627, STC 24295), 1–2.

[74] Fox, *Oral and Literate Culture in England 1500–1700*, 340–63.

[75] Michael Frearson, "The Distribution and Readership of London Corantos in the 1620s," in *Serials and their Readers 1620–1914*, ed. Robin Myers and Michael Harris (New Castle: Oak Knoll Press, 1993), 1–25, here 16–17. For a general description of how written news sparked and was incorporated into oral news in early modern England, see Fox, *Oral and Literate Culture in England 1500–1700*, 363–93.

[76] Paul S. Seaver, *Wallington's World: A Puritan Artisan in Seventeenth-Century London* (Stanford: Stanford University Press, 1985), 45–66, 143–81.

[77] Alastair Bellany, *The Politics of Court Scandal in Early Modern England: News Culture and the Overbury Affair, 1603–1660* (Cambridge: Cambridge University Press, 2002), 129–31; Fox, *Oral and Literate Culture in England 1500–1700*, 393–405; Raymond, *Pamphlets and Pamphleteering in Early Modern Britain*, 89–96.

some notable historical events—the siege of Malta (1566),[78] the sack of Antwerp (1576), the battle of Ivry (1590), and the battle of Kinsale (1602). For reasons of space, they do not include some rather fine, but excessively lengthy news pamphlets. Since I was able to assemble an interesting collection devoted entirely to warfare on land, I have not included any pamphlets on naval warfare.

---

[78] See *Caelius Secundus Curio his Historie of the War of Malta*, ed. H. V. Bonavita, MRTS 339 (Tempe: ACMRS, 2007).

Editorial Notes

This is largely a letter-by-letter edition of these pamphlets. I have preserved not only the spelling but also the typography of the day (e.g., reversed i/j and u/v typography, and "þe" rather than "ye" or "the"). I have, however, spelled out various contractions (e.g., I have represented "+" and "&" as [and], and represented Lieutenaūt as Lieutenau[n]t), turned superscript letters into regular letters ("Sⁱʳ" as "Sir"), transformed the mixture of gothic, roman, and italic typefaces into roman and italic only, and modernized some punctuation for clarity. New pages I have represented as **[TITLE PAGE]**, **[1]**, **[sig. A]**, etc.; where no pagination exists on the pamphlet, or only a sigil, I have used italics to represent the pagination as *[1]*, etc. "|" represents line breaks in the original text.

I have provided notes for each obscure word or phrase once in each pamphlet, but allow later uses of the same word in the same pamphlet to pass unnoted. I have drawn these definitions largely from the *Oxford English Dictionary*. The introductions to each pamphlet provide historical context for the events within, and I have provided a light annotation for persons, events, and references mentioned within the pamphlets. Biblical quotations in the notes use the King James Version. I have not, as a rule, provided annotation for places: I do not judge that the modern spelling of obscure places will greatly enlighten the reader. I have silently emended a small number of transposed letters and other equally minor, obvious typographical errors. My text follows the particular editions listed in the back of the book; it does not attempt to collate all extant variants.

Alastair Bellany helped me untangle some of the more obscure English; Christopher Welser and Sarah Bolmarcich aided me greatly in representing the Latin and the Greek properly; Leslie MacCoull both copy-edited the manuscript and provided sources for a multitude of classical and biblical allusions; Vincent Carey and Robert Tittler critiqued the Introduction; and I received financial support from the Making Publics Project (thanks in particular to the good offices of Robert Tittler and Paul Yachnin), and the Social Sciences and Humanities Research Council of Canada. I am grateful to the critiques of several anonymous readers. All mistakes, of course, are mine alone.

Hereafter ensue the trewe encountre (1513) ||
STC (2nd ed.) #11088.5

In 1512, Henry VIII of England joined the anti-French alliance known as the Holy League; in 1513 he invaded France. James IV of Scotland came to the assistance of his French ally and in turn led a Scottish army into northern England on 22 August. After a brief campaign, during which the Scots took Norham Castle in Northumberland, an English army under the command of Thomas Howard, earl of Surrey, met and fought the Scots at Flodden Field (Branxton) on 9 September. The result was a disaster for the Scots: James IV, most of the higher nobility, and up to ten thousand Scotsmen (one-third of the Scots army) died during the battle, and Scotland was unable to pose a military challenge to England for a generation. Flodden Field was fought in the early stages of the gunpowder revolution: save for an artillery duel, the English and the Scots fought almost entirely without gunpowder. The great majority of combatants were cavalry, archers, billmen, and pikemen, not arquebusiers or musketeers.

This pamphlet is a straightforward account of Flodden Field itself. It includes elements of medieval military custom — the exchange of heralds and pursuivants and the formal challenge to battle — and focuses on the exploits and deaths of noblemen. It also includes what would become standard elements of the military news pamphlet: the list of dead enemy nobles, the list of ennobled victors, the organizational structure of the army, and the exact leadership of each of the army's sections. Of some psychological interest is the pamphlet's laconic mention of the battle rage that led the English to slaughter so many Scots in the aftermath of their victory. On the whole, however, it is of most significance as the earliest surviving English military news pamphlet, rather than for its literary qualities.

Flodden Field is also commemorated in the song "The Flowers of the Forest."

[TITLE PAGE]

Hereafter ensue the trewe encountre or | Batayle lately don betwene .Engla[n]de and: | Scotlande. In whiche batayle the. Scottis- | he .Kynge[1] was slayne.

The maner of thaduau[n]cesynge of my lord of | Surrey[2] tresourier and .Marshall of .Englande | and leuetenu[n]te generall of the north p[ar]ties of th | e same with .xxvi.M. men to wardes the kyn- | ge of .Scotts and his .Armye vewed and nom | bred to an hundred thousande men at the leest.

[*1*] FIrste my sayd Lorde at his beynge at Awnewik[3] in Northumbrelande the iiij. daye of .Septembre the .v. yere of þe Reygne of kynge Henry the .viii.[4] herynge that þe kynge of Scottes thenne was remoued from .Norh[a]me And dyd lye at forde .Castel, [and] in those p[ar]tyes dyd moche hurte in spoylyng robynge, and brennynge,[5] sent to the sayde kynge of Scottes Ruge Cros purseuaunte at .Armes[6] to shewe[7] vnto hym that for somoche as he he sayde kynge contrary to his honour all good reason [and] conscyence And his oothe of Fidelite for þe ferme entartnynge[8] of perpetuall peas between the kyngs hygnes our .Souerayne lorde and hym had inuaded this Raalme, spoylad brente[9] and robbyd dyuers and sondery townes and places in the same. Also had caste and betten downe the Castel of Norh[a]me And crewella had murdered [and] slayne many of the kynnes liege people he was co[m]men to gyue hym bayta[l]. And desyred him þ[a]t for, so moche, as he was a kynge and a great Prynce he wolde of his lusty[10] [and] noble courage co[n]sent therunto and tarye þe the same. And for my sayde Lordes partie his lordeshyp promysed þe assured Accomplysshement and perfourmau[n]ce therof as he was true knyght to god and the kynge his mayster. The kynge of scottes herynge this message reynued[11] and kepte w[i]t[h] hym þe sayd Ruge Cros pursenau[n]ta [and] wolde nat suffre hym at þe tyme to retourne agayne to my sayd lorde.

---

[1] James IV Stuart (1473–1513), king of Scotland 1488 to 1513.

[2] Thomas Howard (1443–1524), earl of Surrey, later 2nd duke of Norfolk.

[3] Alnwick.

[4] Henry VIII Tudor (1491–1547), king of England 1509 to 1547.

[5] brennynge—burning

[6] Ruge Cros purseuaunte at .Armes—the Rouge Croix Pursuivant of Arms in Ordinary was the title of a particular junior heraldic officer in the English College of Arms. Thomas Hawley (?–1557) was the Rouge Croix Pursuivant from 1509 to 1515.

[7] shewe (show)—declare

[8] entartnynge (entering)—entering into an agreement, engaging, pledging

[9] brente—burned

[10] lusty—healthy, strong, vigorous

[11] reynued (renewed)—began again, recommenced. The usage here gives an oddly forcible twist to the word.

The .v. daye of Septembre his lordshyp in his approchynge nyghe to the borders of .Scotlande, mustred at Bolton[n?] in glendayll [and] lodged that nyght therein þ[a]t felde with all his Armye.

The nexte day beynge the vi daye of Septembre the kynge of scottes sent to my sayd lor[d] of Surrey a harolde of his called .Ilaye and demaunded if that my sayde Lorde wolde iustefye[12] the message sent by the sayd purse- [2] uaunte ruge cros as is aforesayd sygnefyinge that if my lorde wolde so doo, it was the thynge, that moost was to his .Ioye end comforte. To this, demaunde, my lord made answere afore dyuers lordes, knyghtes and gentylme[n] nyghe .iii myles from the felde where ys the sayde harolde was appoynted to tarye bycause he shulde nat vewe the Armye that he commaunded nat oonly the, sayde .Ruge cros to speke and shewe the seyde werdes of his message But also gaue and comytted vnto hym the same by .Instruccyon sygned, and subscrybed, with his owne hande, whiche my sayde lorde sayd, he wolde Iustefye, and for so moche as his lordshyp conceyued by the, sayde Harolde, how .Ioyous and comfortab[l]e his message, was to þe sayde kynge of scottes he therfor for the more assuraunce of his message shewed that he wolde be bou[n]den in .x.Mli. [and] good suertes[13] with his .Lordshyp to gyue the sayde kynge batayle by Frydaye, next after at the, furthest, If that the sayde kynge of, scottes wolde, assyne and appoynte any, other Erle or Erles of his, Realme to be bounden in lyke maner that he wolde abyde my sayde, lordes commynge. And for somoche as the sayd kynge of .Scottes recyuued[14] styll with hym Ruge Cros purseuau[n]te and wolde nat suffre hym to retourne to my lorde my, sayde lorde in lyke [and] semblable[15] maner dyd kepe, with, hym the scottesshe Harolde .Ilay and sant to the sayd kynge of scottes with his answere and further offer, as is, afdre rehersed, A gentylman of scotlande that accompanyed and came to my sayde lorde with the sayd Harolde .Ilay. And thus .Ilay contynued and was kepte close tyll the commynge home of, Ruge cros whiche vas the next daye after. And thenne, Ilay was put at large and lyberte to retourne to the kynge of scottes his maystere to shewe my lordes answres declaracyons and goodly, offers as he had hade in euery behalue of my sayde lorde.

[3] The same daye my lorde deuyded his Arme in two bataylles[16] that is to wytte in a vau[n]warde[17] and a rerewarde[18] and ordeyned my lorde Hawarde

---

[12] iustefye (justify)—vindicate by force of arms
[13] suertes (sureties)—pledges, bonds, guarantees
[14] recyuued (received)—kept in his vicinity, kept in his custody
[15] semblable—similar
[16] bataylles (battles)—battalions
[17] vau[n]warde—vanguard
[18] rerewarde—rearguard

Admorall his sone[19] to be .Capitayne of the sayde vaunwarde, and hymselfe to by chefe Capitayne of the rerewarde.

In the breste[20] of þe sayd vaunwarde was w[i]t[h] the sayde Lorde Admorall ix. thousande men and vnder Capitaynes of the sams breste of the batayle was the lord .Lumley, syr Wyll[ia]m Bulmer, the baron of Hylton and dyuerse other of the Bysshopryche of Duresme,[21] vnder .Seynt Cuthberts[22] banner; the lorde .Scrope of vpsall,[23] the lorde Ogle, syr Wyllyam Gascoygne, ser Cristofer Warde, syr John Eueringha[a]m, sir Walter Griffith, syr John Gower, and dyuers other Esquyres and gentylmen of yorkeshyre and Northumberlaed. And in ayther wynge of the same batayle was .iiiM. men.

The Capitayne of the right wynge was mayster Edmonde Hawarde[24] sone to my seyde lorde of Surrey. And with hym was syr .Thomas Butler, syr .John .Boothe, syr Richarde Boolde, and dyuerse other Esquyers, [and] gentylmen of Lancasshyre end Chasshyre.

The Capitayne of the laste wynge was olda syr Marmaduke. Co[n]steble[25] [and] with hym was mayster Wyll[ia]m Percy his sona .Elawe, will[ia]m Constable his broder, syr .Robert Constabla, marmaduke Constable, Will[ia]m Constable his sones, And syr John Co[n]stable of holdernes with dyuerse his kynnesmen Allies and othea Gentylmen of yorkeshyre and Northumberlande.

In the breste of batayle of the sayde rerewarde was .vM. mon with my saide lorde of .Surrey, and vnder .Capitaydes of the same was the lord Scrope of Bolton, syr Philype Ty[l]ney, broder Elawe[26] to my sayd lord of .Surrey, George darcy[27] sone and heyre to the lorde Darcy,[28] say- [4] de beynge Capitayne of the firste batayle of the Scotths fyersly dyd sette vpon maister Edmonde Hawarde .Capitayne of the vttermoste parte of the felde at the west syde. And betwene them was so cruell batayle that many of our partie Chesshyremen and other dyd flee, And the sayd mayster Edmonde in maner lefte alone without socoure and his standerde and berer of the same beten and hewed in peces and hymsel .thryse stryken downe to the grou[n]d. Howbeit lyke a couragyous [and] an hardy yonge

---

[19] Thomas Howard (1473–1554), Lord High Admiral of England, later 3rd duke of Norfolk.

[20] breste (breast)—front

[21] Duresme—Durham

[22] Seynt Cuthbert—St. Cuthbert of Lindisfarne (ca. 634–687) was the patron saint of the Palatinate of Durham.

[23] Henry Scrope (ca. 1480–ca. 1533), 7th baron of Bolton.

[24] Edmund Howard (?–1539). His daughter Catherine became the fifth wife of Henry VIII.

[25] Marmaduke Constable (ca. 1455–1518).

[26] Elawe—in law

[27] George Darcy (1487–1558), later 1st Baron Darcy of Aston.

[28] Thomas Darcy (ca. 1467–1538), 1st Baron Darcy of Temple Hurst.

lusty gentylman he recouered agayne and faught hande to ha[n]de with one sir Dauy home[29] [and] slewe hym with his owne handes. And thus the sayde mayster Edmonde. was in great perell and daunger tyll that the lorde Dacre lyke a good and an hardy knyght releued and cam vnto hym for his socoure.

The seconde Batayle came vpon my lorde .Hawarde. The thirde batayle wherin was the kynge of .Scottes [and] moste parte of the noble men of his .Rea[l]me came fyersly vpon my sayd lord of Surrey, whiche two bataylles by the helpe of elmyghty god were, after a great confydelyete[30] venquysshed ouercomen betten downe [and] put to flyght and fewe of them escaped with theyr lyues. syr .Edwarde Stanley beynge at the vttermoste parte of the sayd rererewarde one heste[31] partie seynge the fourthe batayle redy to releue the sayde kynge of scottes batayle, couragyously and lyke a lusty and an hardy knyght dyd sette vpon the same and ouercame [and] put to flyght all the scottes in the sayd batayle. And thus by the grace socour and helpe of almyghty god victory was gyuen to the Rea[l]me of .England. And all the scottysshe ordena[u]nce[32] wonne [and] brought to .Ettell and Barwykein .Suretie.[33]

Hereafter ensueth the names of sondry noblemen of the scottes slayne at the sayde batayle [and] felde called Brainston moore.

[5]	FIrste þe kyng of scotoes	Lorde .Elweston.
	The .Archebysshop of	Lorde .Inderby
seynt .Androwes.[34]		Lorde .Maxwell
The bysshop of .Thyles.		Mac .Keyn.
The bysshop of .Ketnes.		Mac .Cleen.
The abbot ynchaffrey.		John of graunte
The abbot of .Rylwenny		The maist of .Agwis.
Therle of .Mountroos.[35]		Lorde .Roos.
Therle of .Craforde.[36]		Lord tempyll
Therle of .Argyle.[37]		Lorde .Borthyke.
Therle of lennox[38]		Lorde .Askyll.

---

[29] Sir David Home of Wedderburn (?–1513).

[30] confydelyete — perhaps "confidelity." The meaning is obscure; context suggests "clash."

[31] heste — his

[32] ordena[u]nce (ordnance) — artillery

[33] Suretie (surety) — to be safe from danger (of recapture)

[34] Alexander Stewart (ca. 1490–1513), archbishop of St. Andrews and Lord Chancellor of Scotland. He was the illegitimate son of James IV.

[35] William Graham (1464–1513), 1st earl of Montrose.

[36] John Lindsay (?–1513), 6th earl of Crawford.

[37] Gillespie Archibald Campbell (?–1513), 2nd earl of Argyll.

[38] Matthew Stewart (1488–1513), 3rd earl of Lennox.

Therle of .Lencar.[39]   Lorde .Dawisfie.
Therle of .Castelles.[40]   Sir Alexander Sotlon
Therle of .Boothwell[41]   Sire John home.
Therle .Arell. Constable.[42]   Lorde .Coluiu.
Lorde .Lowett.   Sir .Dauy home.
Lorde .Forboos.   Cuthbert home, of .Fascastell

OVer [and] aboue the seyd p[er]sones there at slayne of the Scottes vewd by my lorde .Dacre the, noumbre of .xi. or .xii. thousande mend And of Englysshme[n] slayne [and] taken prysoners vpon xii.C. dyuers prysoners are taken of þe scottes But noo Notable person saue oonly syr, Wyll[ia]m .Scotte knyght Councellour of the sayde kynge of scottes and as is sayd a gentylma[n] well lerned. Also s[i]r John Forma[n] knyght broder to the Bysshop of Murrey[43] which bysshop as is reported was [and], is moost pryncy[p]all procurour of this warre. And one other called s[i]r John Colehome. Many other scottysshe prysoner, coude and myght haue been taken, but they were soo vengeable [and] cruell in theyr fyghtyng that, whenne Englysshmen had the better of them they wolde nat saue them, though it so were that dyuerse scottes offered great su[m]mes of money for theyr lyues.

It is to be noted that the felde beganne between .iiij [6] and .v. at after Noone and contynued within nyght if it had fortuned to haue ben further afore nyght many mo[re] scottes had ben slayne and taken prysoners. Louynge[44] be to almyghty god all the noble men of Englande tha[t] were vpon the same felde bothe lordes and knyghtes are safe from any hurte, And none of theym awantynge[45] saue oonly maister Harry Gray, syr Huinfeide lyle, bothe prysoners in Scotla[n]de, syr John .Gower of yorkeshyre and syr John Boothe of Lancasshyre both wantynge and as yet nat founden.

In this batayle the scottes hadde many great Auauntagies, that is to wytte the hyghe .Hylles and mountaynes a great wynde with them and sodayne rayne all contrary[46] to our bowes and Archers.

It is nat to be doubted but the scottes fought manly and were determyned outher to wynne þe Felde or to dye. They were also as well apoynted[47] as was possyble at all poyntes with Armoure [and] harneys so that fewe of them were

---

[39] William Sinclair (bef. 1476–1513), 2nd earl of Caithness. This may instead be a reference to Cuthbert Cunningham (1470–1541), 2nd earl of Glencairn. He fought at Flodden, but did not actually die there.

[40] David Kennedy (bef. 1479–1513), 1st earl of Cassilis.

[41] Adam Hepburn (?–1513), 2nd earl of Bothwell.

[42] William Hay (?–1513), 4th earl of Erroll and Lord High Constable.

[43] Andrew Forman (ca. 1465–1521), bishop of Moray, later archbishop of St. Andrews.

[44] louynge (loving) — praise

[45] awantynge (awanting) — missing

[46] contrary — unfavorable

[47] apoynted (appointed) — equipped

slayne with arrowes Howbeit the bylles[48] dyd bete and hewe them downe with some payne and daunger to Englysshemen.

The sayd scottes were so playnely determyned to abyde[49] batayle and nat to flee that they put from them theyr horses and also put of theyr bo[o]tes and shoes and faught in the vampis,[50] of theyr hooses[51] every man for the moost p[ar]tie, with a kene and a sha[r]pe spere of .v. yerdes longe and a target[52] afore hym And when theyr speres fayled and wera spent, then they faught with great end sharpe swerdes makyng, lytell or no noys, vithoue[53] that, that, for the p[ar]tie many of them wolde desyre to be saued.

The felde where þe scottes dyd, lodge was nat to be reprouyd but rather to be co[m]mended greatly for there many and great nombre of goodily tenttes and moche good stuffe[54] in the same [and] in the sayd felde was plentie of wyne [7] bere ale beif mutton salfysshe[55] chese and other vytalles[56] necessary and conuenyent for suche a great Army Albeit our Armye doutynge[57] that the sayd vytallyes hadde ben poysoned for theyr distruccyon wolde nat saue but vtterly distroyed theym.

Hereafter ensueth the names of suche noble men as after the Felde were made knyghts for theyr valyau[n]ce Act, in the same by my sayd lorde therle of Surrey.

Firste, my lord Scrope of vpsall
Sir Will[ia]m Percy
Sir Edmonde Hawarde
Sir george Darcy.
Sir .w. gascoygne þe yo[n]ger.

Sir .will[ia]m. Medlton
Sir will[ia]m. Maleuerdy
Sir Thomas .Bartley
Sir marmaduke .Co[n]stalbe þe yo[n]ger
Sir Xr[ist]ofer .Dacre
Sir .John .Hoothome.

Sir .Guy .Dawny
Sir .Raffe salwayne
Sir .Richarde .Malleuerey
Sir will[ia]m .Constable of Hatefelde
Sir will[ia]m .Constable of Larethorpe
Sir .Xr[ist]ofer .Danby
Sir .Thomas Burght
Sir will[ia]m .Rous
Sir Thomas .Newton
Sir .Roger of Fenwyke
Sir Roger Gray

---

[48] bylles (bills)—concave axes with spikes at the back and shafts ending in spearheads

[49] abyde (abide)—wait for

[50] vampis (vamps)—that part of hose or stockings which covers the foot and ankle, short stockings, socks

[51] hooses (hoses)—leggings, long stockings

[52] target—a light, round shield or buckler

[53] vithoue (withal)—nevertheless, notwithstanding

[54] stuffe (stuff)—provisions of food, munitions of war

[55] salfysshe—salt fish

[56] vytalles—victuals

[57] doutynge (doubting)—fearful

Sir .Nicholas .Appleyarde.
Sire Edwarde .Goorge
Sir .Rauf .Ellercar þe yo[n]ger
Sir .John Wyliyby
Sir .Edwarde .Echingh[a]me
Sir .Edwarde .Musgraue
Sir .John stanley
Sir Walter stonner
Sir .Nyuiane martynfelde.
Sir .Raffe .Bowes
Sir Briane stapleton of wyghall.

Sir .Thomas Connyers
My .lorde Ogle
Sir .Thomas str[a]ngewase
Sir .Henri .Thiuaittes
My lorde lumley
Sir .Xr[ist]ofe[r] .Pekerynge.
Sir .John Bulmer

Emprynted by me
Richarde .Faques dw[e]llyng
In poulys churche yerde

The late expedicion in Scotlande (1544) ||
STC (2nd ed.) #22270

After the death of James V of Scotland in 1542, Henry VIII of England initiated a diplomatic campaign in 1543 to have James's daughter and heir, Mary, married to his own son and heir, Edward; when this failed, in 1544 he initiated an invasion of Scotland, meant to harry the Scots into accepting the proposed marriage. The campaigns, known as "The Wars of the Rough Wooing," were ultimately unsuccessful, but the English were able to raid and burn through lowland Scotland with little effective resistance until the Scottish victory at Ancrum Moor in 1545. The main narrative of this pamphlet describes the debarkation in Edinburgh in May 1544 of an English army under the command of the Earl of Hertford, the successful burning of Leith, Edinburgh, and Holyrood House—and the failure to take Edinburgh Castle—and the English army's return by land through Scotland to Berwick-on-Tweed, pillaging and burning as it went. A second narrative describes the reiving through the Scottish borders in June 1544 by various English noblemen, focusing on a raid to Jedburgh by Sir Ralph Eure.

The pamphlet is notable for its realistic and unapologetic description of Anglo-Scottish border warfare, with a strong emphasis on towns burned and cattle stolen. It also provides a clear description of a mid-Tudor combined-arms campaign, with navy and army acting in cooperation, an attempted siege, and a harrowing of the countryside. Although the spelling departs significantly from modern English, the syntax is recognizably that of modern English prose. The structure of the pamphlet is already that of the military news pamphlet genre, as it would continue for the next century. There are relatively few polemical touches—on occasion, the Scots are "cowardly," but it is, by and large, a laconic and dispassionate narration.

[TITLE PAGE]

The late | expedicion in | Scotlande, | made by the kynges[1] | hyghnys armye, vnder the conduit[2] | of the ryght honorable the | Erle of Hertforde,[3] the | yere or oure Lorde | God 1544.

Londini.[4]

Cum priuilegio ad imprimendum | solum.[5]

[1] *The late expedition in Scotlande sent to the ryght honorable Lorde Russel,*[6] *Lorde priuie seale, from the Kynges armye there by a frende of hys.*

AFter longe soiornynge (my verie good lorde) of the kinges maiesties armye at Newcastele for lacke of commodious[7] windes, which longe hath ben at North Easte, and Easte North Easte: moche to our greife, as your lordshyppe, I doubte not, knoweth. The same as god wolde, who doth all thynges for þe best, the fyrste of Maye, the .xxxvi, yeare of his maiestyes mooste prosperous raigne, vired into the South, and South South weste, so apte and [2] propice[8] for our iorney, beyng of euery man so moch desyred, that it was no nede to haste them forwardes. To be breife, suche diligence was vsed that in two tydes the hole flete being two hundreth sayles at the least, was out of the hauen[9] of Tynmouth towardes our enterprice.

The thyrde day after we arryued in þe Frith,[10] a notable ryuer in Scotlande, hauyng thentry betwene two Islandes, called the Basse and the Maye. The same daye we landed dyuers of our botes at a towne named S[aint]. Mynettes, on the Northe side of the Frith whiche we brente,[11] and broughte from thense dyuers great botes that serued vs after to good pourpose for our landynge. That nyghte thole flete came to an anker vnder þe Island called Inchekythe, thre myles from the hauen of Lyth. The place where we ankered, hath of longe tyme ben called [3] the Englysh rode:[12] þe Scottes nowe taketh the same to be a prophesie of the thynge whiche is hapened.

---

[1] Henry VIII Tudor (1491–1547), king of England 1509 to 1547.

[2] conduit—conduct

[3] Edward Seymour (ca. 1506–1552), earl of Hertford, later 1st duke of Somerset, and Lord Protector of England during the reign of Edward VI, from 1547 to 1559.

[4] Londini—London.

[5] *Cum priuilegio ad imprimendum solum.*—With the exclusive right to print.

[6] Baron John Russell (ca. 1485–1554/55), later 1st earl of Bedford.

[7] commodious—beneficial, serviceable

[8] propice—propitious

[9] hauen (haven)—harbor, anchorage, port

[10] The Firth of Forth.

[11] brente—burned

[12] rode (road)—a sheltered piece of water near the shore where vessels may lie at anchor in safety

The nexte daye beyng the fourth daye of May, the sayde armye landed two myles bewest the towne of Lithe, at a place called Grantame Cragge, euery ma[n] beyng so prompt therunto, that the hole armye was landed in foure houres. And perceyuynge our landynge to be so quyet whiche we loked not for, hauynge our guides redy, we put our selfes in good ordre of warre marchynge forwarde towardes the towne of Lythe in thre battaylles,[13] wherof my lorde Admyral[14] ledde the vantgard, Therle of Shrewesbury[15] tharenregarde, and Therle of Hertford beinge lorde Lieutenau[n]t, the battayll,[16] hauyng with vs certen small pieces of artillary, whiche were drawen by force of men: whiche enterpryse we thought necessarie to be attempted [**sig. A.iii./4**] fyrste of all other, for the commodyous lodgynge of our nauy there, [and] landynge of our artillarie and vittayle.[17] And in a valley vpon þe ryght hande nere vnto the sayd towne, the Scottes were assembled to the nombre of fyue or syx thousande horsemen, besydes a good nombre of fotemen to empeache[18] the passage of our sayd armye, in which place they had layd theyr artyllarie at two strayghtes, thorough the whiche we muste nedes passe, yf we mynded to acheue our enterpryse. And semynge at the fyrste as though they wolde set vpo[n] the vanwarde,[19] when they perceyued our men so wyllynge to encounter with them, namely the Cardynall[20] who was there present, perceyuyng our deuotion to se his holynes to be suche as we were redy to watte our feete for that purpose, and to passe a forde which was betwene vs and them. After certen shotte of ar-[**5**] tillary on bothe sydes, they made a sodayne retrete, and leauynge theyr artyllary behynde them, fledde towardes Edenborrowe. The fyrste man that fledde was the holy Cardynall lyke a valyaunt champyon, and with hym the gouerner,[21] therles of Huntley,[22] Murrey,[23] and Bothewell,[24] with dyuers other great men of the realme. At this passage was two Englishmen hurt with the shot of theyr artillary, [and] two Scottyshe men slayne with our artillary.

---

[13] battayles (battles)—battalions
[14] John Dudley (1501–1553), Viscount Lisle, later 1st duke of Northumberland; effective ruler of England under Edward VI Tudor from 1549 to 1553.
[15] Francis Talbot (1500–1560), 5th earl of Shrewsbury.
[16] battayle (battle)—the main body of the army
[17] vittayle—victuals
[18] empeache (impeach)—impede, hinder
[19] vanwarde—vanguard
[20] Cardinal David Beaton (ca. 1494–1546), archbishop of St. Andrews, leading figure in Scotland from 1543 to 1546, and promoter of Scottish hostility toward England and alliance with France.
[21] James Hamilton (ca. 1516–1575), 2nd earl of Arran, at the time Regent of Scotland for Mary Queen of Scots.
[22] George Gordon (1514–1562), 4th earl of Huntly.
[23] James Stewart (ca. 1499–1544), 1st earl of Moray.
[24] Patrick Hepburn (1512–1556), 3rd earl of Bothewell.

The vanwarde hauynge thus put backe the Scottes and .viii. pieces of theyr artillary brought away by our hackebutters,[25] who in this enterprise dyd very manfully employ them selues, we merched directly towardes the towne of Lythe, whiche
before we coulde come to it, muste of force passe an other passage whiche also was
defended a whyle with certen ensignes[26] of fotemen, and certen [6] peices of artillary, who beyng sharpely assayled hauynge thre of theyr gonners slayne with our
archers, was fayne to gyue place, leauynge also theyr ordinaunce[27] behynd them,
with whiche ordinaunce, they slewe onely one of our men, and hurte an other.

And in this brunt[28] the victory beinge ernestly followed, the towne of Lythe
was entred perforce [and] wonne with the losse onely of two men of owres, and
hurte of thre, where the Scottes had caste greate trenches and dyches purposely to
haue defended it. The same nyghte the armye encamped in the said towne of Lith,
and by reason of the sayde dyches [and] trenches, we made there a stronge campe.
The morow beynge the .v. of May, we caused our shyppes laden with our greate artyllary and vittayles to be brought into the hauen, where we dyscharged the same
[7] at our pleasour. In the sayde hauen we founde many goodely shyppes, specyally
two of notable fayrenes, thone called the Salamander gyuen by the Frenche kyng
at the mariage of his doughter into Scotlande: thother called the vnicorne, made by
the late Scottyshe kynge. The towne of Lith was fou[n]de more full of ryches, then
we thought to haue founde any Scottisshe towne to haue ben.

The nexte daye tharmye went towardes Edenborough, leauyng the lord Stur-
ton in Lithe with .xv.C. men, for the defence of the same. And tharmy beynge
come nere vnto Edenborough, the Prouost[29] accompanied with one or two bur-
geases, and two or thre offycers at armes desyred to speake with the kynges
Lieutenaunt, and in the name of all the towne sayde, that the keys of the towne
shulde be delyuered vnto his [sig. B./8] lordeshyp, condicionally, that they might
go with bagge and baggage[30] and þe towne to be saued from fyer: Wherunto
answer was made by the sayd lorde Lieutenaunt, that where as the Scottes had so
many wayes falsed theyr faythes, and so manyfestely had broken theyr promyss-
es, confyrmed by othes and seales, and certified by theyr hole parliament, as is
euydently knowen vnto all þe worlde, he was sent thyther by the kinges hyghnes
to take vengeau[n]ce of their detestable falshed, to declare and shewe the force of
his hyghnes sworde, to all suche, as sholde make any resiste[n]ce vnto his graces

---

[25] hackebutters (arquebusiers)—soldiers equipped with an early gun called an arquebus

[26] ensignes (ensigns)—troops of soldiers

[27] ordinaunce (ordnance)—artillery

[28] brunt—assault, violent attack

[29] Sir Adam Otterburn (ca. 1480–1548), Scottish notable, at the time the Lord Provost of Edinburgh.

[30] with bagge (bag) and baggage—with all their personal property; with all their
portable military equipment

power sent thyther for that pourpose. And therfore beynge not sent to treate[31] or capitulate[32] with them, who had before tyme broken so many treates: He told them resolutely, that onlesse they wolde yelde vp theyr towne vnto hym frankely[33] without condicio[n], [9] and cause man, woman, and chylde to yssewe into the feldes, submitting them to his wyll and pleasoure, he wolde put them to the sworde, and theyr towne to the fyre. The Prouost answeryng that it were better for them to stande to theyr defence, then yelde to that condicyon. This was rather a false practise of the Prouost and the herauldes, therby tespye the force and order of oure campe then for any zeale they hadde to yelde theyr towne, as it appeared after. Wheruppon co[m]maundement was gyuen to the sayd Prouost and offycers at armes vpon theyr perill to departe. In the meane tyme word was brought by a heraulde of ours (whome the lorde Lieutenaunt had sent to somone the castell) that the erle Bothewell and the lord Hume[34] with the nombre of two thousande horsemen were entered the towne, and were determyned to the defense [10] therof, vpon whiche knowledge the lord Lieutenau[n]t sent with diligence to the vanwarde that they shulde merche towardes the towne. And Syr Cristofer Morice[35] lieutenaunt of thordynaunce, was co[m]maunded tapproche the gate called the Cany gate, with certen Batry peices, whiche gate lay so, that the ordynaunce must be brought vp a brode strete of the suburbes, directly agaynste the sayde Cany gate, whiche was the losse of certen of our gonners. And before that any batry could be made by the sayd ordynaunce, dyuers of the capytains of the sayde vanward (the better to comforthe theyre souldyars) assayled the sayde gate with suche corage, that they repulsed the Scottyshe go[n]ners from the loupes[36] of the same, and there slewe [and] hurte sundry of theyr go[n]ners, and by force drewe one peice of artillary out of one of the sayde loupes. Our ar- [11] chers [and] hackbutters shotte so holly to the batylmentes[37] of the gate and waule, that no man durst shewe him selfe at the defence of the same, by reason wherof, our gonners hadde good leysoure to brynge a Canon harde to the gate, whiche after thre or foure shotte made entry to oure souldiars, who at theyr breakyng in slewe thre or foure hundreth Scottes, of suche as were founde armed. In the meane tyme therle Bothwel and the lorde Hume with theyr co[m]panye fled and saued themselfes by an other waye issuynge out towardes the Castell of the sayde towne: þe situatio[n] wherof is of such strength that it can not be approched but by one waye, whiche is by the hyghe strete of the towne, and the strongest parte

---

[31] treate (treat) — to carry on negotiations
[32] capitulate — to make terms of surrender, to bargain, to parley
[33] frankely (frankly) — without restraint or constraint
[34] George Home (ca. 1506–ca. 1549), 4th Lord Home.
[35] Sir Christopher Morris (ca. 1493–1545), English gunnery expert in the ordnance office, and master and lieutenant of ordnance from 1536 to 1544.
[36] loupes (loops) — the openings in the parapet of a fortification
[37] batylmentes (battlements) — the indented parapets at the tops of walls

of the same lyeth to beate the sayde strete, whiche was the losse of dyuers of our men, with the shot of thordynaunce out of the sayde Ca- [sig. B.iii./*12*] stell, whiche contynually beat alongeste the sayde hyghe strete. And co[n]syderynge the strength of the sayde castell with the situation therof, it was concluded not to lose any tyme nor to waste and consume our munition about the siege therof. All be it the same was courragiously and daungerously attempted, tyl one of our peices, with shotte out the sayde castel, was stroken and dismounted.

And finally it was determyned by the sayde lorde Lieutenaunt vtterly to ruynate and destroye the sayde towne with fyer, which for that the nyghte drewe faste on, we omytted thoroughly to execute on that daye, but settynge fyer in thre or .iiii. partes of the towne, we repayred for that night vnto our campe. And the nexte mornynge very erly we began where we lefte, and continued burnynge all that daye [and] the two dayes nexte ensuinge contynually, so that [*13*] neither within þe wawles nor in the suburbes was lefte any one house vnbrent, besydes the innumerable botyes spoyles and pyllages that our souldyours brought fro[m] thense, notwithstandyng habundau[n]ce whiche was consumed with fyer. Also we brent thabbey called holy Rodehouse,[38] and the pallice adioynynge to the same.

In the meane tyme whyle we held the countrye thus occupyed, there came vnto vs .iiii.M. of our lyghte horsemen from the borders by the kynges maiesties appoyntement, who after theyr co[m]mynge dyd suche exploytes in rydyng and deuastyng the countrie, that within .vii. myles euery waye of Edenborrough they lefte neyther pyle,[39] village nor house standynge vnbrente, nor stakes of corne, besydes great nombres of cattayles which they brought dayly in to the armye, [and] met also with much [*14*] good stuffe,[40] whiche thinhabitau[n]tes of Edenborrough hadde for the sauetie of the same conuayed out of þe towne.

In this meane season syr Nicholas Poyntz[41] by ordre of my lord Lieutenaunt passed the ryuer, and wan by force the towne of Kynghorne, and the same brent with certeyne other townes on that syde.

After this exploytes done at Edenborough and all the countrye there aboutes deuasted, the kynges sayde Lieutenaunt thynkynge the Scottes not to be condyngly ponished for theyr falshed vsed to the kinges maiestie, determyned not to returne without doynge them more dyspleasure, gaue ordre with þe saide syr Cristofer Morice for the reshyppynge of the great artyllary, reseruynge onely certen small peices to kepe the felde, gyuynge also com[m]au[n]deme[n]t to euery Capitayn to receiue [*15*] vittayles out of the sayde shyppes for theyr companyes for .vi. dayes. And for the caryage of the same, caused one thousand of our worst horsemen to be set on fote, and the same horses deuyded egally to euery Capitayn of hundredes, for the better caryage of theyr vittailes. The men that

---

[38] Holyrood Abbey.
[39] pyle—a small castle, tower, or stronghold
[40] stuffe (stuff)—provisions of food, munitions of war
[41] Sir Nicholas Poyntz (ca. 1510–1556), English officer.

rode vpon the saide horses appoynted to attende vpon the sayde vittayls, which was done: besydes dyuers small cartes, which we recouered in the cou[n]try, the whiche with such cattaylles as we had there, dyd great seruice in drawyng of our vittayls, tentes, and other necessaries. These thynges beyng supplyed the xiiii. day of Maye, we brake downe the peire of the hauen of Lythe, and brent euery stycke of it, [and] toke forth the two goodly shyppes, manned them and put them in ordre tattende vpon the kinges maiesties shippes, theyr balast was canon shotte of yro[n] [sig. C./*16*] which we found in the towne to the nombre of .iiii. score thousande: the reste of the Scottishe shyppes mete[42] to serue, we brought awaye bothe they and our owne almost pestered[43] with the spoyle and botyes of oure souldyars and maryners.

That done we abandoned our selues clearely from our shyppes, hauynge firme intent to retorne home by lande, whiche we dyd. And to gyue them better occasyon to shewe them selfes in the felde agaynst vs, we lefte neyther pyle, village, towne nor house in our waye homewardes vnbrent. In the meane tyme of the contynuaunce of our army at Lithe as is afore sayd, our shyps vpon þe sees were not idle, for they lefte neyther shyppe, Crayer,[44] nor bote, belongyng to nether village, town, creke, nor hauen of neither syde the Frith betwene sterlyng and the mouth of the riuer vnbrent or brought away, [*17*] whiche contayneth in length fyftie myles. Contynuynge of tyme they also brent a greate no[m]bre of townes and vilages on bothe sydes the said water, and wan a fortres situated on a strong Island, called Ynchgarue, which they rased and destroyed.

The .xv. daye of Maye we dislodged our campe out of the towne of Lith, and set fyer in euery house, and brent it to the grounde. The same nyght we encamped at a towne of the lorde Setons,[45] where we brente and reased his cheife castell called Seton, whiche was ryght fayre, [and] destroyed his orchardes [and] gardens whiche were the fayrest and beste in ordre that we sawe in al that cou[n]try: We dyd hym þe more despyt, because he was the cheife laborer to helpe theyr Cardynall out of pryson, the onely auctour of theyr calamytie.

The same daye we brente a fayre towne of the erle Bothewelles, cal- [*18*] led Hadyngton, with a great nonry and a house of freres. The nexte nyght after we encamped besydes Dunbar, [and] there the Scottes gaue a smal alarme to our campe, but our watches was in such a redynes that they hadde no vauntage there, but were fayne to recoyle w[i]t[h]out doynge of any harme. That nyght they loked for vs to haue burnt the towne of Dunbar, which we differred tyll the mornyng at the dislodgynge of our campe, whiche we executed by v,C. of our hackbutters beyng backed with .v.C. horsemen. And by reason we toke them in the mornynge, who hauyng watched all nyght for our co[m]mynge, and perceyuynge our

---

[42] mete—fit
[43] pestered—overloaded
[44] crayer—a small trading vessel
[45] George Seton (ca. 1513–1549), 4th Lord Seton.

army to dislodge [and] depart, thought them selues saue of vs, were newly gone to theyr beddes, and in theyr fyrste slepes[46] closed in with fyer, men women and chyldren were suffocated and brent.

[*19*] That mornynge being very mystie and foggie, we hadde perfite knowledge by our espyalles, that þe Scottes had assembled a great power at a strayt called the Pease.[47] The cheife of this assembly was the lordes Seton, Hume, and Bouclugh,[48] w[i]t[h] them the hole power of the Marshe and Teuidall. This daye in our marchynge dyuers of theyr prickers,[49] by reason of the saide myste, gaue vs alarme and came so far within our army, þ[a]t they vnhorsed one betwene the vanwarde and the battayll beynge within two hundreth fote of þe lorde Lieutenaunt. At þe alarme one of theyr best prickers, called Jocke holly Burton, was taken, who confessed that the saide Scottishe lordes were redy at the passage with þe nomber of ten thousand good men. And for asmoch as the myst yet contynued and dyd not breake beynge paste noon, the vanwarde beynge [*20*] within a myle of the sayde passage, enteringe into daungerous waies for an armye to marche in soche wether that one coulde not escrye[50] an other twenty yardes of, we concluded if the wether did not breake vp, to haue encamped our selues vpon the same ground, where we dyd remayne for the space of two houres. And about two of the clock at after noon the sonne brake out, the fogge went awaye, and a cleare daye was lefte vs, wherof euery man receiued as yt were a newe corage, longynge to se the enemies. Who being ready for vs at the said passage, [and] seing vs come in good ordre of battayle as men determyned to passe throughe them, or to leaue our bones w[i]t[h] the[m], abode vs but two shotes of a faucon,[51] but skaled euery man his way to the high mountaines, which was harde at their handes and couered with flockes of their people. The [*21*] passage was soche that hauynge no lette, it was thre howres before all the armye coulde passe it. The same night tharmye encamped at a pyle called Ranton .viii. myles from our borders whiche pyle was a very yll neighbour to þe garison of Berwick. The same we reased and threwe downe to the grounde.

The next daye being the .xviii. of Maye tholle armye entred into Berwicke and ended this viage w[i]t[h] the losse b[e]nneth of forty of the kynges mayesties people thankes be to our lord. The same day at the same insta[n]t that þe army entred into Berwyck, our hole flete [and] nauye of shyppes which we sent from vs at Lyth arryued before Berwycke: as God wolde be knowe[n] to fauour our

---

[46] fyrste slepes (first sleeps) — pre-modern Europeans often divided their sleeping into "first sleep" from dusk until the middle of the night, a period of wakefulness in the middle of the night, and "second sleep" until dawn.

[47] The gorge of Cockburnspath.

[48] Sir Walter Scott (ca. 1495–1552), 3rd Lord of Buccleuch.

[49] prickers — light horsemen, scouts, skirmishers

[50] escrye (descry) — to espy, to scout, to get sight of

[51] faucon (falcon) — a light cannon

maisters cause who euer p[re]serue his most royal maiestie w[i]t[h] lo[n]ge [and] prosperous life, [and] many yeares to reygne in the[m]perial seate of the monarchie of all Bretayne.

[*22*] The names of the cheife borow- | ghes, Castelles, and townes, brente | and desolated by þe kinges army | beynge late in Scotlande, be- | sydes a great nombre of vil- | lages, pyles, and stedes,[52] | whiche I can not | name.

THe borow [and] towne of Edenborough w[i]t[h] thabbey called Holly roode house, and the kynges palice adioynynge to the same.

> The towne of Lythe brent, and the hauen and pere destroyed.
> The castel [and] village of Cragmyller
> Thabbey of Newe Bottell.
> Parte of Muskelborowe towne, w[i]t[h] the chapel of our lady of Lawret.
> Preston towne and the castell.
> Hadington towne with the freres and nunry.
> A castell of Olyuer Sancklers.
> The towne of Dunbarre.
> Laureston w[i]t[h] the grawnge.

[*23*]

Drylawe.	Markle.
Wester Crag	Trapren.
Enderlegh, the pyle [and] the towne.	Kirkland hyll.
Broughton.	Hatherwike.
Thester Felles.	Beston.
Crawnend.	East Barnes.
Dudistone.	Bowland.
Stanhows.	Butterden.
The Ficket.	Quickwod.
Beuerton.	Blackborne.
Tranent.	Raunton.
Shenstone.	Byldy and the towre.

Townes [and] villages brent by the flete vpon the see with a great number of pyles and villages whiche I can not name nor reherse, which be all deuasted and layd desolate.

> Kinkorne. S[aint]. Minetes. The quenes ferry. Parte of Petynwaynes.
> The brent Islande.

---

[52] stedes (steads) — towns, villages, hamlets

Other newe prosperouse adue[n]tures of late against the Scottes.

[**sig. D./24**] AFter the tyme that the Erle of Hertford Lieutenaunt to the kynges maiestie in the north parties of the realme had dissolued the armye whiche lately had bene within Scotland, [and] repayred to the kynges hyghnes: The lorde Eure[53] with many other valiant wise gentylmen abyding in the marches of the North parte, intendinge not by idelnes to surcesse[54] in occasio[n]s co[n]uenient, but to proue whether the Scottes had yet learned by theyr importable[55] losses lately chau[n]ced to them to te[n]der theyr owne weales by true and reasonable vnytynge [and] adioynyng them selues to the kynges maiesties louyng liege people, toke consultation by the aduyse of Syr Raufe Eure[56] his sonne, [and] other sage forwarde gentylmen, vpon the .ix, day of Iune at a place named Mylnefeld, from whence by comen agre- [**25**] ment the said lord with a good number of men made such hast i[n]to Scotland, that by .iiii. of the clocke after the next mydnight he was marched w[i]t[h]in a half myle from þe towne whervnto they tended named Iedworth.[57] Mayntenant[58] after theyr co[m]mynge a messenger was sent to the prouost of the said towne lettyng hym to know that the lord Eure was come before the towne to take it into the kynges allegiaunce by meanes of peace, yf therunto þe Scottes wold truely agre: or els by force of armes to sacke þe same, if therin resiste[n]ce were fou[n]d. Wherunto the prouost euen lyke to proue him selfe a Scot, answered by waye of request, that they myght be respected vpo[n] theyr answer vntyll þe noon tyde, or els to mayntene theyr towne with defence: hauynge hope þ[a]t in tracting[59] [and] dryuyng[60] of tyme, they myghte worke some olde cowardly suttelte. But vpon declaratio[n] made the snake crewlyng vnder þe flowres[61] [**sig. D.ii./26**] easely appeared to the[m] which therin had experience, knowledge also beynge had, that the townesmen had bent[62] .vii. or .viii. peices of ordinau[n]ce in the marketstede.[63] Wherfore þe lord Eure, parte of his co[m]pany beinge into .iii. bandes deuided, [and] abidyng at iii. seueral costes[64] of the same towne, to thend þ[a]t there myght be .iii. entres at one tyme

---

53 Baron William Eure (ca. 1483–1547), a lord of the English Borders.
54 surcesse (surcease)—forbear, omit
55 importable—unbearable, unendurable
56 Sir Ralph Eure (1508–1545).
57 Jedburgh.
58 mayntenant (maintenant)—immediately
59 tracting—prolonging, protracting, delaying
60 dryvyng (driving)—elapsing
61 Perhaps an allusion to Virgil, *Eclogue* 3.93.
62 bent—directed, aimed, cocked
63 marketstead—market-place
64 costes (coasts)—the side or edge of a piece of land

made into the towne: appoynted [and] deuised that the gu[n]ners whiche had battered certen places playne and open, shold entre in one syde, and þe kernes[65] on an other syde, [and] syr Raufe Euers of the thyrd side. But it fortuned that euen vpon the approcheme[n]t of the men to there entrees, the Scottes fledde from theyr ordinau[n]ces leuyng them vnshot into the woodes there about with all other people in the same towne, in þe which flyghte was slayne aboue the no[m]ber of .C.lx. Scottes, hauyng for that reco[m]pence therof the losse of .vi. Englishmen only. The people thus [*27*] fled, and the towne geuen to the Englyshmen by chau[n]ce of warre: þe gunners burned þe abbey, the graye freres,[66] [and] dyuers bastell[67] and fortified houses, wherof were many in that towne: the goodes of þe same towne being fyrste spoyled, whiche layded[68] at theyr departyng .CCCCC. horses, besides .vii. peices of ordinau[n]ce. In theyr retorne likewyse they passed burnyng dyuers places, towres, [and] castelles: as the towre of Callyngcrag, the castell of Sestorth, Otterburn, Cowboge, Marbottel church with many other lyke, vntyll they came to a place called Kyrkyetth[ol]m, beinge .x. myle fro[m] certen villages w[i]t[h]in Englysh grou[n]de named Hetto[n], Tylmouth, [and] Twysell, which appered to them burnyng: for the which cause syr Raufe Eure [and] the capitain of Norh[a]m acco[m]panied w[i]t[h] .CCCCC. horsemen, rode in suche hast towardes the fyer, þ[a]t at what tyme the said syr Raufe dyd set vpo[n] the Scottes, [*28*] whiche had burned the village, he had not with hym aboue .CC. horsemen, neuerthelesse the Scottes vpo[n] the onely sight of þe sta[n]dardes, vsed for theyr defence their light fete, and fledde in so mych haste that dyuers Englysh horses were tyred in þe pursuit, but ouertake[n] there was a great nomber, wherof were slayne many, partly by þe fearsnes of the English men, partly by the giltie cowardnes of þe Scottes. And truely to speake in fewe wordes, in this acte doyng, reason wyl scarsely suffice to p[er]suade the truth: in so mych that there was dyuers Englysh men wherof euery one man had .viii. or .ix. prisonars besyde such whiche was slayne, whose number is certaynly knowen to be aboue a hundreth or mo[re]. And yet in this skyrmish not one Englishma[n] taken nother[69] slayne, thankes be to god. Also further here is to be reme[m]bred that the Englyshe men in theyr returne from the sacke of Ied- [*29*] worth draue [and] brought out of Scotland into England a great no[m]ber of cattel bothe note[70] and shepe.

Furthermore to the apparant co[n]tinuau[n]ce of goddes fauour vnto þe pourposes of thenglishmen it is to be certenly knowe[n], that the .xv. daye of

---

[65] kernes (kerns)—lightly armed Irish or Scottish soldiers. The reference here is to English soldiers from the border with Scotland—unusual, but not inexplicable.

[66] graye freres (gray friars)—Franciscans

[67] bastell (bastille)—a fortified tower, a small fortress

[68] layded—loaded

[69] nother—nor

[70] note (neat)—ox or bullock; cow or heifer

Iune, there was an other Rode[71] made by dyuers Englisshemen to a towne called Synlawes, where as diuers bastel houses was destroyed viii. scottes take[n], [and] .lx. oxen brought away: for þe retorne wherof a no[m]ber of scottyshme[n], pursued very ernestly, who for theyr co[m]myng lost .vi. of theyr lyues, [and] .l. of theyr horsemen.

And vpon tewesdaye next folowinge, syr George Bowes, syr Jhon Witherington, Henry Eure, [and] Leonell Graye roded to þe abbey of Coldyngh[a]m, [and] demau[n]ded the same: but it was denyed ernestly, in so much þ[a]t after an assault made for .v. houres space, it was burnt all, sauyng the church which hauyng fyre in þe one [30] ende smoked so by the dryfte of the wynd toward the Englysh men, þ[a]t it could not co[n]uenie[n]tly the[n] be burned. The stoore of the cattell [and] of þe other goodes there, serued well the spoyle of the souldyours. In this abbey was slayne one monke, [and] .iii. other scottes. And amongest thenglyshe was one only gu[n]ner slayn by a peice of ordinaunce shotte out of þe steple.

Sence this iorney þe .xx. of Iune a co[m]pany of Tyndale [and] Redesdale, w[i]t[h] other valyent men, ventred vpo[n] the greatest towne in all Teuidale, named Skraysbrugh, a towne of þe lorde Hunthylles,[72] where as besydes rych spoyles [and] great plenty of note and shepe .xxxviii. persons were taken, addyng therunto that which is a maruelose truth, that is to saye, these prysoners beyng taken, iii. scottes beynge slayne w[i]t[h] dyuers wounded, no one English man was other hurte or wounded.

In these victories who is to be [31] most hyghest lauded but God, by whose goodnesse the Englyshe men hath had of a greate season notable victories [and] maters[73] wordy[74] triumphs? And for the contynuau[n]ce of goddes fauour towarde vs, let vs pray for the prosperous estate of oure noble good and victorious lorde gouernour and kynge, [et]c. for whose sake doubtelesse god hath spred his blessyng ouer vs, in peace to haue myrth, and in warres to haue victorye.

Imprynted at London in Powls | churchyarde by Reynolde | Wolfe. at the sygne of þe | Brasen serpent. | Anno. 1544.
   Cum priuilegio | ad imprimendum solum.

---

[71] rode (road) — raid
[72] Lord Robert Rutherford of Hunthill (ca. 1490–1544).
[73] maters (matters) — materials for writing, speech, discourse
[74] wordy — worthy

Certayn and tru good nues, from the syege of the isle Malta (1565) || STC (2nd ed.) # 17213.5

Newes from Vienna (1566) || STC (2nd ed.) #24716

In May 1565, some 40,000 Turkish soldiers and sailors invaded and besieged the Christian pirate nest of Malta, defended by the Knights of St. John; after a heroic resistance by the garrison, the Turks abandoned the siege in September—and with it, much of their chances of securing naval dominance in the central Mediterranean.[1] In 1566, the dying Suleiman I the Magnificent led his Turkish troops on a last campaign against the Christian forces in Hungary. While Suleiman I was taking the city of Szigetvár, his vizier, Pertev Pasha, besieged and conquered the city of Gyula. These two conquests secured Ottoman control of the Turkish third of Hungary for the next century. *Certayn and tru good nues, from the syege of the isle Malta* (1565) and *Newes from Vienna* (1566) send news during hopeful moments (for the defenders) in the middle, respectively, of the sieges of Malta and Gyula.

These two works illustrate the international character of the military news pamphlet genre. In contrast to *The late expedicion in Scotlande* (1544), written in English about an English army, presumably by an Englishman, these two pamphlets were translated into English, written by foreigners, and describe the exploits of Catholics against Muslim armies. These illustrate not only the genre similarity of military news pamphlets throughout Western and Central Europe, but also that a mid-century English readership took part in an international community of military news, for which religious division was not an absolute bar. *Newes from Vienna* (1566) also includes what would become a notable feature of the genre—the prayer of thanksgiving at the end, functioning as an editorial comment upon the news of Christian victory.

---

[1] See *Historie of the War of Malta*, ed. Bonavita.

[TITLE PAGE]

[C]ERTAYN AND | tru good nues, fro[m] the syege | of the Isle Malta, wyth the goodly | vyctorie, wyche the Christenmen, by the | fauour of God, have ther latlye obtayned, | agaynst the Turks, before the forteres | of saint Elmo.

Translat owt of Frenche yn to Englysh.

And nuli prented yn Gaunt, | the 27. of August.

M. CCCCC. LXV.

[*1*] The copie of a letter writen, by the ryght honoroble lorde, brother iohn valet,[2] great master ond Comander of the Rodes, now Malta, to the ryght noble [and] worthie Capitayn, don Garcia of Toledo[3] Capitayn general to the kyng of spayn. Contayning the late nues last com from Malta, wyth the horrible [and] pytiful assautes made by the Turks apon the sayd fortressis, and the fayer victori, wych the Christians had before saynt Elmo, the xv. [and] xvj. day of Iune last past.

SYNS I sent vnto your honor the vertuus knyght saluage,[4] I wrat twyes, [and] sent the letters to Gozzo, God grant they may surely pass, and afterward we sent fourth a lyght boot wyth owers, cauled a fregat, wych making all dilige[n]ce to goo [and] co[m], were browght to such necesiti, being abowt .ij. leagues owt yn the sea, that they were fayn to take flight to saue the[m] self, for asmuche as they were chased by thenimies, [and] they cast theyr lettres yn to the sea, [and] so retournyng recouered[5] agayn the la[n]d of Malta, by the grace of God. After the siege of Marzo Sirocco was remoued,[6] [and] I forseyng to be ryght necessari to aduertise[7] your honor, that the hauen[8] ys not yeat so neare enclosed[9] wyth thenimie, I caused to be browght from the land a brigantin, or smal shyp, to Marzo scala, bycause the syege[10] of owr enimies lyeth on the other syde, I hoope the same shall come wythowt [**sig. A2/2**] any stop (wyche God grant) a[n]d that to aduertyse your honor that the .xv. day of Iune, toward euenyng, the

---

    [2] Jean Parisot de la Valette (1494–1568), Grand Master of the Knights of St. John of Jerusalem.

    [3] Don Garcia de Toledo, then Viceroy of Sicily for Philip II, king of Spain.

    [4] Chevalier Rafael Salvage.

    [5] recovered — reached, returned to

    [6] removed — abandoned

    [7] advertise — inform

    [8] hauen (haven) — harbor, anchorage, port

    [9] enclosed — surrounded, hemmed in, blockaded

    [10] syege (siege) — the besieging force

hwole armye or syege wyth all theyr shyps passed by here, that they were easili perceyued of owrs fro[m] the hauen, so that the nyght hyndered vs nothyng, for the great noyse wych the shyps [and] galleis made, wyche were al dysarmed, [and] yll apoynted, hauing left their hole, [and] good shyps at Marzo muscheto, [and] one part of the[m] at saynct Giorgis. Whye the syege of Marzo Muscheto ys raysed, the cause thereof ys lack of fresh water, and yt may be for the great feare they haue of the armye of your lordshyp, for as we vndersta[n]de they be aduertysed how there are yn a reddines at Messina 150. galleis [and] other shyps, therfor they dare not co[m] so fer as saynt Pawles stayers, but lye as neare to their armie (wych ys a lond) as they possible may, neuertheles albeyt that this place lyeth so nye, yeat ys yt not so sure, yf they were yn hast, they myght hardli co[m] to theyr shyps, as thowgh they were ferder of, on the side of Marzo Sirocco ys not one man to be sene, for they haue left yt vp, [and] set fyar on the howsis of saynt Catharins, [and] saynt Ihons, now they be gon from the sayd Marzo to-ward theyr syege, wych ys alway before saynt Elmo, we se playnli that almyghti God purposeth to defend the sayd place of saynt Elmo, for asmuche as yeaster-day in the morning owr me[n] resysted more by miracle, then other wyse, one assault during .iiij. howrs lo[n]g, wyche theni- [3] mies dyd make yn dyuers pla-cis, speciali at a brydge that was bwylt by the[m], wyth the masts [and] decks of .iiij. galeis, on the syde of Marzo muscheto, wyche assault they made .iiij. tymes, [and] so furiusli that at euerie tyme they browght fresh men, [and] at everi tyme were repulst, [and] bet back wyth great loss of theyr men, and not wythout loss of owrs, for of owr syde remayned ded two hundred, and .150. hurt and Capi-tan mirande was slayn wych was great gryef vnto vs, a[n]d of turks were slayne abowt 2000. and as many hurt, and they were left the most part yn the dyches of saynt Elmo, wyth this victori owr men be so encorraged [and] made hardye,[11] that I trust to keape thys place u[n]tyl the comi[n]g of your lordshyps exelence, not wythstanding owr enimies be muche refreshed, [and] more fyers [and] des-perat, the[n] before, as I haue not sene the lyke, for they haue shot wythin .xv. dayes .xiij.M shot of artilarie, neuertheles yf I may ffynd soccours (as I hoop to do) by meanes of owr galleis I dowbt not a whyt, but to keape thys place, for the saff garding of the wych, I haue almost spent all that I haue, goods [and] men, and we are resolued [and] vtterli determined apo[n] this poynt, to dye toguyther, hooping and looking affter ayd, [and] soccours fro[m] your exelence. Consider-ing [and] seyng yn what dangier we may co[m] yn, thorowgh long tarians a[n]d delayes, we beseke your exele[n]ce, not to fayle to gyue vs som asystance, at lest wyth som nomber of valiant men, wyche is easie to be don, by that good [sig. A3/4] meanes I haue certified you, seying the syege ys retyred from Marzo sy-rocco they may la[n]d yn the same syde cauled pietra nigra, all owr comfort [and]

---

[11] hardye (hardy)—courageous

hoope, next God, ys yn your exelence, to the wyche I comme[n]d [and] submyt
my self hwolye, prayng the God almyghti for good auenture,[12] [and] prosperiti.
From Malta the xviij. day of Iune 1565.

Subscribed

By me I. Vallet.

Relation made by ORLANDO MAGRO pilot to the chyff galley of the great
master coma[n]der of the Rhodes, now Malta the wyche aryued at Messina the
.xxvij. day of Iune 1565. And sayth:

HOW THAT HE PARTED from Malta the sonday .xvij. day of the month,
about half an owr after son,[13] and .iiij. companions wyth hym wyth a smal fregat
of iiij. owers, ha-[5]uing letters of the great master of Malta to don Garcia, [and]
sayth that the turks hauyng shot agai[n]st the fortres of saynt Elmo .xviij. dayes
toguyther, wyth .xxiiij. peacis of great artillari [and] assaulted yt sondrye tymes,
at the fyrst asault got the vttmost[14] fortres wythout[15] the dychis, named saynt
Ruelmo the second tyme they went wyth 2000. men and ladders prepared to enter, and last, wych was fryday .xv. day of this month, they hauing made a brydge
wyth the masts [and] d[o]cks of iiij galleis [and] so coming yn to the trenchis,
ryght ouer against where they had made the batterie, hoping [and] thinking by
thys meane, easli to enter, but they fownd them self deceyued, for they wythyn
defended the[m] so valiantli, and the brydge wych the Turks had made, burnt
wyth gon powlder [and] artificiall fyer, and beat the[m] yn soche sort that ther
remayned ded .800. Turks, and 600. hurt, and owr men toke .ij. ensygnes[16] one
of the wyche was, of the general Capitan by lande named Prali,[17] and thother was
of Dragut,[18] yn thys assault were mounted vp .30. Turks an hye ouer the bulwark
and they of the castel of saynt Angelo shot to stryk thes .30 turks, and stroke ded
eyght of owr own men, and afterward charged, and shot agayn, [and] stroke thes
.30. Turks lykwise ded all sauyng one, among the wyche there wer vj. of the hows
of the rayes,[19] [and] one was capitan general of the Rhodes, whose name was Portuch hali, [and] the other dragut wyche remayned onlye alyue.

[6] This assault dured fyue howres toguyther, so muche that the Turks were
forced to retyar back against ther wyll wyth great loss of theyr men. In this asault
dyed of owrs abowt .200. and 150. hurt [and] wonded, and of the Turks wer
slayn abowt .2000. [and] .2000 hurt, of wych the more part were left wythin

---

[12] aventure (adventure)—fortune, luck

[13] son (sun)—sunrise or sunset

[14] uttmost (utmost)—farthest off

[15] wythout (without)—outside

[16] ensygnes (ensigns)—standards, banners

[17] Piali (ca. 1530–?), an admiral of the Ottoman fleet during the siege of Malta.

[18] Dragut (1485–1565), also known as Turgut Reis; Bey of Tunis, and an admiral of
the Ottoman fleet during the siege of Malta. He died during the siege.

[19] rayes (rais, reis)—chiefs, governors

the trenchis [and] dychis of saynt Elmo. Item, that Dragut apon sonday the .xvij day of the month set fyar yn the bulwark, or bastilion,[20] wych they had made. Yn the marketplace of Marzo muscheto, wher they had .iiij. great peacis of artilari. Ite[m] that after the last asault, the most part of the syege, retorned by nyght toward the galleis, and are remayned a land onli abowt 3000. Turks, to gard the artillari, and they shot now wyth no mo[re] then syx piecis,[21] and that they haue shot yn all abowt .13000. stroks[22] or shot. Item, that .ij. dayes before their last assault their syege was retyered from Marzo Sirocco, hauing brent[23] the fortres wych they had mad ther, [and] retyered toward the valey of saynt Paul, where thys pylot leaft them at hys departyng thence. Item, that certayn Christiens taken by the Turks and escaped again affirme, that they sayd yn the Turks armie, that don Garcia had a hundred and fyuetie shyps and galeys to guyther to recounter wyth them, and that the Turks had great feare, a[n]d therfor they went the most part of the[m] by nyght to theyr shyps. Item, that the great master writeth how thei had fownd a quyckspryng[24] of freshe wa- [7] ter wythin the town named Burgo, wych wa[s] thowght as a miracle.

Item the master of the postes of Messina wrat that the galley of portuch hali wyche was slayn yn the assault was bowged[25] and sonck by owr artilarie. Item that the bassa[26] takyng the muster of hys sowdyowrs and nauie, fownd fower galleys lackyng, of hys nomber.

Item, we vndersta[n]d by other letters, that when owr enymies came to offer to set thys brydge wych they had made vearie artificiali[27] owr men wyche were wythin were yn great dowbt [and] feare, yn so muche that they were ons determyned to render the place, but thorowgh good inspiration and the grace of God, [and] by the hardines of one valiant knyght hauing a two handed swerd yn hys hand, saying that he wold dye for the Cristian fayth, gave to all the rest suche currage, that they obtayned at last the victori. Item that the great master was veari sorrowful for the death of Capitayn mirande.

FINIS.

---

[20] bastilion (bastillion) — a small fortress or castle; a fortified tower
[21] piecis (pieces) — cannon
[22] stroks (strokes) — discharges
[23] brent — burned
[24] quyckspring (quick-spring) — a running spring
[25] bowged (bulged) — to have the bottom staved in
[26] bassa — pasha
[27] artificiali (artificially) — skillfully, artfully

[TITLE PAGE]

Newes from Vi- | enna the .5. day of August .1566. of the | strong Towne and Castell of Iula in Hungary, | xl. myles beyond the riuer Danubius, which was cruelly | assaulted by the great Turke, but nowe by Gods | mighty working re-lieued, [and] the sayd Turks | marueylouslye discomfited and ouer- | throwen. Translated out of hye | Almaine[28] into English, and | printed in Augspurge | by Hans Zim- | merman.

Imprinted at Lon- | don by Iohn Awdeley, dwelling in | litle Britaine streete without[29] Alders- | gate. The .21. of September. | 1566.

[sig. Aii/*1*] Newes from Vienna the .5. day of August .1566. of the Turkes ouerthrow:

AFter that the Emperour of Turkie[30] had besieged with an army of thirty thousand horseme[n] and footemen, the famous town and stro[n]g Castel of Iula in Hungary, lying .xl. dutch myles beyo[n]d the ryuer Danubius, which City had by the space of .vi. weekes sustayned many greuous assaultes: God through his great mercy and goodnes so comforted the sayd towne of Iula and the poore Christians therein, at their earnest praiers, that the Turke with all his host was driuen backe, by the handes of the General called Keretshim Laslawe[31] and hys valiant company. Who not onelye defended the sayd Towne, but also con-strayned the cruell Turkes to retyre, to their great shame and confusion, w[i]t[h] the slaughter of a great number of their Turkish rable. For the which the euerli-uyng God be praysed for euer. The manner of their ouerthrow was thys.

As the foresayd Generall Keretshim did se his aduauntage, wyth Captayne George and other horsmen of Schesians[32] and Hungary, he set vpon the arere-ward[33] of the Turkes, and kylled about .8. thousand of them, and tooke also some of their ar- [*2*] tillery, and followed them so fast, that the Turkes were con-strayned to flee into a marrish grounde, and to breake the wheeles of the rest of their artillery, to saue them selues: which the Christians also tooke, and haue re-seued and taken besydes from the Turkes a great nomber of Christia[n] prisoners, and therewyth a very rych bootye.

The like also hath done that valiant man Magotsrhie the Captayne of Erla, the which making toward the Turkes, did encounter with the Tertarians, setting most valiantly vpon them, and killed about eyght hundred of them.

---

[28]   hye Almaine (high Almaine) — German
[29]   without — outside
[30]   Suleiman I the Magnificent (1494–1566), emperor of the Ottomans from 1520 to 1566. He died during this Hungarian campaign, at the siege of Szigetvár.
[31]   László Kerecsényi.
[32]   Schesians — probably the Saxon soldiers of Transylvania
[33]   arereward — rearguard

A few dayes past the Earle of Serin[34] did encounter with a Turkish Capitayne called Begen, the which Capitaine then had with him a thousa[n]d fresh horsmen, then comming out of Turkye, to go to a towne called Fynffekyrchen. Which Earle did set vpon them in the night, and killed the Captain, and tooke .viii. Camels, and .viii. Moyles[35] laden wyth treasure, and got also twoo read Gwydons,[36] wyth a whole great peece of rych cloth of gold, and also a very fayre and straunge Iewel or token of the field. This foresayd Earle dyd sende vnto the Emperours Maiesty[37] to Vienna for a present, the foresayd Captaynes horse, the which was not onely a very fayre one and good, but also betrapped[38] [and] decked[39] moste rychly. For fyrst the pomel[40] [and] the back part of the saddel was couered ouer with plate of fine Arabick gold, and the rest of the saddel besyde the sytting place, was drest wyth syluer plate, very [sig. A.iii./3] fayre gilded, which sitting place was couered with a fine purple veluet, and þe trappers[41] [and] bridle beset w[i]t[h] litle Turkies[42] and Rubies. The Earle would very fayne haue saued the sayd Capitayne, but the turkish Ianyssery[43] defended themselues so manfully, thinking to haue caryed away safelye their Capitaine, þ[a]t the said Earle w[i]t[h] hys company was constrayned to kyll both them and their Captayne.

Also this valiant Earle of Serin hath got amongest other great prices from the Turkes .xv. thousand Turkish and Hu[n]garish Ducates, which money was brought for the payment of the Turkishe men of warre, which are in the towne called Fynffkyrchen. Thus not onely this said Earle had got to himselfe rich and great prices, but also hys Souldiours haue met with very rich prayes and spoyles.

And now to declare the Mahometical and turkish cruelty of these hellish Turks, which they vse agaynst the Christians (which cannot be declared without weeping and sorowfulnes of mynde) is this in effect. Where euer they ouercome the Christians and take them captiues, they take the yong and lusty[44] men tying

---

[34] Nikola Šubić Zrinski (1508–1566), Ban of Croatia. He died in the defense of Szigetvár; his actions in that defense are the subject of the Hungarian epic *The Peril of Sziget* (1651), written by his great-grandson Nikola Zrinski.

[35] moyles (moils)—hornless cows

[36] gwydons (guidons)—flags or pennants

[37] Maximilian II Habsburg (1527–1576), Holy Roman Emperor from 1564 to 1576.

[38] betrapped—adorned with a trap, a cloth or covering spread over the saddle or harness of a horse

[39] decked—clothed

[40] pomel (pommel)—the upward projecting front part of a saddle

[41] trappers—coverings put over a horse or other beast of burden, made of metal or leather for purpose of defence, or of cloth for shelter and adornment

[42] turkies—turquoises

[43] janyssery (janissary)—an elite Turkish infantry, recruited as tribute from Christian children

[44] lusty—healthy, strong, vigorous

them to their horses [and] famishe[45] them to death. The old men and women they cut in peeces, deflouring the maydens and young women very villanously. The sely[46] Infants and yong Babes lying in their cradels smyling vpon them, they take out very cruelly and sticke them on long poles and so gore them to death without pitye or [4] mercy, and this very spitefully they do in the sight of the Infantes Parentes. The residue of them which they keepe alyue being men, they vse as beastes for all kynde of drudgery and toyle, more cruelly entreating them then their brute beastes. To the women and children whych they keepe alyue, they vse such Sodomish[47] abhomination and tyranny, as may not for shame be knowen, nor wythout harty sorow be declared. Wherefore it behoueth al Christian Princes and good Christians to wythstand thys cruel Turckish enemy, [and] to set to theyr helpyng handes, such as can to helpe to resist hym with some power of warre: and suche other good Christians as cannot helpe these our Christian brethre[n] (so cruelly assaulted) by this kinde of meanes: yet at least to helpe them with their godly praiers. For if thus he proceede forwarde to take the vpper land,[48] it wyl redound to the great plague and ruine of whole Christendome. Wherefore that thus it may not come to pas, let vs not cease to cal vpon our heauenly father for his mightye defence, who so mercifully hath heard the praiers of his poore afflicted children. And also geue him hartye thankes for this great ouerthrow of thys his Christes and our cruell enemy.

[5] A Prayer [and] thankes | geuyng, for the defence of the Chri- | stians agaynst the cruel Turke.

O Eternal God and most mercyfull father, we geue thee harty thanks for this thy mightye woorking in ouerthrowing that cursed and cruell Turke, the enemy of thy deare sonne Christ Iesus, and hys deare Christians, and for relieuing his poore afflicted members,[49] in deliuering them from his and their bloody handes: Wherefore (deare father) we beseche thee to continue in this thy merciful defending them, and in ouerthrowing his tirannical power, that they hereby may wel feele and know, that ther is none other God besides thee[50] [and] thy sonne Iesus Christ our Sauiour. Preserue (O Lord) those godlye [and] Christian Princes which venter their liues against this thi enemy, as namely the Emperours Maiesty with his two brethren, and all hys whole nobility, geuing them prosperous succes [and] victorious conquest. Grau[n]t this O Father for thy deare sonnes sake Iesus Christ our Sauiour. So be it.

---

[45] famishe (famish)—starve
[46] sely (silly)—helpless, defenceless, pitiable, miserable
[47] Sodomish (sodomitical)—characterized by sodomy; i.e., unnatural sexual intercourse
[48] upper land—this may be a misprint of "upper hand," or it may refer to the unconquered parts of Hungary, upstream along the Danube
[49] members—members of the Christian community. Cf. 1 Corinthians 12:27.
[50] Cf. Isaiah 44:6, 45:21.

*A discourse of such things as are happened in the armie of
my lordes the princes of Nauarre, and of Condey* (1569) ||
STC (2nd ed.) #11269

The third of the French Wars of Religion began in September 1568 when the
Huguenot (Protestant) leaders, Prince Louis de Condé and Admiral Gaspard de
Coligny, fled from the threat of assassination by the Catholic government, and
rallied a new Huguenot army in La Rochelle. The Huguenots would be defeated
by the king's army at Jarnac in March 1569, but the royal offensive ran out of
steam thereafter; the Peace of Saint-Germain, relatively favorable to the Huguenots, was signed in August 1570. All in all it was an inconclusive war that ended
in a stalemate. This pamphlet narrates the fortunes of the main Huguenot armies
in the autumn of 1568. These were engaged during these months in a series of
minor and generally inconsequential skirmishes with the royal armies; they are
rendered here as a series of Huguenot triumphs.

The pamphlet is translated from the French, and was, presumably, originally a Huguenot pamphlet. As such, it served also as Huguenot propaganda for
a French readership, as it described the successes of virtuous Huguenot leaders
against cowardly, despicable Catholics. To some extent, therefore, the English
audience were the accidental recipients of domestic Hugenot propaganda; but to
some extent they were the deliberate targets of a Huguenot plea for sympathy and,
ultimately, friendly intervention. We see here one of the first salvos of a decades-
long propaganda war, by which French and Netherlandish Protestants used military news as a means to woo their English co-religionists. Ironically, the pamphlet
also served to illustrate the bloody nature of the wars in France: although likely intended to promote English intervention, it probably reinforced the wariness
Englishmen felt about committing themselves to any sort of war abroad.

[TITLE PAGE]

A discourse of | such things as are | *happened in the armie* | of my lordes the prin- | *ces of Nauarre,*[1] *and of* | Condey,[2] since the | moneth of | September last. | 1568.

Seene and allowed.

Imprinted at | London, by Henry Byn- | neman, for Lucas | Haryson. | 1569.

[sig. A.iii./*1*] *A Discourse of things hap-* | pened in Fraunce, since the | *Moneth of September.* | Anno. 1568.

WHan Gods' goodnesse and prouidence, with manifest help and fatherly care had withdrawn (as al me[n] know) the Prince of Condyes grace, and my Lord the Admiral[3] from the extreme perill, and almost vnaduoydable daunger of their liues, in whiche they were at *Noyers* and *Tanlag,* he guyded and conducted them to *Rochel*: (from one parte of the Realme to the other) without any harme or daunger, with their wyues and children, yea their cradles and nourses, with small trayne,[4] and greate iourneys, by bye wayes [and] villages, vnhandsome and ill appoynted. Not long after, continuing his goodnesse and fauour towardes Monsieur *Dandelot,*[5] [*2*] which was in Britayne, so assisted him, that thoughe he were pursued by the Lordes *Montpensier*[6] and *Martigues,* accompanied with great strength both of footemen and horsemen, to hynder his ioyning with the prince, this notwithstanding, beyonde al expectation he passed ouer the riuer of *Loyre,* with all his troupe in their sight, at a foorde, whiche was neuer marked or knowen of the dwellers them selues. The fauour of God appeared also in the passage of the Queene of *Nauarre*[7] and Prince hir sonne, whiche went through the whole countrey of *Gascoigne* passed the riuer of *Garonne* [and] *Dordoigne,* with other riuers, foordes and perillous streights though they were straightly[8] followed by the Lordes of *Montluc, Terides, Descare,* and *Losses* with great force, without any hyndrance at all. The like was seene also in the passage of Monsieur *Dacier*[9] whiche marched

---

[1] Henri de Bourbon (1553–1610), then prince of Navarre; later Henri IV of France from 1589 to 1610.

[2] Louis I de Bourbon (1530–1569), prince de Condé, Huguenot leader during the 1560s, until his death in 1569 at the battle of Jarnac.

[3] Admiral Gaspard de Coligny (1519–1572), Huguenot leader during the 1560s and 1570s, until his murder at the St. Bartholomew's Day Massacre.

[4] trayne (train) — retinue, suite

[5] François de Coligny (1521–1591), Seigneur d'Andelot, brother of Admiral Gaspard de Coligny. A Huguenot notable.

[6] Louis II de Bourbon (1513–1582), duke de Montpensier. A Catholic notable.

[7] Jeanne d'Albret (1528–1572), queen of Navarre, and leader of the Huguenots.

[8] straightly — immediately

[9] Jacques II de Crussol (1540–1586), later baron d'Acier. A Huguenot notable.

with all his troupe thorough the whole countreys of *Dalphine, Languedoc* and *Gas-coigne*, to meete with [**sig. A.iiii./3**] my lordes the Princes, in the sight and knowl-edge of the Lorde *Ioyeuse*,[10] which had expresse charge to stay hym: so that in de-spite of the sayd Princes enemies, they haue gathered together from all corners of this realme, to the number of fiue and twenty thousande hargebouziers,[11] and fiue or sixe thousande horsemen, notwithstanding the order taken by their sayd ene-mies at all portes, bridges, straights and passages, and hauing their armie ready foure monethes before, wherwith (God be thanked) they coulde neuer touche the sayde Lordes princes, or let them from taking of their townes of *S[aint]. Maxant, Fontenay, Nyort, Coignac, Xantes, S[aint]. Iohn d'Angely, Angoulesme, Ponts, Bourg, Taillebourg, Taillemont*, and other townes, from the riuer of *Gyronde*, vnto the sub-urbes of *Salmure* vpon *Loyre*, some by composition[12] and other some by force. And though the same were done in the sight of all men, but onely that the sayde Lorde Princes were at the siege before the sayd towne [4] of *Ponts*, they were aduertised[13] that the sayde Lord of *Assier* was arriued with his troupe at *Aubeterre*, whiche was with a hundreth and three score enseignes[14] of footeme[n], beyng in number a fourtene thousand harguebouziers, and sixe thousande pikemen, [and] twelue hundreth horsemen: and that the enimies had sodenly taken the Captayne *Mauuance*, and the Captayne *Pieregourdis*, and had ouerthrowen them with cer-tayne number of their souldiers, whiche caused the sayde Princes, fearyng some greater mischief, to marche with their armie towardes the sayde place of *Aubeterre*, myndyng to fyght with the enemies yf they woulde stande to it: who so soone as they had newes of the Princes comming, remoued incontine[n]t.[15] And bicause they vnderstoode they toke the way to *Poitiers*, they determined to ouertake them if it might be with as great iourneys as was possible, seeking al meanes to make them come to the battayle, wherein they vsed suche diligence, that [**sig. B.i./5**] the thirde day they were so nygh them, that where the fore warde[16] of the sayde Princ-es lodged, the enemies were vnlodged a little before: and oftentimes they found their bread, munition and cariage, so that seing them selues pursued so nygh, they were constrained to retire to *Chastellerault* and those partes, where they entrenched them selues and their artillerie, and mette with Monsieur the kinges brother[17]

---

[10] Guillaume II de Joyeuse (1520–1592), viscount de Joyeuse, then commander of the royal (Catholic) armies in Languedoc.

[11] hargebouziers (arqubusiers) — soldiers equipped with an early gun called an ar-quebus

[12] composition — terms of surrender

[13] advertised — informed

[14] enseignes (ensigns) — troops

[15] incontinent (incontinently) — immediately

[16] fore warde — vanguard

[17] Henri de Valois (1551–1589), then duke d'Anjou, later Henri III of France from 1574 to 1589.

with new force. And for that it was reported by the Gentlemen that wer sent to descry[18] them neare, that the commyng to them was so daungerouse and harde, that it had bene to no purpose, and without reason to assayle them in their campe, whiche they had so well fortified with trenches, and so well prouided with munition and artillery, whiche dyd so beate the sayde commers therto, that it had ben vnpossible to kepe aray[19] without great losse of men: it was determined to present them selues to the sight of the army, to see if they would come out of their fort, whiche was done [6] by the lord Admiral with his fore ward whiche he kept a whole day in battayle raye[20] on the top of a hill, from whence they might see the sayde towne of *Chastellerault*, but the enemies made no cou[n]tenance[21] of comming out to them. For this cause deuising howe they might get them out of their forte, to a place where the sayd princes might fight with them, they caused their army to marche towardes *Mirebalois*, whiche is a very good and frutefull countrey, and whence their enemies had their most commoditie[22] of vittayles,[23] [and] where the said princes might best vittayle[24] their men to the hinderance of their enemies. And drawing thetherward, it hapned that the enimies appoynted to lodge at the same place where the Princes army was appointed. And that monsieur the *Admiral* and Monsieur *Dandelot* his brother approchyng nyghe their lodgyng, accompanyed wyth foure or fiue Hundreth horsemen at the most, they discryed their enimies whiche had all their [sig. B.ii./7] horsemen of the fore warde, to the number of two thousande horse. So that the sayd Admirall sent incontinently on all partes for al the troupes of horseme[n], as well of the battayle[25] as of the foreward, delaying still tyll the sayde Princes began to appeare with their battayle and other troupes of the fore warde, which somewhat abashed the enemies, [and] then they caused certayn harquebouziers to approche nygh the enimies, and there was shot on bothe sides: but bicause it was vpon the closing in of day, and beganne to waxe very darke, the battayle was deferred tyll the next day, at which tyme the sayd Princes with al their armies began to marche by breake of day straight to the place where they had left their enemies the euen before, and the sayde princes perceyuing that they were departed, caused certayne cornettes[26] of horsemen to post after the said enemies, to descry whiche way they toke, and to assay[27] once againe if they coulde prouoke them to fight. Whiche they dyd to a vil- [8] lage named

---

[18] descry — to espy, to scout, to get sight of
[19] aray (array) — arrangement (of soldiers) in lines or ranks
[20] battayle raye (battle array) — the order of troops arranged for battle
[21] countenance — show, appearance
[22] commoditie (commodity) — convenient access, supply
[23] vittayles — victuals
[24] vittayle — to victual, to feed
[25] battayle (battle) — the main body of the army
[26] cornettes (cornets) — companies of cavalry
[27] assay — to put to the test

Sausay, where the lordes of *Guyse*, *Martigues*, *Brissac*, *Tauannes*, *Sansac*, and diuerse other had lyen that night, who were not the last that toke their heeles, and that with such hast, that they left all their cariage behinde them, whiche was not lesse woorth than two hundreth thousand crownes, and eyght or nyne score drawing horses,[28] with certayne pouder. The sayd Princes being aduertised that all the fore warde of the enemies was out of aray and confused, and that *Mountsalan* amongest others was put to flight, and the most part of his company slayne and taken, and had their cornettes[29] and enseignes,[30] they began to marche as fast as they coulde after them to ouertake them, whiche they coulde not do till they came to a village named *Iazeneuil*, into whiche the enemies retyred, and where the Kings brother had fortified and trenched himselfe with his artillerye. Where the Princes gaue them the brauest skirmishe that euer was geue[n] by memory of ma[n], which [sig. B.iii./9] lasted no lesse than fower or fyue long houres, where was shot on bothe sides, aboue fourescore thousand harquebouze[31] shot, and three hundreth seuen and thirtie great shot[32] on the enemies syde only, for that the Princes great shot was not brought from the siege of *Ponts:* and it was found by þe co[n]fession of the enimies themselues, þ[a]t they lost at this skirmishe fiue or sixe hundreth Soul-dioures, and fiftene or sixtene Captaines: and on the Princes side there were two hundreth hurt and slain. Yet it was written to the Queene[33] by some of hir trusty seruaunts that are in the enimies campe, that neuer French kings so[n]ne was in so great danger, as my Lord the kings brother, for the space of three dayes and three nights: and in deede it is moste certaine that at the same skirmish, the said Princes footemen wanne the trenches twise or thrise, and set vpon the Artillerie, and killed some at their peeces, yea that many of the Souldioures entred into cer-taine houses which were within the e- [10] nimies Fort, and brought away armor, and eate and dranke, whereof they had great nede: for that three dayes togither they wanted vitailes, yet were they so pacie[n]t, and so desirous to fight, that they forgatte the hunger that they suffred. This skirmish being ended, by þe means of the night, the saide Princes ordained that the next day by breake of day, they should present them selues in the same place of *Iazeuenil*, to see if they coulde prouoke the enimie to fight. Which was done, but none of þe enimies durst shew their heades, sauing a hundreth or sixe score horsemen, and that so nighe their fort, þ[a]t it was impossible to buckle[34] with them. Since they had newes that they were retired to *Luzignon*, and thence to *Poitiers:* which caused the said Princes to

---

[28] drawing horses—draught-horses
[29] cornettes (cornets)—standards, banners
[30] enseignes (ensigns)—standards, banners
[31] harquebouze (arquebus)—an early gun
[32] great shot—cannonballs
[33] Catherine de Medici (1519–1589), queen dowager of France, and power behind the throne of her son, Charles IX de Valois (1550–1574), king of France from 1560 to 1574.
[34] buckle—to come to close quarters, to grapple, to engage

lodge their armie in the Countrey of *Myrebalois*, wher they found great qua[n]titie of bread and munitio[n], that the enimies had caused to be prouided, and vndersta[n]ding that they wer come to lodge at *Ausance*, which is within a league of [*11*] *Poitiers*, and foure leagues fro[m] the place wher the said Princes lodged, they prepared them suche an enterprise, that the saide Lord Admirall with a thousande horsme[n] and only two thousand harquebouziers, droue the said enimies into þe sayd village of *Ausance*, bet them from a bridge which was there, and put all þe armie to flight, who retired into *Poitiers* in great disorder and confusion with the losse of many of their men [and] of all their cariage. And although things passed in this wise, yet are the said enimies so shamelesse, that they giue out rumours wholly contrary to the truthe, yea they sent letters to the Court wherein they were not ashamed to send worde, þ[a]t they withstoode the said Princes, where continually they put the[m] to flight, [and] sought all meanes possible to prouoke them to fight. Whereto the said Lords Princes seeing their enimies haue so little lust,[35] by reson of the ill successe that they had in the former encounters, to enforce the[m] to fight, and (will they nill they) to pre- [*12*] uent such subtilties and disguisings as they co[m]monly vsed, this other day in the sight of their enimies, and of all theyr campe, they toke a towne and castle belonging to one of the principall heads of their armie, although the sayd Towne was funished with men, artillerie, [and] all other kinde of munition, as he to whom it belongeth, hathe had good meane and leisure to do: the taking whereof shalbe so cleare and euident witnesse of it self, of the faint courage that they haue to fight, that they shall neuer be able hereafter to disguise [and] coloure their cowardise as they haue done heretofore. Afterward the said Lord Princes, seeing that neither the taking of the sayde towne [and] castle, nor anye other occasion that they could giue to the enimies, could prouoke them to fight, and that they kept them selues alwayes on the farther side of the river of *Clain*, whyther they fled when they were driuen from *Ausance*, hauing further a good riuer before them, [and] sonke all the boates to hinder any enterprise [**sig. C.i./*13*]** that might be attempted against them: giuing out þ[a]t they taried for the strength that came with the Seigneur of *Ioyeuse* which they saide was of sixe thousande hargebouziers [and] fiftene hundreth horsemen: and then they determined to fight with the armie of the said princes. This caused the Princes (to giue them newe occasion to passe the river, [and] to encrease their will and desire to fight) to force[36] in their sight the town of *Salmure*, which is a passage of the Riuer of *Loire*, which draue the enimies into suche a ielousie, that they prepared themselues to hinder the said Princes from taking of that towne, and for this cause they marched forth their armie, lodging their fotemen in one of the Suburbes, but when the batterie was readie, tidings came þ[a]t the ennimies had passed ouer the Riuer of *Clain*, making a countenaunce to come to the rescuing of *Salmure*, with the forse of the Lorde of *Ioyeuse*, which was arriued two or

---

[35] lust—desire, inclination
[36] force—take by force

three dayes before, which [*14*] made the saide Princes immediately to raise their siege from *Salmure*, causing their armie to marche straight vpon the enimies, which was easie to be done, for that there was no riuer betweene them and the said enimies which they mette before the towne of *Loudun*, which were appointed to lodge in the Suburbes, where their lodging was ordained, from whence my Lorde the Admirall raised them, so that they retired and camped in the places [and] villages about the saide *Loudun*. The next day the two armies faced one an other, their scoutes being within an hundreth paces the one of the other. They shot their Ordinaunce on bothe partes, and so passed all that day with certain small skirmishes only. And although the enimies had encamped the[m] selues to the vauntage, which commonly they do that chose their place first, and might haue approched the sayd Princes armie without any daunger, which the said Princes could not doe to them, yet [**sig. C.ii./***15*] when they stept two paces, the Princes armie stept foure to ioyne with them: two dayes after the sayd two armies met againe in the same places, as they likewise did the day after þ[a]t. But þe Princes could neuer gette them from theyr vauntage, which is maruellous, considering the bruites[37] that they gaue abrode, that they were so strengthned with the Lord of *Ioyeuses* power, that they determined not to depart the places till they had fought with the said Princes army, and said also that they had expresse commaundement so to doe, or at the least to raise them from that place, for thereon depended the honor of both the armies. But how soone this hot corage was cooled, is easie to be iudged by their sodain retiring a league backe from the place which they had taken, [and] getting a brooke betweene them, and the said Princes armie. Who being not content wyth the vauntage that they wanne of their sayd enimies, in raising them from the place [*16*] that they sayd they chose to fight on, folowed them to the second place, and althoughe the sayd enimies had a great vauntage by reason of the brooke which made them hard to be come by, yet what with cannon shot and continual skirmishes that they gaue them, they constrained them againe to leaue that seonde place, [and] to retire, (yea the kings brother himself) towards *Chinon*, [and] to passe the riuer of *Vienna*, leauing all their sicke behinde them, and much of their cariage [and] munitions. The Princes seeing this, appointed certaine troupes of horsemen and footemen to follow them which set vpon one place of the enimies where there were seuen Ensignes, whereof foure were put to flight, and the other three wholly discomfited, and theyr ensignes were burned in a house, where some of the souldiours had withdrawne them selues. Afterwarde the said Princes seeyng all meanes of fighting to be taken away, by reason of a great and [**sig. C.iii./***17*] strong riuer betwene them, determined to marche with their army towardes *Towars* and *Montreuilbellay*, as well to refreshe them and for commoditie of vitayles, whereof they had great neede for fiue or sixe dayes, as to coast[38] the army of the enemies, which being thus retired, diminisheth and breaketh away

---

[37] bruites (bruits)—reports, tidings
[38] coast—to march on the flank of

dayly by litle and litle, so that we heare from diuers places, that they talke of passing ouer the riuer of *Loyre* agayne: to place part of their Armie in all the townes that lye on the sayd riuer, and to border it with warriours at all the brydges, gates, passages and villages, and the other part to send towardes the campe that the King leuyeth against the Prince of *Orenge*,[39] and the Duke of *Swebrug*.[40] Which causeth the sayd Princes nowe to determine, that as soone as they haue receiued those ten thousand footemen, and twelue hundreth horseme[n] that the foure Vicountes of *Bourniquel, Poulin, Monclay* and *Calmont*, bring vn- [18] to them to strengthen them, and which are almost arriued at their campe, to marche forewarde to the siege of some one of those townes on the sayde riuer, that they may with all expedition ioyne with the prince of *Orange*, [and] the duke of *Swebrug*. From whom they haue receiued newes by certayne Gentlemen that they haue sent vnto the[m], that they are not lesse than fiue and twentie or thirtie thousande horsemen, and three score thousande footemen when they be al mette. In the meane whyle the sayde Lord Princes haue 35. enseignes[41] of footmen and twelue guydons[42] whiche they haue wonne of the enemies, besides the seuen enseignes[43] of companies of footemen that were discomfited, at the departing from before *Loudun*, which wer burnt in the lodgyng to haue the Souldiers that were within. On the other side, the sayde foure Vicountes lost no time where they were, but toke and put to fire and sworde the towne of *Gaillac* [sig. C.iiii./*19*] in whiche diuers cruelties with maruellous stoutnesse[44] had bene committed against those of the Religion,[45] and also the lowe towne of *Carcassonne* was taken by them, with twelue or fiftene other townes. Monsieur of *Grammont* in the countrey of *Basque* hath also disco[m]fited the seigneur of *Luye* which had raised foure thousand me[n] against those of the Religion, [and] won certayne peeces of artillerie from him. The Cardinal of *Lorayne*[46] perceyuyng that al things we[n]t not on his side as he hoped and purposed, caused the Quene to send out Mo[n]s[ieur]. *Portall* the generall receiuer, to make some motion of peace, to the sayd Princes, to whom the lyke aunswere was made, that was made to þe maister of requestes *Malassise*, that was also sent by the Quene to the lyke ende, whiche is this, that as long as the Cardinall of *Lorayne* ruled and vsed suche tiranny over Fraunce, and namely the kinges counsel, out of whiche they have driuen [20] away my Lorde the

---

[39] William I "the Silent" (1533–1584), prince of Orange-Nassau from 1544 to 1584, leader of the Netherlanders' rebellion against Spain from 1568 to 1584.

[40] Wolfgang of Bavaria (1526–1569), duke of Pfalz-Zweibrücken, mercenary general.

[41] ensignes (ensigns) — probably "standards," but possibly "troops"

[42] guydons (guidons) — flags or pennants

[43] ensignes (ensigns) — probably "troops," but possibly "standards"

[44] stoutnesse (stoutness) — pride, haughtiness, arrogance

[45] Reformed (Calvinist) Protestants; in France, Huguenots.

[46] Charles de Guise (1524–1574), Cardinal of Lorraine, and leader of the Catholic League of France.

Chancelour,[47] and the principall Officers of the crowne, they woulde accept no letters nor messages made vnder the name of his maiestie, but onely as commyng from the forge and inuention of the sayde Cardinall, and that they had vsed so muche vnfaithfulnesse in the treaty of peaces heretofore, that those of the Religion are driuen to this extremitie, to beleue that there is none other safetie for them, but by the meane of the sworde.

Since that tyme the companye of Monsieur *Dinoy*, tooke the last of Decembre in the suburbes of *Chynon* four score *Switsers* with the Prouost of the Kings Brothers garde, whiche was on the far syde the water, from whence the armye fled in great hast. This is the happy successe that it hath pleased God hitherto to giue to the affaires of the sayd Princes, and the reward and reco[m]pence that the enemies haue receyued for their treason and vnfaithfulnesse, [**sig. D.i./21**] which is more then sufficiently verified by the contentes of the Popes Bull,[48] whiche they sewed for in the Month of Iune [and] Iuly last, [and] dispatched at *Rome*, the last of August folowing, which sayd sute shal alwayes euide[n]tly co[n]uict them, þ[a]t they neuer intended but to breake the faith and publique safetye, both promised and sworne, [and] further to reuoke the Edict:[49] whiche came forth anon after, and in substance hath relation to the sayd Bull. Wherby they reuoke all the Edictes whiche haue been heretofore made in the fauour of those of the Religion, as being made in the assemblies of men hyred or brybed therto: thoughe it be well knowen, that it was done in the solemnest assemblye that euer was made in this realme, namely the Edict of Ianuarie, where all the Princes and Lordes of the Councell of both Religions, with the greatest and most notable personages of all the highe Courts of this Realme were present, and fur- [*22*] ther beinge made at the Request of the Estates. And for sufficient proofe to all those of the Religion, that they neuer ment but to abolish [and] bring to naught þe said Religion, they declare in expresse wordes by the same Edict, that they neuer mynded or inte[n]ded any other thing, notwithstanding any co[m]mande- ments, Lettres patents, and declarations that haue been giuen forth or otherwise, and notwithstanding the great assurance of words, that his Maiestie hath giuen, as wel to his subiects, as to straunge Princes.

[*23*] *Imprinted at London, by* | Henrie Bynneman, dwelling in Knight | *Rider streate, at the signe of* | *the Marmayde, for Lu-* | *cas Haryson.* 1569.

---

[47] Michel de l'Hôpital (ca. 1505–1573), chancellor of France from 1560 to 1568.

[48] *In coena domini* (1568), published by Michele Ghislieri (1504–1572), Pope Pius V from 1566 to 1572.

[49] The Edict of January (1562). The Edict established, in highly regulated form, the right of the Huguenots to worship, and gave the Reformed religion recognition by the French crown.

George Gascoigne, *The Spoyle of Antwerpe* (1576) ||
STC (2nd ed.) # 11644

In the autumn of 1575, Philip II of Spain, his finances stretched thin by war, suspended interest payments on Spain's debts to its bankers. Without new loans to keep Spain's finances going, the state was unable to pay its armies in the Netherlands, and in July 1576 they began to mutiny. The mutineers attacked Antwerp in November 1576, overwhelmed the defenders, and sacked the town. "The Spanish Fury" was bloody enough, and the Spaniards slaughtered at least several hundred citizens of Antwerp, but it was immediately played up in Protestant propaganda as an unparalleled slaughter of thousands. This was a seminal moment in the creation of the "Black Legend" of Spanish cruelty and murderousness, which helped sustain anti-Catholic and anti-Spanish sentiment for centuries, among Protestants generally and Englishmen in particular.

George Gascoigne (ca. 1534/5–1577) was a soldier, man of letters, and government agent. He was probably educated at Trinity College, Cambridge, led a financially precarious life in his young adulthood, wrote and published in a wide variety of literary genres, including the somewhat scandalous anthology of his works, *One Hundreth Sundrie Flowres* (1573), and served as a soldier against the Spanish in the Netherlands in the early 1570s. In November 1576 he traveled to Antwerp as an agent of the English government, and was trapped in the city during its sack. Upon his return to England, he whipped out an anonymous account of what he had witnessed — marvelously vivid in its account both of the sack and of Gascoigne's psychological state at the time, and also a foundational libel in the aforementioned Black Legend of Spanish cruelty.

[TITLE PAGE]

The Spoyle | of Antwerpe.

Faithfully reported, | by a true English- | man, who was pre- | sent at the same,

Nouem. 1576.

Seene and allowed.

Printed at London by Richard Iones.

[sig. *.i./1] *Faultes escaped, to be considered of the Readers: and to be amended, as fol-loweth.* [1]

In .A. the third leafe, the second syde, and last lyne: for, *Fuora villiauo:* reade, *Fuora villiacco.*

In .A.4. leafe .2. syde, and .7. lyne: for, take Caues: reade, take Armes.

In .A.6. leafe, the first side, and 20. lyne: for, West or Southwest: reade, East or Southeast.

In .B. the first leafe, and first syde, the 22. lyne: for, west syde: reade, east syde. And in the same leafe, the .2. side, and .7. lyne: for, Southwest syde: reade, Southeast syde. And in the .15. lyne: for, East syde: reade, West syde.

In .B.4. leafe .2. syde .9. lyne, for *aeste ville:* reade, *ceste ville.* And in the .13. lyne, for Trumpete: reade, Trumpetter. And in the .17. lyne: for *Cauaille:* reade, *Canaille.*

In .C.1. leafe .2. syde .1. lyne: for fleeing: reade, flaying.

[2]   To the Reader.

I Shall earnestlye *require thee (gentle Reader) to correct the errors passed and escaped in printing of this Pamphlet, according to this table. And furthermore, to vnderstande that this victorye was obteyned with losse but of fyue hundreth Spanierds, or sixe at the moste: of whome I hearde no man of name recoumpted, sauing onely,* Dom Emanu-ell. *Thus muche [3] (for haste) I had forgotten in the treatye,* [2] *and therefore thought meete to place it here in the beginning: and therewithall to aduertise* [3] *thee, that these outrages and disordered cruelties done to our nation, proceeded but from the co[m]mon Souldiers: neither was there any of the twelue which entred the englishe house, a man of*

---

[1] Some of these emendations were made in the original pamphlet; the others I have made myself, noting where I have done so, and referring back to this note.

[2] treatye (treaty) — treatise

[3] advertise — inform

any charge⁴ or reputacion. So that I hope (these extremyties notwithstanding) the king,⁵ their Maister, will take [4] such good order for redresse thereof, as our countrymen in the end, shall rest satisfyed with reason, and the amytye betweene our moste gracious Soueraigne⁶ and him, shal remain also firme [and] vnuiolate: the which I pray God speedely to graunt for the benefyt of this Realme. Amen.

Note in the Modell:⁷ that the trowpe of *A*lmayncs by the ryuers side, should be footemen. *A*nd also that the trowpe next the windemyl should be horsemen.

[**sig. A ii/5**] The Spoyle | *of Antwerpe.*

S*Ince my hap*⁸ *was* to bee present at so pitteous a spectakle, as the sackyng and spoyle of *Antwerpe,* (a lamentable example whiche hath alredy filled all *Europe* with dreadfull newes of great calamitie) I haue thought good for the benefit of my countrie, to publish a true report thereof. The which may aswell serue for profitable example vnto all estates of sutche condicion as suffred in the same: as also, answer all honest expectations with a meane truthe, set downe beetween thextreme surmises of sundry doubtfull mindes: And encreased by the manyfolde light tales whiche haue been engendred by feareful or affectionate⁹ rehersals.¹⁰ And therwithall, [6] if the wickednesse vsed in the sayde towne, doo seeme vnto the well disposed Reader, a sufficient cause of Gods so iust a scorge and Plague: and yet the furie of the vanquishers doo also seeme more barbarous and cruell, then may become a good christian conquerour: let these my few woords become a forewarnynge on bothe handes: and let them stande as a Lanterne of light beetween two perillous Rockes: That bothe amendyng the one, and detestynge the other, wee may gather fyre out of the Flint, and Hunny out of the Thystle.¹¹ To that ende, all stories and Chronicles are written: and to that ende I presume to publishe this Pamphlet: protestyng that neither mallice to the one syde, nor parciall affection to the other, shall make my pen to swarue any iote from truth of that which I will set down [and] saw executed: For if I were [**sig. A iii/7**] disposed to write maliciously agaynst the vanquishers: their former barbarous cruelty, insolences, Rapes, spoyles, Incests, and Sacriledges, committed in sundrie other places, might yeeld mee sufficiente matter without the lawful¹² remembrance of this their late stratageme: or if I would vndertake to mooue a

---

⁴ charge—importance
⁵ Philip II Hapsburg (1527–1598), king of Spain from 1556 to 1598.
⁶ Elizabeth I Tudor (1533–1603), queen of England from 1558 to 1603.
⁷ modell (model)—map. A map apparently accompanied the original pamphlet, but it does not survive.
⁸ hap—chance, fortune, luck
⁹ affectionate—biased, partial
¹⁰ rehersals (rehearsals)—accounts, narrations
¹¹ Cf. Matthew 7:16.
¹² lawful—justifiable

generall compassion, by blazynge[13] abroade[14] the miseries and callamities of the vanquished: theyr longe susteyned iniuries and yokes of vntollerable bondage: theyr continual broyles[15] in warre: their doubtful[16] dreades[17] in peace: theyr accusations without cause: and condempnations without proofe: might enable a dome stone to talke of their troubles, and fetche brinysh teares out of the most craggy rocke: to lament and bewayle the burning houses of so neare neighbours. But as I sayd before, mine onely entent is to set downe a plaine truthe, for the satisfiynge of sutche as *[8]* haue hetherto beene caried aboute with doubtfull reportes: and for a profitable example vnto all sutche as beeyng subiect to like imperfections, might fall thereby into the like calamities.

And to make the matter more perspicuous,[18] I must deriue[19] the beeginnyng of this discourse a litle beeyonde the beeginnynge of the massacre: That the cause beyng partly opened,[20] the effect may bee the more playnly seene.

It is then to bee vnderstoode that the sackyng [and] spoyle of *ANTWERPE* hath been (by all lykelyhoode) longe pretended[21] by the Spanyerds: And that they haue done nothing els but lien in wayte continually to fynde any least quarrell to put þe same in execution. For proofe whereof, their notable rebellion and mewtinye beegun in the same, when theyr watche woorde was *Fuora villiaco*,[22] might sufficiently **[sig. A iiii/9]** beewray theyr mallicious and cruell intente. And though it were then smoothly colloured ouer,[23] and subtilly appeased, by þe craftie deuisers of the same, yet the coles of their choller[24] beynge but raked vp in the Imbers of false semblance, haue now founde out the wicked windes of wilinesse [and] wrath: Whiche meetynge together haue kindled sutch a flame, as gaue open way to theyr detestable deuices. For thestates of al the low countries[25] beeyng ouerweried with the intollerable burden of theyr tyrannies: and hauynge taken armes to withstande their mallice and rebellyous Mewtinyes, the towne of *Antwerpe* (beeing left open and subiecte vnto the Cytadell) did yet remayne quiet, and entred not into any martiall action. Whereat the Spanyerdes beeinge mutch moooued, and hauinge not yet oportunity to woorke their will

---

[13] blazynge (blazing)—proclaiming
[14] abroade (abroad)—at large
[15] broyles (broils)—tumults, quarrels
[16] doubtful—questionable
[17] dreades (dreads)—apprehensions
[18] perspicuous—clear or easy to be understood
[19] derive—trace the origin
[20] opened—made known
[21] pretended—intended
[22] Emended from *"Fuora villiauo"*—see Note 1. *Fuora villiaco*—"Away, villain!"—possibly with the implication of "Kill the villains!"
[23] colloured over (colored over)—speciously and plausibly disguised
[24] choller (choler)—anger
[25] Low Countries—the Netherlands

so colourably[26] as they wisshed, beestowed [*10*] certayne Canon shot out of the saide Castle, and slew certayne innocent soules, with some other small harme and dammage done to the edifices: Thinking thereby to harden þe harts of the poore Flemynges, and to make them take Armes[27] for theyr iust defence: whiles they therby might take occasion to execute theyr vniust pretence.[28] And this was doone on the xix. or .xx. of October last.

Now to answere all obiections, I doubt not but it wilbee alledged, that the Castle beestowed the said Canon shot at þe Towne, because they of the Towne did not shote at the prince of Orenges[29] Shippes, which lay within syght thereof: But alas it is easy to finde a staffe, when a man woulde beate a dogge.

For the truth is, that those Ships did no greater hurt, either to þe towne or Castle, then frendly to waft[30] vp al manner of Grayne and victualles, for [*11*] the sustenance of þe said towne: which euen then began to want sutch prouision, by reason that the sayde Spanyerds had builte a Forte on Flaunders syde vpon the same Riuer: And thereby stopped all sutch as brought Victuall to the sayd Towne: burnynge and destroyinge the countrie neare adioynyng, and vsynge all terrour to the poore people, to the intent þ[a]t *ANTWERPE* might lack prouision.

And about the same time also the Spanierds cut of a Brydge, which was the open passage beetween *Antwerpe* and *Machlen*, at a village called *Walem*. A manifest proofe of their playne intent to distresse[31] þe sayd town, and to shut vp the same from all the rest of *Brabant*. Since they were walled in with the Riuer on the one syde, and on that other the Spanish horsemen occupied all the countrie, and so terrified þe poore people as they durst not bring theyr co[m]modities to þe same. [*12*] All this notwithstandynge, the chiefe rulers of the sayde Towne of *Antwerpe*, appeased[32] the people and put vp these iniuries vntill they might bee better able to redresse them. Soone after the Spanierdes (assysted by the treason of certaine high Duches)[33] entred the towne of *Maestrecht* vpon a sodeyne, and put the same to sacke: killynge, and destroying great numbers of innoce[n]t people therein: a thing to be noted. For that *Maestrecht* had neuer reuolted, but stoode quiet vnder their garisons as faithfull subiectes to the kinge. And the one halfe therof perteyned[34] also vnto þe bishop of *Liege*, who had yet medled nothing at all in these actions. The cheife rulers and people of *Antwerpe* perceiuing therby the

---

[26] colourably (colorably) — with a fair appearance, speciously, plausibly

[27] Emended from "Caues" — see n. 1.

[28] pretence — design

[29] William I "the Silent" (1533–1584), prince of Orange-Nassau from 1544 to 1584, leader of the Netherlanders' rebellion against Spain from 1568 to 1584.

[30] waft — convey

[31] distresse (distress) — to subject to pressure, to harass

[32] appeased — pacified

[33] high Duches (high Dutchmen) — Germans

[34] perteyned (pertained) — were subject to

cruell entent of the Spanyerds, and doubtinge their Dutche garyson which was of the Counte *Euersteines* regiment (as they were also which betrayed *Maestricht*,) beegan to aban- *[13]* don the towne, leauyng their houses [and] goods beehinde them: and sought to withdraw themselues into some place of safer abode. Whereat the estates[35] beynge mooued with compassion, and doubtynge[36] that the towne would shortly bee left desolate, leuied a power of three thousand footemen, and eight hundreth, or one thousand horsemen, and sent the same vnder the co[n]duct of the Marquise *d' Haurey*, the yonge Counte *d'Egmont*,[37] *Mounser de Capres, Mou[n]s[ieur]. de Bersel, Mou[n]s[ieur]. de Goo[n]nie*, and other nobles [and] gentlemen to succour [and] defend the towne of *Antwerpe*, agaynst the cruell pretence of the sayd Spanierdes: And they came beefore the gates therof on Friday the second of this instante: at a Porte[38] on the east or southeast[39] syde thereof called *Kybdoerporte*: Wherat the Spanierds beeynge enraged, discharged sundrie shotte of greate Artillerie from the Castle, but to small purpose. At last *[14]* *Mouns[ieur]. de Champaigne*, who was gouernour of the Towne: and the Counte *d'Euersteine* which was Colonel of the Garysone, demaunded of the States wherefore they approched the towne in sutch order: who answered þ[a]t they came to entre the same as freinds, [and] to entrenche [and] defend it from þe Spanyerds: protesting furder, þ[a]t they wold offer no manner of violent domage or iniury to the persons or goods of any sutch as inhabited the same. Hereupon þe sayd *Mou[n]s[ieur]. d'Champaigne* and Counte *d'Euersteine* went out vnto them and conferred more priuately together by the space of one houre, and returned into the towne leauing the estates power[40] at a village called *Burgherhout*.

On the morrow beeing the third of this instant, they were permitted to enter, and came into the towne .xxi. ensignes of footemen, and .vi. cornets of horsemen. Immediatly after their *[15]* entrie, þe inhabitantes brought them sackes of wooll and other sutch prouision, wherwith thei aproched þe yeard or playne grounde which lieth beefore the Castle. And placing the same at thendes of fiue streets which lye ope[n] vnto the sayd Castle yearde, entrenched vnder them with sutch expedicio[n] that in lesse then fyue howers, those streetes endes, were all reasonably well fortified from the Castle for any sodaine.[41] At this time and .xii. dayes beefore I was in the sayde towne of *Antwerpe* vpon certeine priuate affaires of myne owne: so that I was enforced to become an eyed witnes of their entry and all that they did. As also afterwards (for all þe gates were kept fast shut [and] I

---

[35] estates — the States General (the parliament) of the Netherlands

[36] doubtynge (doubting) — fearful

[37] Philip, Count Egmont (1558–1590). Son of the Dutch national martyr, Lamoral, Count Egmont.

[38] porte (port) — gate

[39] Emended from "west or southwest" — see n. 1.

[40] power — army

[41] sodaine (sudden) — sudden danger

could not departe) to beeholde the pittifull stratageme which folowed. The Castle thondred with shot at the towne: but it was a very mysty day, so that they could neither finde their markes[42] very wel, nor [16] yet see how the streetes endes were entrenched. It was a straunge thing to se the willingnes of þe inhabitants, and how soone many hands had dispatched a very great peece of worke: for beefore midnight they had made the trenches as highe as the length of a pike: and had begun one trenche for a Counterskarfe[43] between al those streets [and] the Castle yearde: the which they perfected[44] vnto the halfe way fro[m] S[aint]. Georges Churchyearde vnto the waters side by S[aint]. Michels, [and] there left from worke, meaning to haue perfected it the next day. That Counterskarfe had been to mutch purpose if it had been finished, as shall appeare by a Model of the whole place, which I have annexed to thend of this treaty: by view wherof þe skillfill reader may playnly perceiue thexecution of euery particularitie. These thinges thus begonne [and] set in forwardnes, it is to bee noted that the Spanyerds (hauing [17] intelligence of the states power when it set forwards from *Bruxelles*: and perceuing that it bent towards *Antwerpe*) had sent to *Maestricht*, *Liere*, and *Aelst*, to drawe all the power[45] þ[a]t could be made vnto the Castle of *Antwerpe*.

So þ[a]t on Sunday, the fourth of this instant in the mornyng, they al met at þe sayd Castle. And theyr powers[46] (as farre as I could gather) were these.

There came from *Maestricht* very neare to a thousand horsemen, led by *Dom Alonso de Vergas*, who is the generall of the horsemen: [and] fyue hundreth footemen or more, gouerned by the Campemaster[47] *Francesco de Valdes*.

There came from *LIERE*, fiue hundreth footemen or more, gouerned by the Campemaster *Iuliane de Romero*.

There came from *Aelst* two thousa[n]d footemen, which were the same that rebelled for their pay [and] other vnresonable demau[n]ds immediatly after the winning of *Zierickzee*. These had none [18] other conductour[48] then their *Electo*[49] (after the maner of sutch as mewtine [and] rebel) but were of sundry companies: as *Dom Emanuels* [and] others. Neuerthelesse I haue ben so bould in þe Model as to set downe þe sayd *Dom Emanuell* for their leder: bothe because I think that (their mewtiny notwithstanding) he led them at þe exployte, and also because, he was slayn amongst them at their entrie. Thus the numbre of spanierds was .iiii.M. or there aboutes, besides some help that thei had of the garison within

---

[42] markes (marks)—targets
[43] counterskarfe (counterscarp)—the outer wall or slope of the ditch, which supports the covered way; sometimes extended to include the covered way and glacis
[44] perfected—completed, finished
[45] power—(military) forces
[46] powers—troops
[47] campemaster (camp-master)—a staff officer
[48] conductour (conductor)—leader
[49] electo—a leader or commander chosen by mutineers (in the Spanish armies)

þe castle: And besides a M. high Almaynes,[50] or more, whiche came from *Mae-stricht, Lyere,* and those partes. And were of three sundry regiments: *viz. Charles Fuckers, Poelderuills* and *Froemsberghs:* but they were led all by *charles Fucker.* So þ[a]t the whole force of þe Spanierds [and] their co[m]plices, was fiue .M. and vpwards: the which asse[m]bled [and] met at þe castle, on þe said fourth day about .x. of þe clocke before dinner.

[**sig. B.i./19**] And (as I haue hearde credibly reported) would neyther stay to refresh themselues (hauing marched all night and the day before) nor yet to con-ferre of any thing, but only of the order how they should issue and assaile, pro-testing and vowing neyther to eat nor drinke vntill they mighte eate and drinke at liberty and pleasure in *ANTWERP*: the which vowe they performed contary to all mans reason and expectacion. Their order of entry into þe Castle yarde, and of their approch to the trenches, I did not see, for I could not get out of the town: neyther did I thinke it reasonable to be *Hospes in aliena republica curiosus*:[51] Yet as I heard it rehearsed[52] by sundry of them selues, I wil also here rehearce it for a truth. The Horsemen and footemen, which came fro[m] *Maestrecht* and *Lyere,* came through a village on the east syde of the town called *Burgerhout,* about ten of the clock before noone, as before sayd: The Go- [**20**] uernour and estates being thereof aduertised, sente out presently parte of their Horsemen and Footemen to discouer and take knowledge of them: But before they could issue out of the gates, the Spanyardes were passed on the Southeast[53] syde of the towne dyche, and entred at a gate which sta[n]deth on the Counterscarfe of the castle yeard, called the Windmil porte: there entred the Horsemen, and al the footemen, sau-ing the high Almaynes, who marched round about the Castle, by a village called *Keele* and trayling their pikes on the ground after them, came in at a small Pos-terne[54] on the Brayes[55] by the Riuer, and on the west[56] side of the Castle.

Those which came from *Aelst,* came through the sayd vyllage called *Keele,* and so through the Castle: issued out of the same at the fore gate, which sta[n]deth to-ward the towne. Being thus passed, and entred into the Castleyard [**sig. B.ii./21**] about eleuen of the clock, they of *Aelst* and of the Castle, cast them selues into foure Squadrones: they of *Maestricht* and *Lyere,* into two Squadrones: and their Horsemen into a trowpe behind them: and the high Almayns into one Squad-rone, or Batallyon, by the ryuers side. Being thus ordered, and appoyntment giue[n] where euery Squadrone should charge and indure, they cast of certayne

---

[50] high Almaynes—Germans
[51] *Hospes in aliena republica curiosus*—an inquisitive guest in a foreign state. Cf. Ci-cero, *De Officiis* (1.34.125).
[52] rehearsed—recounted, related, narrated
[53] Emended from "Southwest"—see n. 1.
[54] posterne (postern)—back door, side gate
[55] brayes (braes)—the steep bank bounding a river valley
[56] Emended from "east"—see n. 1.

loose shot, from euery Squadrone, and attacqued the scarmouch: [57] the which continewed not one hower, before they drew their Squadrones so nere vnto the Counterscarfe and trenches, that they brake [and] charged *pell mell*. The Castle had all this while, played at the Towne and trenches, with thundring shot: But now vpon a signall geuen, ceased to shoote any more, for feare to hurt their owne men: wherin I noted their good order which wanted no direction, in their greatest furye. The Wallonnes, [58] and [22] Almaynes, [59] which serued in the Trenches defe[n]ded al this while very stoutly. And the Spanyerds with their Almaynes, contynewed the charge with such valure, that in fyne they won the Counterscarf, and presently scaled the Trenches, with great fury. The Wallonnes and Almaines hauing long resysted without any fresh reliefe or supplye (many of them in this mene while being slayne and hurte) were not able any lo[n]ger to repulse the Spanyerds: so that they entred the trenches about twelue of the clock, and presently pursued their victory down euery streate. In their chase, as faste as they gained any crosse streate, they fla[n]ked the same with their Musquets, vntill they saw no longer resistance of any power: and then proceeded in chase, executing all such as they ouertooke. In this good order they charged and entred: in this good order they proceded: and in as good order their lackeyes and Pages [**sig. B.iii.**/*23*] followed with Firebrands, and wyldfyre, [60] setting the houses on fyre, in euery place where their maysters had entred. The Wallonnes and Almaynes, which were to defend the town being growen into some security, by reason that their Trenches were so high, as seemed inuincible: and lacking sufficient Generals [and] directors, were found as far out of order, as the Spanyerds were to be honored for the good order and direction which they kepte. For those which came to supplye [and] relieue the tre[n]ches, came stragling and loose: some came from the furdest side of the towne: some that were nearer came very fearefully: and many out of their lodginges, from drinking and carousing: who would scarsely beleeue that any conflicte was begonne, when the Spanyerdes nowe mette them in the streates to put them out of doubt that they dallyed not. To conclude, their carelesnesse and lack of foresyght was [*24*] such that they had neuer a *Corps du gard* [61] to supply and relieue their tre[n]ches, but only one in þe market place of the town whiche was a good quarter of a myle from their fortifycations: and that also was of Almaynes, who (when they spied the Spanyerds) did gently kneele

---

[57] scarmouch (skirmish) — body of skirmishers

[58] Wallonnes (Walloons) — the French-speaking inhabitants of the Netherlands

[59] Almaynes — without further specification, this can apply to people we would now call Flemings, Netherlanders, or Germans

[60] wyldfyre (wildfire) — a composition of highly inflammable substances, readily ignited and very difficult to extinguish, used in warfare

[61] *corps du gard* (*corps de garde*) — a small body of soldiers stationed on guard or as sentinels

down letting their Pykes fall, and crying *Oh lieue Spaniarden, lieue Spaniarden.*[62] Now I haue set downe the order of their entrye, approch, charge, and assaulte: together with their proceeding in victory: and that by credible report, both of the Spanyerdes them selues, and of others who serued in their company: let me also say a litle of that which I sawe executed. I was lodged in the Englishe house *vt supra,*[63] and had not gone abroade that morning by reason of weighty businesse which I had in hand the same day. At dinner tyme the Marchauntemen of my Countrey whiche came out of the towne, and dined in my chamber, told [sig. B.iiii./25] me that a hote scarmouch was begon in the Castleyeard, and that the furye thereof stil increased. Aboute the middest of dinner, newes came that the shot was so thick, as neyther ground, houses, nor people could be discearned for the smoke thereof: and before dinner were fully ended, that the Spaniardes were like to win the trenches. Whereat I stept from the table, and went hastily vp into a high Tower of the sayd English house: from whence I might discouer[64] fyre in fower or fiue places of the towne, towardes the Castleyeard: and thereby I was wel assured that the Spanyerds in deede were entred within the Trenches. So that I came down and tooke my cloake and sword, to see the certainty thereof, and as I passed toward the Bource,[65] I met many, but I ouertoke none: And those which I mette were no Townsmen, but Souldyeres: neither walked they as men which vse [26] traffique,[66] but ran as men whiche are in feare: Wherat being somwhat greued,[67] and seeing the townesmen stand euery man before his doore with such weapons as they had, I demaunded of one of them, what it mente? Who aunswered me in these wordes, *Helas mounsieur, il ny a poynt de ordre, [et] voila la ruine de ceste ville.*[68] *Aiez courage mon amy*[69] (quoth I,) and so went onwardes yet towards the Bowrce, meeting all the way more [and] more which mended their pace. At last, a Wallon Trompeter on horsback (who seemed to be but a Boy of yeres) drew his sworde, and layd about him crying, *Ou est que vous eufuiez canaille? faisons teste pour le honeur de la patrie.*[70] Wherewith, fyfty or three score of them turned head, and wente backewardes towardes the Bource. The which encouraged mee

---

[62] *Oh lieue Spaniarden, lieue Spaniarden*—Oh, kind Spaniards, kind Spaniards

[63] *vt supra*—as before

[64] discouer (discover)—observe for the first time

[65] bource (bourse)—an exchange, or place of meeting for merchants; the money-market

[66] use traffique (traffic)—pass to and fro in an everyday manner

[67] greved (grieved)—troubled

[68] *Helas mounsieur, il ny a poynt de ordre, [et] voila la ruine de ceste ville.*—Alas, monsieur, there is no degree of (military) order here, and behold the ruin of this town.

[69] *Aiez courage mon amy.*—Have courage, my friend.

[70] *Ou est que vous eufuiez canaille? faisons teste pour le honeur de la patrie.*—Where are you fleeing, scum? Hold your ground for the honor of the country.

(*per companie*)[71] to proceede: But alas, this comforte indured but a while: For by that time I came on the farder syde of the [27] Bource, I might see a great trowpe comming in greater haste, with their heads as close togeather, as a skoule of yong frye,[72] or a flocke of Sheepe: Who met me on the farder side of the Bource, toward the market place: And hauing their leaders formost (for I knewe them by their Iauelines, Borespeares, and Staues) bare me ouer backwardes, and ran ouer my belly and my face, long time before I could recouer[73] on foote. At last when I was vp, I looked on euery syde, and seeing them ronne so fast, began thus to bethinke me. What in Gods name doe I heare which haue no interest in this action? synce they who came to defend this town are content to leaue it at large, and shift for themselues: And whilest I stoode thus musing, another flocke of flyers came so fast that they bare me on my nose, and ran as many ouer my backe, as erst[74] had marched ouer my guttes. In [28] fine, I gotte vp like a tall[75] fellow, and wente with them for company: but their haste was such, as I could neuer ouertake the[m], vntil I came at a broad crosse streate which lyeth betweene the English house [and] the sayd Bource: there I ouertooke some of the[m] groueling on the ground, and groning for the last gaspe, and some other which turned backwards to auoyd the tickling of the spanishe Musquets: who had gotten the ends of the sayd broad crosse streate, and flanked it both wayes: And there I stayde a whyle till hearing the shot increase, and fearing to bee surprysed wyth suche as mighte follow in tayle of[76] vs, I gaue aduenture[77] to passe through the sayde crossestreate, and (without vaunte[78] be it spoken) passed through fiue hundred shotte, before I could recouer the English house.

At my comming thether, I founde many of the Marchauntes standing [29] before the gate: Whom I would not discomforte nor dismay, but sayd that the Spanyerdes had once entred the towne, and that I hoped they were gone backe agayne: Neuerthelesse I wente to the Gouernour, and priuily perswaded him to drawe in the company and to shut vp the gates: The which he consented vnto, and desyred me because I was somewhat better acquaynted with such matters then the Marchauntes, to take charge of the Key: I tooke it willingly, but before I coulde well shut and barre the gates, the Spanyardes were nowe come forewards into the same streat: And passing by þe doore, called to come in? bestowing fyue or sixe Musquette shotte at the grate where I aunswered them, whereof one came very neare my nose, and pearcing thorowe the gate, strake one of the

---

[71] *per companie*—by their company
[72] frye (fry)—young fish
[73] recover—get back
[74] erst—earlier
[75] tall—quick, prompt
[76] in tayle (tail) of—in the train of, following
[77] gave adventure—ventured
[78] vaunte (vaunt)—boasting

Marchants on the head, without any greate or daungerous hurt: but the heate of the [*30*] pursute was yet such, that they coulde not attend the spoyle, but passed on in chase to the new towne: where they slew infinite nombers of people: And by three of the clocke, or before retourned victors, hauing slayne or put to flight all their ennemies. And nowe to keepe promise, and to speake wythout parciality: I must needs confesse, that it was the greatest victory, and the rou[n]dlyest[79] executed, that hath bene seene, red, or heard of, in our age: and that it was a thing myraculous, to co[n]sider, how Trenches of such a height should be entred, passed ouer, and won both by Footemen, and Horsmen: For immediately after that the Footemen were gotten in, the Horsemen founde meanes to follow: and being many of them harquebuziers[80] on horseback, did passe by their owne Footemen in the streates, and much hastened both the flight of the Wallones, and made the [*31*] way opener vnto speedy execution.

But whoseuer wil therein most extoll the Spanyardes for their vallure and order, must therewithall confesse that it was the very ordinance of god for a iust plague and scourge vnto the Towne: For otherwise it passeth all mens capacity, to conceiue howe it should be possible. And yet the disorder and lacke of foresight in the Wallons did great helpe to augment the Spanish glory and boast. To conclude, the County *de Euersteine* was drowned in the newe Towne: the Marquise *de Haurcy* and *Champaigne* escaped out of the sayd new Towne, and recouered the Prince of Orenges shippes: only the yong Counte *de Egmont* was taken fighting by S[aint]. Myghels. *Mouns[ieur]. de capres*, [and] *Mouns[ieur]. de Goonie*: were also take[n]: but I heard of none that fought stoutly, sauing onely þe said Counte *de Egmo[n]t*, whom the *Colonel Verdugo*,[81] a spanyard [*32*] of an honorable compassion and good mind, did saue with great daunger to himself in defending the Counte. In this conflicte there were slayne sixe hundred Spanyerds or thereaboutes: And on the Thursday next folowing, a view of the dead bodies in the town being take[n]: it was esteemed at .17000 men, women, and children. A pittifull massacre though God gaue victory to the Spanyerdes. And surely, as their vallyaunce was to be much commended, so yet I can much discommende their barbarous cruelty, in many respectes: For me thinkes, that as when God geueth abundaunce of welth, the owner oughte yet to haue regarde on whome he bestow it: euen so, when God geueth a great and myraculous victory, the co[n]querours ought to haue great regard vnto their execution: and though some, which fauour the Spanish faction, will aleadge sundry rea- [*33*] sons to the contrary: yet when the blood is cold, and the fury ouer, me thinkes that a true christian hearte should stand content with victory, and refrayne to prouoke Gods wrath by sheadding of innocente blood. These things I rehearce (the rather)

---

[79] roundlyest—most thoroughly

[80] harquebuziers (arquebusiers)—soldiers equipped with an early gun called an arquebus

[81] Francisco Verdugo (1536–1595), Spanish officer.

because they neither spared age, nor sexe: time nor place: person nor countrey: profession nor religion: yong nor olde: rich nor poore: strong nor feeble: but without any mercy, did tyrannously tryumphe when there was neither man nor meane to resist them: For age and sex, yong and old, they slew great numbers of yong children, but many mo[r]e wome[n] more then fowerscore yeares of age: For time and place, their furye was as great ten dayes after the victory, as at the tyme of their entry: and as great respect they had to the church and churchyeard, (for all their hipocriticall boasting of the catholique religi- [34] on) as the Butcher hath to his shambles or slaughter house: For perso[n] and Country, they spared neither friende nor foe: Portingal nor Turke: for profession and religion, the Iesuites must geue their ready coyne: and all other religious houses both coyne and plate with all shorte endes[82] that were good and portable. The ryche was spoyled because he had: [and] the poore were hanged because they had nothing: neither strength could preuayle to make resystaunce, nor weakenesse moue pitty to refrayne their horrible cruelty. And this was not onely done when the chase was hotte, but (as I earst sayd) when the blood was colde, and they now victors without resystaunce. I refrayne to rehearce the heapes of deade Carcases whiche laye at euery Trench where they entred: the thicknesse whereof, did in many places exceede the height of a man.

[**sig. C.i/35**] I forbeare also to recount the huge nombers, drowned in þe new Toune: where a man might behold as many sundry shapes and formes of mans motio[n] at time of death: as euer *Mighel Angelo* dyd portray in his tables of Doomes day.[83] I list[84] not to recken the infinite nombers of poore Almains, who lay burned in their armour: som thentrailes skorched out, [and] all the rest of the body free, some their head and shoulders burnt of: so that you might looke down into the bulk [and] brest and there take an Anatomy of the secrets of nature. Some standing vppon their waste, being burnte of by the thighes: [and] some no more but the very toppe of the brain taken of with fyre, whiles the rest of the body dyd abide vnspeakable tormentes. I set not downe the ougly [and] filthy polluting of euery streete with the gore and carcases of men and horses: neither doo I complaine, that the one lacked bu- [36] ryall, and the other flaying,[85] vntyl the ayre (corrupted with theyr caryon) enfected all that yet remained alyue in the Towne: And why should I describe the particularitie of euery such anoiance, as commonly happen both in campes [and] Castels, where martiall feates are managed: But I may not passe ouer with sylence, the wylfull burning and destroying of the stately Townehouse, [and] all the monuments and records of the Citie: neither can I refraine to tel their shamful rapes [and] outragious forces presented

---

[82] shorte endes (short ends)—odds and ends
[83] Michelangelo Buonarroti's painting *The Last Judgment* (1534–1541), in the Sistine Chapel in Rome.
[84] list—choose
[85] Emended from "fleing"—see n. 1.

vnto sundry honest Dames [and] Virgins. It is a thing too horrible to rehearse, that the Father and Mother were forced to fetche their yong daughter out of a cloyster (who had thether fled as vnto Sanctuary, to keepe her body vndefyled) [and] to bestowe her in bed betweene two Spaniards, to worke their wicked and detestable wil with her.

[sig. C.ii/37] It is also a ruthfull[86] remembrance, that a poore English march-ant (who was but a seruaunt) hauing once redeemed his Masters goods for three hundreth crownes, was yet hanged vntyl he were halfe dead, because he had not two hundreth more to geue them: and þe halter being cut downe, and he com-men to him selfe againe, besought them on knees with bytter teares, to geue him leaue to seeke [and] trye his creditte and friendes in the Towne, for the rest of theyr vnreasonable demaund. At his returne because he sped not (as indeede no money was then to bee had) they hong him again outright: and afterwards (of exceeding curtesie) procured the Friars *Minors*[87] to burie him.

To conclude, of the seuentene thousande carcases, which were viewed on the Thursday, I thinke in conscience, that fiue thousand or fewe lesse, were mas-sacred after their victorye, [38] because they had not readye money, wherewith to raunsome theyr goods at such prices as they pleased to set on them: At least all the world wyll beare mee witnes, that ten (yea twenty dayes) after, whosoeuer were but poynted at, and named to bee a Wallon, was immediatlye massacred without furder audience or tryall. For mine owne part, it is wel known that I did ofte[n] escape very narrowly, because I was taken for a Wallone. And on Sunday, the eleuenth of this insta[n]t (which was the day before I gat out of the Towne) I saw three poore soules murdered in my presence, because they were poynt-ed to be Wallons: and it was well proued immediatly that one of the[m] was a poore artyficer,[88] who had dwelt in the Towne eight yeares before, [and] neuer managed[89] armes, but truely folowed his occupatio[n]: Furthermore the seede of these and other barbarous factes [sig. C.iii/39] brought forth this crop [and] fruite: that within three daies Antwarpe, which was one of the rychest Townes in *Europe*, had now no money nor treasure to be found therein, but onely in the hands of murderers and strompets: for euery *Dom Diego*[90] must walk ietting[91] vp [and] downe the streetes with his harlotte by him in her cheine and bracelettes of golde. And the notable Bowrce which was wont to be a safe assemblie for Mar-chaunts, and men of all honest trades, had nowe none other marchaundize there-in, but as many dycing tables as might be placed round about it al the day long.

---

[86] ruthfull (ruthful)—causing sorrow or pity
[87] Friars Minors—Franciscans
[88] artyficer (artificer)—craftsman
[89] managed—bore
[90] Dom Diego—a derisive personification of the Spanish soldier
[91] ietting (jetting)—parading, strolling jauntily

Men wyll boast of the Spanierds that they are the best [and] most orderlye Souldiours in the world: but sure, if this be their order, I had rather be coumpted a *Besoigner*,[92] then a braue Souldiour in such a bande: neither must wee thinke (although it hath pleased God for some secreete cause [40] only knowne to his diuine Maiestie, to yeelde Antwarpe and *Maestrecht*, thus into their handes) that he wyll spare to punish this theyr outragious crueltie, when his good wyl and pleasure shall be to doo the same: for surely their boasting and bragging of iniquitie, is ouer great to escape long vnskorged.

I haue talked with sundry of them, and demaunded why they would co[m]maund that the Townehouse should be burned: And their aunswer was, because it was the place of assembly where all euyll counselles were contriued. As though it were iust that the stockes[93] [and] stones should suffer for the offence of men. But such is their obstynate pride and arrogancie, that if they might haue their wyll, they woulde altogether raze [and] destroy the Townes, vntyll no one stone were left vppon another. Neither doeth their stubborne blindnes suffer them [41] to perceiue þ[a]t in so doing they should much endomage the King their Master, whome they boast so faithfully to honour, serue and obey.

As for the iniuries done by them vnto our owne nation particularlie, I wyll thus set downe asmuch as I knowe. We were quiet in the house appointed for the mansion of English Marchaunts vnder safe conduct, protectio[n] and Placard[94] of their King: hauing neither medled any waye in these actions, nor by any meanes assisted the estats of the countrey with money, munition, or any kinde of aydc. Yea the Gouernor and Marchauntes (foreseeing the daunger of the tyme) had often demaunded pasporte of the Kinges gouernours and officers to depart.

And all these with sundrie other allegations, wee propounded and protested vnto them before they entred the English house: desiring to be [42] there protected according to our priuiledges and graunts from the King their Maister. And that they would suffer vs there to remaine free from all outrage, spoile or raunsome, vntill wee might make our estate knowne vnto the Castellane,[95] and other head officers which serued there for þe sayd King. All which notwithstanding, they threatned to fyre the house, vnlesse we would open the doores: and being once suffred to enter, demaunded presently the raunsom of twelue thousande crownes of the Gouernor: Which summe, being not in deede in the house, neyther yet one third part of the same: they spared not with naked swordes and daggers to menace the sayde Gouernour, and violently to present[96] him death because he had not wherwith to content theyr greedie mindes. I wyll not boast

---

[92] besoigner (besongner)—a woman
[93] stockes (stocks)—timbers, the wooden frameworks of buildings
[94] placard—an official document or proclamation, often written or printed on one side of a single sheet, posted up, and publicly displayed
[95] castellane (castellan)—the governor or constable of a castle
[96] present—show; here, "show" implies "threaten with"

of any helpe afforded by me in that distresse: but I thanke the Lorde God, who [43] made mee an instrument to appease their deuillish furies. And I thinke that the Gouernour and al the company wyll confesse that I vsed mine vttermost skyll and ayde for the safegarde of theyr lyues, aswell as mine owne.

But in the ende, all eloquence notwithstanding, the Gouernour being a comlie aged Man, and a personne, whose hoarie heaires might moue pittie, and procure reuerence in any good minde, (especiallye the vprightnesse of his dealing considered) they enforced him with great danger to bring forth all the money, plate, and iewelles, which was in the house: [and] to prepare the remnant of twelue thousand crownes, at such dayes, and tymes as they pleased to appoynt. And of the rest of our Nation, which had their goodes remaining in their seuerall packehouses,[97] [and] lodgings elsewhere in the Towne, [44] they tooke such pitty, that fowre they slewe, and diuerse other they most cruelly [and] daungerously hurt: spoyling and raunsoming them to the vttermost vallewe that might be made or esteemed of all their goodes. Yea, some one they enforced to raunsome his goodes twise, yea thrise: and all that notwithstanding, tooke the sayd goodes violentlye from them at the last.

And al these iniuries being opened vnto their chiefe Gouernors in time conuenient, [and] whyles yet the whole summe set for seuerall raunsomes of our countreymen and the English house in generall, were not halfe paide: so that iustice and good order might partly haue quallified[98] the former rygors proffered by the Souldiours, the sayde gouernours were as slowe and deafe, as the other were quicke and light of hearing to finde the bottome of euerie bagge in the [45] Towne. So þ[a]t it seemeth they were fullye agreed in all thinges: or if any contention were, the same was but stryfe who or which of them might do greatest wrongs. Keeping the sayd Gouernor [and] Marchaunts there styl (without graunt of passeport or safeconducte) when there is scarcely any victualles to bee had for any money in the Towne, nor yet the sayd marchaunts haue any money to buye it, where it is. And as for creditte, neither creditte nor pawne can nowe finde coyne in Antwarpe. In these distresses I lefte them the twelfth of this instant Nouember 1576, when I parted from them, not as one who was hastie to leaue and abandone them in such miserye, but to solycite their ruefull causes here: and to delyuer the same vnto her Maiestie and councell in such sort as I beheld it there.

And this is in effecte the whole [46] trueth of the sacking and spoyle of so famous a Towne. Wherein is to be noated, that the Spanyerdes and their faction, being but fyue thousande, the trenches made againste them of suche height as seemed inuincible: the power within þe Towne fifeteene or sixteene thousand able fighting men well armed, (I meane the Townesmen ready armed being coumpted:) it was charged, entred, [and] wonne in three howres. And before sixe howers passed ouer, euery house therein sacked or raunsomed at the vttermost vallew.

---

[97] packehouses (packhouses)—warehouses
[98] quallified (qualified)—moderated, made less violent, made less severe

The which victory being miraculous and past mans capacitie to co[m]pre-hend how it should be possible, I must needs attribute vnto Gods iust wrath pow-red vpon the inhabitants for their iniquitie, more then to the manhoode and force of the Spanyerdes: and yet I meane not to robbe them of their deserued glorie, but to [*47*] confesse that both their order [and] vallure in charging and entring was famous[99]: And had they kept halfe so good order, or shewed the tenth part of such manly corage, in vsing theyr victory, and parting of their spoyle: I must then needes haue sayde that *Caesar* him selfe had neuer any such souldiours. And this must I needs say for them, that as theyr continual training in seruice doth make them expert in all warrelyke strategeme: so their daily trade in spoiling hath made them the cunningest ransackers of houses, and the best able to bring a spoyle vnto a quicke market, of any Souldiors, or Mastertheeues that euer I heard of.

But I leaue the skanning[100] of theyr deedes vnto God, who wyll bryddle theyr insolencie, when hee thinketh good and conuenient: And let vs also learne out of this rewfull[101] tragedie to detest [and] auoyde those synnes, and [*48*] prowde enormyties, which caused the wrath of God to be so furiouslye kindled and bent against the Towne of Antwerpe: let vs also (if euer wee shoulde be driuen to lyke occasion,) (which God forbidde) learne to looke better about vs for good order [and] dyrection, the lacke whereof was theyr ouerthrow. For surely the in-habytantes lacked but good guides and leaders: for hauing none other order ap-pointed, but to stand euerye man armed in readynes before his doore, they dyed there (many of them) fighting manfully, when the Walloners and high Duches fled beastly. Let vs also learne to detest the horrible cruelties of the Spanyerdes in all executions of warlike stratagemes, least the dishonour of such beastly deedes, might bedymme the honour wherewith Englishe Souldiours haue alwayes bene endowed in theyr victories. And fynally let vs praye to God [*49*] for grace to amend our lyues, and for power and foresyght to withstande the mallyce of our enemyes: that remayning and continewing in the peaceable protection of our most gratious Soueraigne, we maye geue him the glory, and all due and loyall obedience vnto her Maiestie, whome God nowe and euer prospere and preserue. *Amen.*

Wrytten the .xxv. daye of *Nouember* .1576. by a true English man, who was present at this pytteous massacre. *Vt supra.*

---

[99] famous—illustrious, admirable
[100] skanning (scanning)—passing of judgment
[101] rewfull (rueful)—lamentable, doleful, dismal

Thomas Churchyard, *A Plaine or moste true report of a daungerous seruice* (1580) || STC (2nd ed.) #5247

In 1580, the Spanish armies and their collaborators were advancing against the rebel Netherlanders on several fronts, and during that year they gained territory in Flanders and Overijssel. During a year of general retreat, English troops in Netherlandish service, under the command of John Norreys, recaptured Mechelen in Brabant from the Spaniards in April; the Englishmen's sack of the town, in echoing tribute to the Spanish sack of Antwerp in 1576, was known as the "English Fury."

Thomas Churchyard (1523?–1604), like George Gascoigne, was also a soldier, man of letters, and government agent—and also, like Gascoigne, financially strapped for much of his life. He served as a soldier in wars from the 1540s to the 1580s, including a stint in the Netherlands in the early 1570s, and pursued a literary career from the early 1550s to the year of his death. He was a persistent seeker after fame and patronage.

The pamphlet is notable for the elaborate explanations and justifications Churchyard wrote, which help to place military news pamphlets in their social and literary context within the world of English patronage and social hierarchy. The pamphlet is clearly a means for Churchyard to seek the patronage of his dedicatee, Henry Lord Norreys, by means of his flattering celebration of the exploits of Lord Norreys' son John. Churchyard also complimented English national feeling in his popular audience by celebrating an English martial valor purportedly slighted in Dutch reports of the battle—reminding us that these pamphlets also participated in the polemics of nations. As did *A discourse of such things as are happened in the armie of my lordes the princes of Nauarre, and of Condey* (1569), it also served as soft propaganda to increase the English audience's sympathies for Protestant forces fighting Catholic enemies.

[TITLE PAGE]

A PLAINE OR | moste true report of a daun- | *gerous seruice, stoutely attempt-ed, and* | manfully brought to passe by English | *men, Scottes men, Wallons*[1] *[and] other worthy sol-* | diours, for the takyng of *Macklin* on the sodaine, | a strong Citee in Flaunders: sette forthe at | large with speciall pointes to bee | noted: by *Thomas Church-* | *yard gentleman. 1580.*

Imprinted at London by Ihon Pe- | *rin, dwellyng in Paules Church-* | *yarde, at the Signe of* | *the Angell.*

[1]   [The Epistle.]
TO THE RIGHT | honorable my singuler good | *Lorde, the Lorde Norrice:*[2] *Thomas* | *Church-yard wisheth blessednesse of* | life, muche honor in the worlde | and the beste happe[3] can | bee desired.

MY good lorde the fauor and Noble dealynges towards me in the dayes you were lorde embassadour in Fraunce, when your aide and pollicie[4] *(by meane of a passeport) conuayed me from danger to the Prince of Orrange,*[5] *made me often remember that sutche courtesies with good will or seruice should bee re-* **[2]** *quited. But hauyng small power for the publishyng of duetie,*[6] *and little abilitie to requite a good tourne (watchyng occasion to bee gratefull) I take sutche matter as tyme doeth minister for a furtherer of my expectation,*[7] *and a meane to encrease my credite with your lordship. And consideryng whe[n] dolefull newes was brought of one of your cheefest sonnes dedde in Irelande,*[8] *I wrote a heauie*[9] *Epitaphe, I thought now hearyng greate and good newes of an other (both in nature and valliancie brother to the eldest who GOD hath called) to make a pece of ame[n]ds, for the saluyng of my first presumption, [and] the throughly expressyng of my present desire of duetifull doyng. So my good Lorde leauyng* **[3]** *circumstance of wordes and filed*[10] *phrases of florishyng ceremonies, I fall to my purposed matter. It hath been an olde maner, and a newe finenesse*[11] *in this cunnyng worlde, that sutche as could*

---

[1] Wallons (Walloons)—the French-speaking inhabitants of the Netherlands
[2] Henry Norreys, 1st Baron Norreys (1525–1601), English notable, and ambassador to France in the 1560s and early 1570s.
[3] happe (hap)—fortune, luck
[4] pollicie (policy)—political sagacity, prudence, skill; but possibly here "stratagem"
[5] William I "the Silent" (1533–1584), prince of Orange-Nassau from 1544 to 1584, leader of the Netherlanders' rebellion against Spain from 1568 to 1584.
[6] publyshing of duetie (publishing of duty)—public declaration and acknowledg-ment of obligation
[7] expectation—expectant waiting (here, of an opportunity to repay Lord Norris)
[8] Sir William Norreys (ca. 1547–1579), English soldier.
[9] heauie (heavy)—sorrowful
[10] filed—polished, smoothed, neatly finished off or elaborated
[11] finenesse (fineness)—cunning; stratagem

purchace praise or commendation by their owne practises (either by pen or tong) would
reape the glorie thei could get to themselues, and leaue out the fame of others, if trothe
by tract[12] *of tyme reueled not rightfull causes, and gaue eche well doer the reward of*
their workes, then if those maners of menne, finenesse of the worlde, [and] greedinesse
of glorie runnes awaie with hast to their owne commoditie,[13] *and no benefite to others:*
Blame not any nation (properly giuen to their priuate praise) to tread doun the laude
[4] and honor of any strange people, neither borne in their Countrey, nor commyng to
their soile, but to serue for money [and] sutche report of fame, as the Countrey maie spare
from them selues to the Soldiours, that serue for these twoo causes before rehearsed.[14]
Notwithstanding because the eager myndes of menne (that bites at euery blaste of fame)
shall not breed by their boldnesse, neither abuse nor ill custome, whereby the estimation
of forwardmen should be hindered, nor the quicke forwardnesse of vainglorie should not
finde too mutche occasion to triu[m]ph on the aduantage of tyme, I haue now tyme as I
thinke with trothe and good laisure, written sutche intellige[n]ce[15] *to the worlde of the*
taking of Macklin, [5] as I hope shal serue for a testimonie that my penne is euer honestly
occupied, and that no writer maie willingly (if lice[n]ce permit) suffer further report of
newes to be published, then the wise of the world alloweth, [and] the generall opinions
of men maie embrace. Thus wishing truthe alwaies (as a torche to burne on the topp of
a hill) to bee looked on, and affections of men to bee tried and wrested to the beste con-
structions of that whiche beste becomes a good worlde to heare, I present to your Lord-
ship the true reportes I haue heard for the winnyng of Macklin, and sutche thynges as
there happened at Macklins mischance:[16] *written not for that sutche matter (or a greate*
deale greater) can bee hid from a noble [6] man of your callyng. But presented to keepe
my acquaintaunce with my good freendes, and cause the worlde to imagine I was borne
vnder a Marcial planet and signe: and neither spareth pen, studie, nor paines to pre-
farre Marciall people, and honour the worthiest sorte of men. So hopyng your Lordship
lookes on my willyng mynde to dooe well, and turnes your face fro[m] the defectes of my
base phrase[17] *and writyng: I wishe your honor daiely to encrease, with the blessyng of*
God vpon your house and children. From Westminster the laste of Aprill: your Lord-
shippes at commaundement.

Thomas Churchyard.

[sig. b.i./7] *Macklins mischance.*

AS eche Countrey and Nations seekes their owne credite and aduauncement, so
hardly any forrain soldier reapeth fame in a strange soyle he serueth in: I meane
an Englishe man seruyng out of his owne Countrey (ioyned with straungers in

---

[12] tract—duration, lapse
[13] commoditie (commodity)—advantage
[14] rehearsed—recounted, related, narrated
[15] intelligence—news
[16] mischance—ill luck, disaster, calamity
[17] phrase—manner or style of expression

action) standes at reward of common report, or is subiecte to the affection of
the people where he serueth, who regardes more their owne estimation, then
the fame of a forraine Soldier, which soldier rather for fame then rewarde, goes
from the natiue soile he was borne in, and serueth a straunge people for a small
peece of money, but yet a great portion of praise and good [*8*] renowne. This not
spoke[n] nor applied to the discredite, and hindrance[18] of any straungers well
doyng, but in the defence and seruice of the Englishe Nation, whose labour,
charge,[19] courage, readinesse, and warlike mindes, is not inferiour to the greatest
neighbours, (or furthest of you can name) nere vs, in any Marciall order, maner,
discipline of warre, or hazard of life.

And for a profe of these special pointes herein rehersed, the moste warres
of christendome beares suche testimoniall and witnesse of their forewardnesse
(though here at home God bee praised is peace) that few or none hath been so
forward in the feeld, nor more daungerously serued. Then iniurie it were, and
cleane against good nature of men, and order of armes, that any nation for their
owne glory (vaine as a shadowe) should eclips the dezartes and valiauncie, of the
Englishe now seruyng in Flanders, drawne thether [**sig. b.ii./9**] for fame (and
their owne desires to do well) and liue from debt of the worlde and daunger of
the Lawe. In whose commendation, and for the trothe of matter now penned,
vnder good will of the wise, and sounde iudgemente of the world, I enter into a
discourse and plaine order of the takyng of *Macklin*, dispraisyng no Nation at the
seruice, nor leauyng out no matter is true, because trothe is to bee embraced, and
matter depending of flatterie or affection, is vtterly to be disalowed.

It happened I beyng at the Court (where the trothe of many thynges is moste
certain) I sawe a letter written out of Flaunders, from the handes of a gentilman,
whose eyes beheld to every seruice and enterprise, and the winnyng of the great
towne of *Macklin*, and the letter was so well penned, [and] went so directly to the
matter (in euery point and order) touchyng the particulars and generall takyng of
the same citie, [*10*] that I was forced by the credite of the gentilman that wrote
(and by the probable confirmation of sonderie other reportes) to beleue the letter to be moste true, and worthie the rehearsall to the open world. But amased
at the strangenesse of the hazard,[20] and wonderyng not a little at the attempt
(which was maruelous) I bethought me how the Spanyardes vpo[n] a resolution emong themselues sodainly set vpon *Antwerp*, and in a smal season had
the people at their mercie, and toune at their pleasure: and yet me thought this
enterprise for the winnyng of *Macklin*, surpassed all the exploites that euer before I heard of, or in deede throughly vnderstode. Tha[n] waiyng how sleightly I
had gone ouer the Seruices of Flaunders, in a booke called my *Choice*[21] knowyng

---

[18] hindrance—injury
[19] charge—responsibility
[20] hazard—venture
[21] Thomas Churchyard, *A Generall Rehearsall of Warres, called Churchyardes Choise* (1579).

that I had forgotten bothe maister Norris,[22] maister Ca[ven]dish, maister Yorke, and a number of others verie valiaunte gentilmen, that merites [*11*] more praise then my pen can giue the[m]. I thought to make amendes with the nexte woorke I should set out, and so peisyng[23] in the ballance of an vpright iudgemente, the weight and value of the valiauncie of men, and the inuinsible courages that reso-lute soldiours dooeth shewe. I tooke an accasion to publishe the letter I haue spo-ken of, and to stretche out the fame and honour of my countreymen, that other-wise might be darkned by disdaine, or drouned in forgetfulnesse, for want of true recorde that proceadeth from the penne of an honest writer, who iustlie maie be bold without blushyng, to report that he heareth, and maie be proued to be true. In the warrs betwene the Prince of Orrange and the *Mallecontants*,[24] for causes I nede not to touch *Mounsire de Fammai, and Mounsire de Temple*, beyng as some saie, the drawers[25] of a drift,[26] [and] to be at some execution of the practice, as appeareth by many mens [*12*] opinio[n]s, the ix. of Aprill eerely at a determined howre, by the consentes and deuises of suche as gouerned in Marciall affaires. Maister Ihon Norrice with seuen Enseantes,[27] beeyng but eight hundreth Eng-lishmen (or somewhat more) he Collonell of those companies, with the aide of the Scottes and Wallons fower hundreth, approched in orderly marche and man-ner (without sound of Dromme) nere the walles of *Macklin, Monsire de Famai* promisyng before that the Soldiours (on his honor) should haue fiue monethes paie for their further encouragemente to that and all other the like seruices.

And these whole companies approched, and deuidyng them selues some for the skalle[28] in one place, and some in an other, the one parte with Boates well manned, and the other wadyng verie depely to enter vpon the skalyng Ladders, some negligence or haste by some not spoken of, had almoste dis- [*13*] couraged the whole attempte: And in the ende failed their footyng, and forced Maister Nor-rice and the power with hym, to aduaunce them selues towardes the enemie, and dwell vppon their gard (with the losse of some tyme) before the face of the Toune, whiche by meanes of noyes and *Alarum* the daie beyng come, was in a readinesse for defence, and shotte of their peeces to their moste aduauntage, and the assail-antes discourage, defendyng a Courtaine[29] verie stoutly, against the whiche Cour-tain maister Ihon Norrice was faine to drawe fiue hundreth shotte, not meanyng thereby to enter. For the Boates by mischaunce of vnladyng of them were drouned,

---

[22] Sir John Norreys (ca 1547–1597), English soldier, later a notable English general.
[23] peisying (peising) — weighing
[24] mallecontants (malcontents) — the Catholic opponents of William the Silent
[25] drawers — devisers
[26] drift — scheme, plot, design
[27] enseantes (ensigns) — troops
[28] skalle (scale) — scaling ladder; or possibly "ascent"
[29] courtaine (curtain) — the plain wall of a fortified place; the part of the wall which connects two bastions, towers, gates, or similar structures

and the fiue hu[n]dred shot was drawne to this one place, to procure the people in
the toune to repaire thether, whiles some apointed for purpose, at an other place
should enter with more ease and lesse daunger. But those that were putt to [14]
the plonge for to wade, found the water so deepe, that it came aboue their shul-
ders: a matter to bee marueled at, a harde aduenture, and a sore escape: But by
that meanes thei found a waie to enter by Ladder at a Gate, where thei passed fiue
seuerall tymes with some small power,[30] but could enter no more but one persone
at once. Yet hap[31] serued so well, no resistaunce in that corner was made, till three
hundreth of the Englishe soldiours had possessed a peece of the toune: And then
the Albanoies[32] horse menne, thinkyng to breake through the force of footemen,
charged them. So suche as foolishely aduentured to farre of the footemen, fell into
the daunger of the Albanoies, whereon the horsemen gaue an other charge, and
tastyng with their boldenesse the pushe of the Pike,[33] and seeyng the Englishe
stande stoutly at defence, the Albanoies wheeled about, and forsooke that maner of
fighte, with the [sig. c.i./15] losse of diuers of their horsemen.

After which repulce the Albanoies had no mynde any more to come so nere
daunger, whereby the Burgoes[34] of the toune beganne to quaile, and stoode in a
little mase[35] and doubt of the matter. Then the whole tounes men and soldiours forsooke the rampiers[36] and manned bothe brigges and streates as well as thei might:
in this season and hard fight bothe doubtful and dangerous. The Englishe, Scottish,
and all the other Soldiours for that attempt presente, hauyng passed ouer the gates,
walles, and places of readiest entrie, marched forewardes (criyng a noble woorde)
and founde great resistaunce at the ende of euery streate by whiche sharpe encounter thei were faine by little and little (as Fortune serued their hopes) to winne their
ground with some losse of Soldiours who mynded[37] more victorie, then cowardlie
to retire, and at the laste with [16] mutche a doe and long bickeryng (the tounes
menne for their libertie and liues, and the assailantes for fame and conqueste) thei
came in vewe of the Market place, where the tounes men and their stoutest companies stood in order of battaile, euery waie flancked with ordinaunce:[38] But as
the French man saieth, *Il falloie aualler cela*,[39] the Soldiours meanyng to trie what

---

[30] power—number of troops
[31] hap—fortune, chance, luck
[32] Albanoies—Albanian
[33] the pushe (push) of the pike—the confrontation of pikemen (or soldiers generally) face-to-face, pushing and stabbing at each other with pikes until one side or the other
breaks and runs. Actually and proverbially fierce and trying combat.
[34] burgoes—burghers
[35] mase (maze)—a state of bewilderment
[36] rampiers—ramparts
[37] mynded (minded)—considered important
[38] ordinaunce (ordnance)—artillery
[39] *Il falloie aualler cela*—It must be swallowed

Fortune durste dooe, gaue a lustie[40] charge, and by Gods helpe, and the greate courage of sonderie stoute gentilmen, and officers of credite and value, thei had the vpper hande of their enemies, with whom thei made as short worke as thei might: But in deede before apparaunte victorie could any waie bee knowne, greate strug- gling and stoute sturre[41] on bothe sides was seen, and maister Ihon Norrice was matched with a lustie Limlifter,[42] a breachlesse[43] Freer called Brother Peter, the onely manne that made and maintained [sig. c.ii./17] all the broile[44] and businesse, who had put on a resolute mynde, either to kille Maister Norrice, or els to bee slaine hym self, and dealt blowes so brauelie in this his determination, that he hitt maister Norrice with a Halbert[45] two full thwackes on the Curate,[46] whiche blowes wer sone reuenged by maister Norrice, who dispatched þe Freer, and gaue hym a dedde paie[47] in recompence of his paines. This gallaunte Freer thus slain, ended all the strief and blodie braule: for then euery one cried *Misericorde*,[48] and fell piti- fully at the feete of the Soldiours, who findyng victorie vsed not mutche extremitie. For the nomber of all those that were slaine were not aboue twoo hundreth per- sones: one letter declareth that the gouernoure with the Albanoizes, dispairyng a little before the ouerthrowe fledde (out at a backe Porte[49] or Posterne)[50] to Louain and so saued their liues: an other letter saith the gouernor [18] was taken prisoner. Oure Englishe Nation loste in their companie a fifteene Commoners,[51] but as I beleeue thei were all gentilmen Soldiours.[52] For to the number of thirtie Englishe men were slaine, and fower score sore hurte: whiche argues of eight hundreth, one hundreth and more were likelie to haue paied their liues for their enterprise. And further the losse or hurtyng of so many oure Nation, manifestly declares that thei did most of the seruice, and deserues therefore the moste honor: how so euer the printyng of the firste newes bee taken and vnderstoode, one Maister Smithe, twoo valiaunte Lieutenantes, Maister Humfrey Turner an Enseante,[53] Maister Iones a

---

[40] lustie (lusty)—vigorous

[41] sturre (stir, stour)—tumult, commotion, armed conflict

[42] limlifter (limb-lifter)—fornicator

[43] breachlesse (breechless)—without breeches (i.e., dressed in a friar's robes); but with the contemptuous implication "naked about the buttocks"

[44] broile (broil)—tumult, quarrel

[45] halbert (halberd)—a combination of a spear and a battle-axe

[46] curate (cuirass)—body armor

[47] dedde paie (dead pay)—pay continued in the name of a dead soldier, and appro- priated by his commanding offcier

[48] Misericorde—Mercy

[49] porte (port)—gate

[50] posterne (postern)—back door, side gate

[51] commoners—probably, "common soldiers"

[52] gentilmen Soldiours (gentlemen soldiers)—gentlemen serving in the ranks rath- er than as officers

[53] enseante (ensign)—standard bearer

gallant yong Soldiour, were worthely seen serue, and slaine in the action. By a misfortune after the fight Maister Whitchurche, and Maister Heddleis brother of the Garde was slaine: and of all the other [19] Nations that came with the English, as yet can be knowne was but twoo persones slaine in the enterprise.

Nowe yet I praie you, heare what an other man of good credite wrote of this matter, who stoode and plainely behelde the seruice from the beginning to thende. The power of twelue hundreth in all, whereof eight hundreth were Englishmen, set forward from Filforde and came to *Macklin*, as eager as Haukes that seeketh their praie, wadyng to the chinne, and climyng ouer Iron gates, as men that cared not for life, so fame might be gotten. Yea surely saieth he, the strengthe of the toune considered, there was neuer vnder the cope[54] of heauen, suche an enterprise taken in hand, and brought to so glorious a victorie. For saieth he though very good captaines might after long fight [and] hurtes forsake the assault, these soldiers wer so desirous of seruice, that thei would not in any cace [20] at no tyme retire, and beeyng entered the toune but a very fewe, thei fought it out so manfullie, that maister Roulande Yorke stept into the water, wadyng after them to their succour: And at the present displaiyng of his Enseant,[55] he loste his Lieutenant, his Sergeante, and Maister Iones his Enseante bearer, and he hym self shotte through his Dublette, and Maister Norrice not as a Collonell, but as a common Soldiour, ledde his Soldiors the waie through thike and thin, where moste daunger appeared. And encountered Frier Peter, who was cheef leader of all the Priestes in the toune, he was in daunger to be slaine, for the Frier firste shotte of his peece,[56] then he tooke him to his Pike or Halberte, and laste fell to his sworde, and so like a couragious Confessour valliauntly lost his life. And when all the broyle was in a maner ended, he saith that looked vpon all these dooynges, [21] *Mounsire de Temple*, [and] *Mounsire de Fammai* came to the toune, or were peraduenture[57] about the toune nere the seruice, for the aunsweryng their hope, and furthering of the matter expected. Yet haue thei no sutche cause to bee written of, as those that wer the onely executioners of the seruice in deede: wherfore the firste printed booke of this newes must be wayed, accordyng to the trothe and vmore[58] of the matter.

After the toune was wonne, Maister Norrice did what he might too keepe his people from pillage, but in the meane while Temples men ioynyng with the Scottes gotte the best booties: wherevpon the Englishmen fell to take that easely might bee had, either of Churchmen or Cloister houses, but especially thei

---

[54] cope—vault
[55] enseant (ensign)—standard, banner
[56] peece (piece)—gun or cannon
[57] peraduenture (peradventure)—perchance
[58] umore (humor)—temperament, disposition. The implication is of unreliable partiality.

searched the Cloisters and Religious places, saiyng thei were Inquisitors[59] for to
seeke out Copes,[60] Surpleses[61] and Vestmentes,[62] and to take so good an order
by [22] their Commission, that no Masse should bee songe nor saied in *Macklin*
many a long yere after, for wante of gilted Challices, and golden Copes.

And the Shrine of Sainct Toinball was so terriblie handeled, that it was bothe
remoued out of his place, and left not worthe a pennie. And the Soldiours were so
wealthie, that the olde custome of the Spaniardes was taken vp againe, for Dice
plaie began so merrilie on the toppe of Drommes heddes, that money could not
tarrie in the bothome of mens purses. Men that haue by their forwardnes found
sutche good Fortune, are to bee excused, though thei merrilie passe a little money awaie at Dice: Declaryng by that pastime whiche standeth on good happe to
winne, or euill lucke to lose. The whole life of manne standeth but on hazarde
and chance: a matter that soldiours doe mutche marke, and the worlde can not
denie. But for all their [sig. d.i./23] plaiyng at Dice (whiche Soldiours will not
bee barred from) their Capitaines and Leaders, as it is reported, had more regard
to that whiche was so hardly gotten, and yet to redeeme a Capitaine out of prison,
maister Norrice hath paied a greate somme of money, whiche money was moste
noblie employed: my freende good Capitaine Morgane[63] that now is in *Macklin*,
will I warrant you confesse the same whe[n] he is asked. An other poincte of hon-
or is to bee spoken of. For when a Nonrie in the toune was readie to be spoiled,
Maister Norrice hearyng that some Englishe women were emong the Noonnes,
defended them from harme, and sette them free, and vsed other courtesies more,
that is worthie the noting. When I heard of this noble parte of a Soldiour, I remembred how a greate conquerour,[64] in a maner of the moste parte of the worlde,
hauing *Darius*[65] wife[66] and a nomber of gal- [24] launte Ladies vnder his mercie:
vsed hymself so honourably towardes his captiues, that for feare to bee tempted
with their beauties, he would not scarce come where thei were, and yet were the
prisoners so reuerentlie and honestly vsed (beyng women of greate callyng and
birth) that *Darius* thought hym self happie (though vnfortunate Prince he was) to
bee conquered of sutche a noble kyng as *Alexander*, who could not onely conquer

---

[59] inquisitors — members of the Roman or Spanish Inquisitions; proverbial figures
of hatred or fear for Protestants, with a reputation for brutal efficiency

[60] copes — the long cloaks or capes worn by monks, friars, and ecclesiastics; or possibly "cups"

[61] surpleses (surplices) — loose vestments of white linen worn by clerics and others
taking part in church services

[62] vestmentes (vestments) — priestly garments

[63] Possibly Sir Thomas Morgan (ca. 1550–1595), a noted English soldier of the period. He served at Mechelen, but with a higher rank than Captain.

[64] Alexander the Great.

[65] Darius III (ca. 380 B.C.–330 B.C.), Emperor of Persia from 336 B. C. to 330 B.C.

[66] Stateira (?–331 B.C.)

his owne affections, but winne his enemies hartes by his fauourable and Princelie dealynges: And surely greater honor is gotte[n] by vsyng victorie wiselie, then by ouerthrowyng a multitude with manhoode, without shewyng mercie and gentilnesse. A conquerour by repressyng crueltie by courtesie, is hadd in admiration of his verie enemies, and a victor without vertue and pitifull consideration, is hated emong his freendes, and despised generally emo[n]g [sig. d.ii./25] all kinde of people. Nowe you muste note that the Englishemen, and suche as entered the toune by hazard, furie of shotte, danger of sworde, and pushe of the Pike, are not a little to bee honoured and praised, and more to bee commended then thousandes of those that stood a farre of, and gaue but the lookyng on. And you maie see by the same some menne are happie, not onely to passe through many perilles, but likewise to liue long, and make them selues and their soldiours ritche: and cause the fame of their Countrie to be spred as farre as the winde can blow, or the Sunne maie shine. And the more happie be our Englishemen and Scottes men, with all the reste of this attempte, that thei dwell as yet in the place thei haue taken, and mynde not to parte there fro[m], till the poore Soldiours bee pleased. And the keepyng the saied Toune in their handes all this while, argues thei haue deserued [26] too haue the charge thereof, though *Mounsire Fammai* beare the name to bee the Gouernour of *Macklin*.

Thus haue you heard the effecte [and] rehersall of two letters, sent into Englande from those in Flaunders, that sawe *Macklin* bothe wonne and loste, which commyng to light and to the open eye of the worlde, showes that all tounes, fortresses, and holdes[67] (bee thei neuer so stro[n]g) are subiect to sodain ouerthrowes, and in the deuine disposition of the Almightie, who visiteth a number of our neighbours, with many kindes of callamities, to make vs beare in mynde his Omnipotente power, and our owne dueties to GOD and our Prince. This peece of seruice I haue touched, because euery Nation prefarres their owne Countriemen, and the Englishe doe thei neuer so well, and be the first at a breach[68] (or at the saulte of a Toune) thei are the last shalbe spoken of, and the worst [27] rewarded) especially where beste thei deserue, and moste should be made of. I feare it is some mennes Deastenie, neither at home nor abroade to reape no benefite of their labours. So for this season I bid you farewell, myndyng hereafter to shewe other seruises that are forgotten in my booke of *Choice*, that was ouer hastely Printed, and must be runne ouer againe, bothe for the fame of some therein lefte out, and the troth of some matters I was wrong instructed of. And to keepe the people in some good likyng of me and my woorkes, I am presently settyng out a discourse of the late yeartquake,[69] not touched of any writer in Englishe here tofore: Though some haue touched many good pointes to bee noted, bothe

---

[67] holdes (holds)—strongholds
[68] breach—a gap in a fortification, made by artillery fire
[69] Thomas Churchyard, *A warning for the wise, a feare to the fond, a bridle to the lewde, and a glasse to the good: Written of the late earthquake chanced in London and other places* (1580).

learnedlie and louynglie with duetifull order, declared to God and the worlde. Thus once againe crauyng your pacience and iudgemente, to read before you condempne, I [*28*] bid you *adue*,[70] and goe aboute the Printyng of my booke presently promised.

Finis.

---

[70] adue (adieu) — farewell

A. M., *The True Reporte of the prosperous successe which God gaue vnto our English Souldiours* (1581) ||
STC (2nd ed.) #17124

In 1570, Pope Pius V had excommunicated Elizabeth I of England; his successor, Pope Gregory XIII, encouraged Philip II of Spain to invade and dethrone Elizabeth, and lent his support to an attempt to raise a revolt against her in Ireland. In July 1579, the Irish rebel James Fitzmaurice Fitzgerald landed in Dingle with 700 Spanish and Italian troops recruited under papal auspices, and much of Munster and Leinster soon rose up against the English government, under the auspices of the earl of Desmond. English counter-attacks, however, soon broke the back of the rebellion, and the last city in Ireland they reconquered was Smerwick, held by six hundred late-arriving papal reinforcements. The town surrendered in November 1580, and most of the papal troops were butchered by the English. The last sparks of the rebellion were extinguished in 1583.

This pamphlet relies very largely on a letter to Elizabeth from Arthur Grey de Wilton, lord deputy of Ireland and commander of the English expedition to Smerwick. The pamphlet, which covers the relatively under-reported theatre of Ireland, is most notable for the matter-of-fact way it describes the slaughter of the surrendered Catholic garrison of Smerwick. This slaughter was justified on the grounds that the soldiers were aiding rebels against the English crown, but it may have been made easier by the fact that the slaughtered were Catholics fighting in Ireland. The pamphlet includes an introductory poem, by way of editorial comment. It also contains a considerable amount of anti-Catholic polemic.

[TITLE PAGE]

The true reporte of the prosperous successe | *which God gaue vnto our English Souldiours a-* | gainst the forraine bands of our Romaine[1] enemies, lately ariued, | (but soone inough to theyr cost) in Ireland, in the yeare .1580.

Gathered out of the Letters of moste credit and | circumstaunce,[2] that haue beene sent ouer, and more at large | set foorth then in the former printed Copie.

For a singuler comfort to all godly Christians, [and] true harted sub- | iectes, and an exceeding encouragement to them to persist valiantly in | their true Religion and faithe towards God, their due obedience and | looue to their Prince,[3] and to repose their whole assured confidence | in the strengthe of the Almight-ie, as moste safe vnder | the Shield of his protection.

Seene and allowed.

Imprinted at London for Edward White, dwelling at the little North | doore of Paules Church, at the signe of the Gunne.

[1]   WHo wayeth well each point of this discourse,
        How crooked hap[4] encounters canckred[5] minde:
        How rightfull cause subdueth wrongfull force,
        How he is caught that layes the snare: shall finde,
        Naught bootes[6] it then to trust to any ods,
        Who Giantlike doo fight against the Gods.[7]

        To rob all Princes of their rule and right,
        God of the glory due to him alone:
        Man of his soule, and Sathan of his might,
        To boulster Rebelles, gainst their Princes throne:
        To seeke Gods truthe and Gospell to suppresse.
        Let all men iudge if this be *holynesse*.

---

[1] Romaine (Roman) — Roman Catholic
[2] circumstaunce (circumstance) — circumstantiality of detail
[3] Elizabeth I Tudor (1533–1603), queen of England from 1558 to 1603.
[4] hap — chance, fortune, luck
[5] canckred (cankered) — infected with evil, corrupt, depraved, malignant, spiteful
[6] bootes (boots) — avails
[7] According to Greek myth, the giants rose up in a war against the gods, but were defeated.

O *Roome*, the roome, where all outrage is wrought,
The Sea of sinne, the beast with seuenfold head:[8]
The Shop wherein all shame is sould and bought,
The Cup whence poison through the world is spred.[9]
Well maist thou draw the simple with a Dreame,
And ween to winne, yet striue against the streame.

Who fauours, feares, or followes with desine,
Thy state, thy strength, thy vaine and wicked reed:
Deserues, dislikes, and iustly dooth acquire,
The swoord, thy swaye, destruction for his meed.
Let Pope, let Turke, let *Sathan* rage their fill:
God keepeth vs, if we doo keepe his will.

Esto Honor [et] gloria Domini.[10]

[2]   *To the Reader.*
BEcause there go many and diuers reports of the late conflict in *Ireland*, proceeding of sundry Letters sent ouer, which, although they agree in effect and sub-
staunce of the matter, yet haue not euery one the same, nor any one the whole
circumstaunce of the manner thereof: And hauing considered how that it is not
onely vsuall among the people, to be desirous to know newes, but also necessary
that this happy newes should be knowen vnto all (aswell to the true religious and
obedient subiect, for his comfort, as to the supersticious disloyall recusant,[11] for
his vtter dismaying and confusion): I haue thought it not amis to bestow some
light paines of my little leisure, in gathering one sound discourse out of those
sundry fragments which haue come to my hands, some presented vnto me in
writing out of *Ireland*, and some imparted vnto me (by the aduertisements[12] of
men of good credit) out of those letters which were sent vnto her Maiestie,[13] the
true collection whereof I present vnto the well affected Reader, in such order as
the time would serue me to dispose them.

---

[8] "And I stood upon the sand of the sea, and saw a beast rise up out of the sea, having seven heads and ten horns, and upon his horns ten crowns, and upon his heads the
name of blasphemy": Revelation 13:1. The beast is the Antichrist; hence to Protestants of
the time, the pope or the papacy.

[9] Allusion to Revelation 17:4.

[10] *Esto Honor [et] gloria Domini.* — Let it be to the Lord's honor and glory.

[11] recusant — a(n English) Roman Catholic who, breaking the law, refused to attend
the services of the Church of England

[12] advertisements — informations, notifications

[13] Elizabeth I.

[sig. A iii./3]   Newes out of *Irelande.*

THe enimies lying (as it seemed) very surely entrenched in the Forte which they had made, which they called, *Il Castel del Oro*,[14] and sufficiently manned with Soldiers, to withstand a farre greater force then our Englishe men were, they beeing in number sixe hundreth within the Forte, and our men but eyght hundreth abroade:[15] which is a verie vnequall match (as they knowe well, which are skylfull, and haue bene exercised in those affayres) considering the ods of place, the one beeing vnder couert,[16] well fortified, and hauing theyr Ordinaunce,[17] placed at all aduauntage, the other naked,[18] vtterly without Municion, or opportunity of placing any Ordinaunce, wherby to auoyde[19] theyr enimies, beeing them selues continually subiect to their annoyaunce. The Lord Deputie,[20] beeing (in so great disaduauntage) almost in dispayre of dooing any good, was soone recomforted[21] with the happy arriuall of the Queenes Shippes, which it is to be thought that the verie great and woonderfull prouidence of God (quite beside their expectation) sent thither so luckely for their succour. [**MARGIN:** The *Swift sure*, one of the Queenes Maiesties ships, ariued at *Smitherick* xvii. daies before the rest of her fellows in which time, the enemy shot 30. shot a day, and neither could hit Ship nor man.] They beeing arriued, there were certayne great Peeces[22] brought out of the Shippes, and a Trench made, [and] that great Ordinaunce planted about fowre hundreth paces from the enimies Forte, to batter it: which Ordinaunce was so well plyed all that day (beeing the ninth of Nouember) that they galled[23] the enimie greeuouslie, and beat them away from plying theyr Ordinaunce.

On the tenth day in the morning, they cast[24] an other Trench for small shotte,[25] within an hundreth, and three score paces of the Forte, and began a freshe batterie, and espying certayne Peeces within the Forte, that were lyke to annoy the Campe, planted theyr Ordinaunce against them, and dismounting two of theyr Demicanons,[26] brake and defeated the rest, to the number of foureteene or fifteene great Peeces. And the same night made a third Trench for small shotte, within a hundreth and twenty foote of the Fort. Afterward perceyuing

---

14 *Il Castel del Oro*—the Castle of Gold
15 abroade (abroad)—out of doors, out in the open air; probably here, "outside the Fort"
16 covert—cover, concealment, protection
17 ordinaunce (ordnance)—artillery
18 naked—badly clothed; exposed to assault
19 avoyde (avoid)—to rid, to remove, to empty out
20 Arthur Grey (1536–1593), 14th Baron Grey of Wilton, Lord Deputy of Ireland from 1580 to 1582.
21 recomforted—inspirited with fresh courage
22 peeces (pieces)—cannon
23 galled—harassed
24 cast—dug
25 small shotte (shot)—musket bullets
26 demicanons (demi-cannon)—a cannon usually of about 6 ½ inches bore

that the *Spanish* Musket shot was the hottest, and espying a house of boordes, where they were bestowed: they beat [4] that downe with the Ordinance, and scattered the Muskets:[27] Which doone, the enimies finding them selues thus dismembred,[28] and vtterlie dispoyled of theyr cheefe force, whereto they trusted: beganne to chaunge theyr countenaunce, and hung out theyr banners of Truce, quietly calling for Parle.[29] Then issued out a braue *Italian*, who beeing demaunded by my Lord Deputie, who sent him thether? answered, The holy Father: Wyll you (sayd my Lord) aduenture in the seruice of a shaueling,[30] an Antichrist,[31] a murtherer bothe of soule [and] body, against such a Prince as my Mistresse is? You shall haue the iust reward of your seruice. And requiring him to bring foorth the cheefe of the *Spaniardes*, he asked the sayd *Spaniarde*, who sent him thether? He sayd he could not tell. Whether the King of *Spaine*? He sayd no: Whether with the Kinges knowledge? He aunswered no: But (sayd he) at *Porto* in *Portugall*, the Gouernor there co[m]maunded mee, to goe to such a place, where I should receyue my chardge, which I dyd, but whether I should goe, or against whome I knew not, and so brought to this place as blindfold, and (as I see now) vtterly betrayed. Then (quoth my Lord) if you be not sent by the King, you come as a runnagate, and must receyue the lyke hyer.[32] They desiring to depart with the honor of Soldiers, it was denied them. Then resolued they to surrender vp the Fort, to yeelde theyr money and Iewels, and other things of price, into the Lord Deputies handes, and them selues to his mercy: Whereof he accepting, receyued three of them pledges vntyll the next morning, when according to that conclusion, they returned, and the cheefe of them (whome it is needlesse to name, they onely remayning a lyue) to the number of twenty were saued. The rest to the number of fiue hundreth and sixe were slaine, and seuenteene hanged. The poore English Soldiors that lacked hose [and] shooes, and were barely cloathed, by means of this medley,[33] fou[n]d to apparell them, *Al modo Italiano*.[34] Wine and Bisket they met with good store, and other victuals for a good space: fowre thousand Armors, with many good Peeces, and (as they say) some reasonable share of Ecclesiasticall *Italian* money. In all this conflict there were onely two hurt of our men, whereof the one was Maister *Iohn Cheeke*, who is thought vnlikely to recouer. [MARGIN: Maister *Iohn Cheek* my Ladie *Cheekes* sonne.] Thus may we see how God fighteth for vs, and subdueth our enemies, who by all mans rea- [sig. A.iiii./5] son and

---

27 muskets—musketeers
28 dismembred (dismembered)—divided, cut off from one another
29 parle (parley)—negotiation of terms of surrender
30 shaveling—a contemptuous epithet for a tonsured ecclesiastic
31 Antichrist—an opponent, or the great and final opponent, of Christ; often applied by Protestants to the Pope
32 hyer (hire)—pay, reward
33 medley (mêlée)—combat, skirmish
34 *Al modo Italiano*—in Italian style

likelyhood were not to be ouerthrowne by ten times the nomber that our men
were, in that vnreasonable inequalitie of defence and Furniture.[35] For our men
were in that opinion, that if they had beene within the Forte so well appointed[36]
of great and small shot as the enemies were, it would haue cost 10000. lyues before it would haue beene wonne. But by the good prouidence and assistaunce of
God (notwithstanding their great aduantage) the Lord Deputie with his worthy
endeuor by land, and our ships (through their fortunate ariuall) by water did so
coupe them vp on euery side, that they could no way escape. They sayd that if
our Ships had stayed but two dayes longer, out of that Harboroughe, they would
haue beene gone. For at their first ariuall, there came syxe sayle of them, being
of men in number about 800, who so soone as they beheld the barrennesse of the
Countrey, and the brutishnes of the people, two of the greatest Shippes departed
home againe, with about 300. men in them, and left the rest to taste of the good
entertainement that they looked for there: which (thanks be to God) they found
not so satisfiable to theyr wicked expectacion, as agreeable to their iust desarts,
which would be incited by a blasphemous Antichristian Prelate, against a true
zealous Christian Prince, wrongfully to inuade her rightfull inheritaunce and
possessions, and to assist her disobedient and rebellious Subiects, against their
most gracious renowmed Soueraigne. Wherein, although the Popes[37] holines
forsoothe followed the footesteps and example of his Predecessors, which haue
beene euer sowers of sedition, raisers of Rebellion, maineteyners of disobedience,
Authors of infinite bloudshedding, which is euen growne to be the Badge of their
Catholike (or rather *Cacolike*)[38] profession, and the true Cognisance of their ho-
linesse: yet these Gallants should haue had more wit, to haue looked or they had
leapt, and sounded the depth, ere they had entred the shore of a forraine Princes
dominion. But as theyr greedynes of gaine, or superstitious deuocion towardes
an infamous Foole, hath brought them to the Shipwracke of theyr lyues (at the
least) so hath their vnaduised rashnes vtterly sunck, all excuse of theyr guiltines,
and pittie of theyr miscarying. They confessed vnto my Lord Deputie, that the
Pope theyr paymaister, whose Ensignes[39] they spread on theyr Fort, with [6]
his Crownes, Miters,[40] Croskeyes,[41] and other lyke trumperie, promised to send
them a greater power, for which cause they brought much Treasure with them,
beeing appoynted to stay for that supplie, for which our Englishmen were not
greatly sorie. It is reported that eyther they or other, were already comming at

---

[35] furniture—munitions
[36] appointed—equipped
[37] Ugo Boncampagni (1502–1585), Pope Gregory XIII from 1572 to 1585.
[38] κακός is Greek for bad or evil; hence Cacolike is an insulting wordplay on Catholic.
[39] ensignes (ensigns)—standards, banners
[40] miters (mitres)—ecclesiastical headdresses
[41] croskeyes (cross keys)—the papal insignia is of crossed keys of silver and gold, representing the pope's power to bind and loose on Earth and in Heaven (Matthew 16:19)

that tyme: for the fowreteenth of Nouember, there was escried a Pynnis,[42] to-wardes the coast of *Irelande*: but I take it to be rather an opinion or imagination of some co[m]ming, conceyued through that former report: then any true appa-raunce of the verie persons approching. Howsoeuer it be, it is no great matter, for our Soldiers stay there, and certayne of our Ships this winter, to welcome them.

The Earle of *Desmond*,[43] and his brother *Iohn*,[44] were co[m]ming towards the reskew of the *Spaniards* [and] *Italians*: but hearing how the Forte was taken, and what was become of theyr assistaunts, they thought it wisdome to beware by theyr exa[m]ple and to keepe them selues out of such sharpe clawes, and so re-tyred them backe, [and] are fled into the Mountaynes. Our good cou[n]tryma[n] of the Deuils owne dubbing, Doctor *Saunders*[45] (an Apostata towards his Saui-our, and Archtraytor to his Soueraigne) is there in the countrey, but where, it is vnknowen. One of his me[n] was take[n] in the Fort, [and] a Preest of that order, who were hanged [and] quartered in the Forte. Thus much hath bene certified out of *Ireland*, of what was doone there before the fifteene day of Nouember last past. For which ioyfull and happy newes, let vs render harty thankes vnto our almighty protector, attributing the whole prayse thereof vnto his omnipotencie, beseeching him to preserue our most gratious Princes, vnder whose prosperous gouernment we haue receyued bothe this [and] other infinite blessings at his hands: to strengthen our good Captaines and Soldiors, with force and power to ouercome our bodily foes, and vs al with his grace, to withstand the assaultes of the Deuill, and the tyranny of Antichrist his dearling (our spirituall enemy) [and] to serue our Redeemer in true feare and holynesse, and his true Minis-ters with due looue and reuerence, to be faithfull vnto him, loyall to her Maies-tie, lyke minded and charitable one to an other, to the glorie of his name: vnto whome all glorie, power, and dominion belongeth.

FINIS.

---

[42] pynnis (pinnace)—a small, light vessel

[43] Gerald Fitzgerald (ca. 1533–1583), 15th earl of Desmond, leader of the Second Desmond Rebellion from 1579 to 1583.

[44] Sir John Fitzgerald (ca. 1540–1582), brother of the earl of Desmond, leading par-ticipant in the Second Desmond Rebellion from 1579 to 1582.

[45] Dr. Nicholas Sander (ca. 1530–1581), Catholic controversialist, and papal emis-sary to Ireland during the Desmond Rebellion.

A Discourse and true recitall of euerie particular of the
victorie obtained by the French King, on Wednesday the
fourth of March, being Ashwednesday (1590) ||
STC (2nd ed.) #13131

In 1589, Henri III of France was assassinated; his successor was the Protestant Henri IV. Henri IV's accession to the throne sent much of Catholic France into rebellion, led by the house of Guise; Henri IV would have to conquer much of his kingdom. From his base in southwestern France he marched north to win the battle of Arques in September 1589, then took much of Normandy in December. An army of the Catholic League, under the Duke de Mayenne, began to challenge Henri IV for control of Normandy early in 1590; on 14 March 1590, the Protestant and Catholic armies met at Ivry, and Henri IV won a decisive victory. Thereafter Henri IV was able to dominate the countryside around Paris, but, since he was not strong enough to assault the city, he settled in for a long siege.

This pamphlet, like *Discourse of such things as are happened in the armie of my lordes the princes of Nauarre, and of Condey* (1569), was translated from the French; it likewise was Huguenot domestic propaganda doubling as propaganda intended to influence an English audience. It also served to promote in England the Protestant warrior-king legend of Henri IV, which would be so rudely shattered in 1594 by his conversion to Catholicism. Voss has explored the importance of these news pamphlets as the grounds for literary production in the 1590s;[1] this pamphlet is an excellent example of the heroic image of Henri IV that formed the basis for Shakespeare's Navarre, Marlowe's Henri, and Spenser's Burbon.

---

[1] Voss, *Elizabethan News Pamphlets.*

[TITLE PAGE]

A | Discourse and true | recitall of euerie particular of the | *victorie obtained by the French* | King,[2] on Wednesday the | fourth of March, being | Ashwednesday.

Also of his good successe that he hath had | since that time, in taking of cer- | taine Townes.

Out of French into English.

Seene and Allowed.

AT LONDON,

Printed by Thomas Orwin, for Richard Oliffe, and are | to be sold at his shop in Paules Church-yard, at the | Signe of the Crane. 1590.

[**sig. A 3/1**] A Discourse and true recitall of | *euerie particular of the victorie ob-* | tained by the King of *France*, on | *Wednesday the 4. of March be-* | *ing Ashwednesday.*
    YOV vnderstood by my last aduertisement[3] how God had giuen victorie to the king ouer his enemies: since which time I haue endeuoured my selfe to learne the truth of all things, as neere as I could, of such as were present at the fight, who say the victorie as it fell out, was a miraculous worke of God: for the forc-es of the Duke *de Maine*[4] were 4500. horse, aswell armed as possible, amongst which were 1600. Launces, and the rest Petronells[5] armed, and 18000. footmen, and the forces of the King were 2000. horse, and 12000. foote. The King was aduertised that the Duke *de Maine* was passed the Riuer at *Maunte*, and that he iornied with great boldnes towards him: wherevpon it was aduised in counsell to raise his siege before *Dreux*, which had sustained two assaults, and so vpon monday the 2. of March the King raised [**2**] his siege, [and] encamped himselfe so neere the Duke, that the same night certaine Marshalls of the Duke lodged in certaine Villages were dislodged by the King, and there lodged himselfe by force. The next morning the King did put himselfe into the field in a faire plaine, and sawe that the Duke was returned betweene Saint *Andre* and *Yury* nere *An-net*, three quarters of a mile further than he was the day before, which troubled the King much to seeke him so farre; which was great aduantage to the enemie,

---

    [2] Henri IV de Bourbon (1553–1610), king of France from 1589 to 1610.
    [3] advertisement—information, notification
    [4] Charles de Guise (1554–1611), duke de Mayenne, leader of the Catholic League during the French Wars of Religion.
    [5] petronells (petroneliers)—soldiers armed with a petronel, a kind of large pistol or carbine often used by cavalrymen

and perill to the King to approach them, which made them to leaue a Village that they held. This day was nothing performed but skirmishes. The Wednesday morning the King caused euerie man to bee put in aray,[6] he himselfe ordered the whole, and gaue order that so soone as they heard one peece of Ordnance[7] shot of, they should prepare themselues to the battaile.

The Duke by his Espialls had discouered the signe of the Cannon, but vnderstood it had been to haue prepared for their departure, and therefore sought by all meanes to knowe which way the King ment to flee, and trussed[8] vp his baggage[9] to followe: but it fell out otherwise, for at this signe euerie man was prepared.

The Tuesday before, the Duke sent to knowe how the King was apparelled, whereby to knowe him, the better to lay[10] to kill him. The King being aduertised[11] hereof, sent a Tru[m]pet to tell him, that he was sorie he took so much paine, [and] that he would ease him of that care, and that he gaue him to vn- **[3]** derstand, that (if he had desire to see him) he should finde him mounted vpon a gray horse, with a great white feather in his crest armed in blew and black, and desired to knowe how he would be armed and mounted, for that he desired to speake with him verie neere; vnto the which he answered, he would be armed in red, but the gallant was armed in black. The King hauing commaunded all into battaile aray,[12] did command euerie one to pray, which they all gladlie did in particular.[13] This done, the king began to march forward with some part of his Cornet[14] of horse, and caused one of the squadrons of his horse to approach behinde him, in the which was the Artillerie, which was shot with such furie amongst the *Reisters*,[15] thrice out of euerie Cannon, that he made at euery shot a faire breach:[16] notwithstanding they did not let to come to the charge,[17] where they were well receiued; and of the Cannons which the enemie discharged, there was but one shot that hurt, wherewith was slaine of the Kings Cornet foure or fiue persons. The Cornet of the King was so hardlie[18] assailed by 1600. horse in 4. parts, that he that bare the Cornet[19] was throwne downe, [and] all that troope

---

[6] aray (array) — arrangement (of soldiers) in lines or ranks
[7] ordnance — artillery
[8] trussed — packed
[9] baggage — portable military equipment
[10] lay — lie in wait with malicious intent
[11] advertised — informed
[12] battaile aray (battle array) — the order of troops arranged for battle
[13] in particular — invidivually, separately
[14] cornet — a company of cavalry
[15] Reisters (Reiters) — German cavalry soldiers
[16] breach — gap or disruption in the line of soldiers
[17] they did not let to come to the charge — probably means "they did not fail to make a charge"
[18] hardlie (hardly) — severely
[19] cornet — standard, banner

forced to retire. The King which was in another Cornet than in his owne, hauing left *Chiccot* apparelled like himselfe, sauing he had two Foxe tailes hanging in his Helmet, was merueilously charged, thinking it had bin the king, for the which *Chiccot* did mock them, [and] defended himselfe valiantlie. The King seeing the said Cornet so hardlie assailed, came to the head of the ene- **[4]** mie encouraging his Armie, which began to retire, crying *A moy enfans*,[20] it is I that am the King, and his feather being high mounted, serued for a standard, and then euerie one began to returne to the King, and charged the *Spaniards* and *Wallons*,[21] which shewed themselues valiant men: but it it had not been for the comming of the King, all his men had fled. Vpon which returne and charge, the *Spaniards* and *Wallons* sodainlie began to flee, who were presentlie pursued by the King and his men, who gaue them no time, once being broken, to ioyne againe, charging them in sundry places. The Marshal *Daumont*[22] charged the *Reisters*, and passed and repassed twise through them: wherevpon the said *Reisters* seeing the *Spaniards* and *Wallons* flee, which were 1600. Launces[23] wel mounted, fled also. The Marshal *Daumont* pursuing them, met the Launce Knights,[24] who charged him, and caused him to stay to fight: but the Launce Knights stood but a while, and retired into a small Wood, whether the footmen of the King went to them, and put the[m] al to the sword.

While this battaile was fighting, the Lord of *Humieres* of *Picardie* arriued with 300. horse to the King, who charged also the *Wallons*, and came in good time. The King fearing at the first he and his companie had been enemies that had come to charge him: but when he sawe them to assaile the *Spaniards*, hee reioyced and was glad, and then sent to knowe what he was, and it was answered, that it was *Humieres*. This man helped the King much to ouerthrowe the *Spaniards* and *Wallons*, who **[sig. B/5]** stood well valiantlie before, and to saie trueth, there was none that fought well of the enemies side that day but they: By the opinion of those that were at the battaile: that first without the helpe of God, and secondarelie, the valiantnes of the King, and thirdlie the happie comming of *Humieres*, the battaile had been lost on the Kings side. But marke a notable miracle, in a moment our men retired, in a moment againe returned, [and] after in a moment put the enemies to flight: for so soone as the King had gathered againe his men together, setting vppon them, the feare of God strooke them, (for by the iudgement of men, they had no other occasion) and so fled: also it was thought

---

[20] *A moy enfans*—To me, countrymen

[21] Wallons (Walloons)—the French-speaking inhabitants of the Netherlands

[22] Jean d'Aumont (1522–1595), count of Châteauroux, Marshal of France. A moderate Catholic, he fought against the Huguenots until Henri IV became king in 1589, at which point he swore allegiance to Henri and fought against the Catholic League

[23] launces (lances)—lancers

[24] launce knights (lance knights, landsknechts, lansquenets)—(German) mercenary soldiers, usually armed with a lance

they feared the Marshall *Byron*,[25] who all this while stood in a heape with 600. Horse[26] to sustaine and giue helpe to the weakest parte of the Kings battaile,[27] but when the King sent him word to giue helpe to his Cornet which was sore oppressed, he made answere, that his lying still did giue more terror [and] feare to the enemie making signe euerie mynute to set vpon the[m], than if he had entred the battaile, for if he had charged the enemie, they should no longer haue feared, seeing all the Kings forces to bee imployed. There were three Cornets of the Kings, which at the first retired, of the which S. *Bonet* which bare the cornet of Captain *Rowlet* was one. The said *Rowlet* remained still in the Kings Camp onlie with 12. Lances, but afterwards did put himselfe into another Cornet to fight. *Gerponnite* who carried the Cornet of the Gouernour of *Deepe* fel vnder his horse, where- [6] vpon one of the greatest and ritchest Barons of *Caux*, being the commanders Lieftenant ran to the baggage to keepe it obtaining thereby great honour. In briefe, there were many astonied,[28] and surelie had it not been thorough the great endeuour of the King who with Marshall *D'aumont* and others hauing their hearts [and] minds fullie bent, stil incouraging his people all had been lost. *De Maine* seeing this hard onset,[29] stayed not the charging of himselfe although he had with him 500. horse but betooke him to his spurres, by *Deuery* vpo[n] the river of *Eury*, which stoode by good hap for him. The Knight *D'aumal*[30] and *D'namures*[31] without fight ran awaie, then euerie one pursued the enemie by the commandement of the King. The footemen seeing the Tragedie, (that is to saie) the *Frenchmen* and *Switzers*, kept their place, [and] holding downe their pikes cried for mercie. The King sent to take away their Ensignes,[32] and then took them to mercie: the Lance Knights were all put to the sworde for their Treason at *Arkes*.[33] *De Maine* ran away by the bridge of *Deuery*, and cast awaie his Cassock[34] and tooke a Mandilian[35] of a Soldier, and passing through his owne men slew foure or fiue whereby more easielie to passe, and caused a Barricado to bee made

[25] Armand de Gontaut (1524–1592), baron de Biron, Marshal of France, Huguenot notable.

[26] horse — cavalrymen

[27] battaile (battle) — the main body of the army

[28] astonied — stunned, bewildered, dismayed

[29] onset — attack

[30] Charles de Guise (1555–1631), duke d'Aumale, and notable figure in the Catholic League.

[31] Charles Emmanuel de Savoie (1567–1595), 3rd duke de Nemours, and notable figure in the Catholic League.

[32] ensignes (ensigns) — standards, banners

[33] The Battle of Arques (21 September 1589), won by Henri IV. Henri IV's Swiss pikemen had defected from his army at the last minute.

[34] cassock — a cloak or long coat

[35] mandilian (mandilion) — a loose coat, worn by soldiers as an overcoat

at the bridge and placed soldiers there to defende[36] the pursuite, the King comming to the said Barricado, and seeing some let[37] beeing conducted[38] by *Chiccot*, who assured him that hee knew the waie, did returne to passe by a shallowe, and pursued *De Maine* to the Suburbes of *Maunte*, which was 7. leagues **[sig. B2/7]** from the place. The Duke *de Maine* was an houre at the gates intreating entrie, which at the first they denyed, telling him they feared least the King should enter with him in the pursuite, whereupon hee sware hee had killed the King with his owne hands, but in trueth had lost the battaile, by which meanes he entred, [and] if he had staied but one quarter of an houre longer he had been dispatched, and had it not bin for the Barricado at the bridge of *Deuery*, which letted[39] them, and his speedie departure from the battaile, he had been either slaine or taken. He saued himselfe from thence to *Pontois* and so to Saint *Denis*: hee caused all the Pesants to rise by the reporte of his men that were prisoners, to kill al them that should flee: he commanded all the nobilitie of *France* to be slaine without sparing any: he ordered also meanes to kil the King, in which God hath changed his purpose. There were taken in the place of the battaile foure Cannons and other small peeces,[40] all his baggage, powder and munition, a great number of Charriots[41] and horses of the *Reisters Germaines* and *Wallons:* in briefe, the Pesants are by that meanes rich, a great number of the soldiers were drowned. The Barricado of *Deuery*, was after taken by the Kings side, and many men slaine there. In the battaile were slaine not past 1500. but in the pursuite of the flight was the great slaughter. The confusion was so great, that the baggage of *Monsieur* the Prince of *Conte* were carried away by the enemie fleeing to *Vernone*, but afterwards were recouered. There were 60. Ensignes [and] 40. Cornets **[8]** taken, the white Cornet of *de Maine*, the King (hauing slaine the bearer) tooke himselfe. The King hath licensed the *Switzers* to depart, and hath giuen them a co[n]voy to their Cantons, allowing them six pence a day during their trauell home, with aduertisement[42] that they should come no more against the Crowne of *France*. There is 6000. footmen *French*, which haue sworne seruice to the King, cursing *de Maine* that he left them to the butcherie of the Victor, praising greatlie the King for his great mercie. The King as yet will not accept of their seruice. The Countie *Egmond*[43] was slaine there by the hands of Marshal *Daumont*, who was Colonell of the *Wallons*. The Duke of *Brunswicke* cannot bee found, but is thought to be

---

36 defende (defend)—ward off, repel
37 let—hindrance
38 conducted—dealt with
39 letted—hindered, obstructed
40 peeces (pieces)—cannon
41 charriots (chariots)—coaches, carts, wagons
42 advertisement—warning
43 Count Philip Egmont (1558–1590). Son of the Dutch national martyr, Lamoral, Count Egmont.

dead: *Fountden Martell* dead, *Bassonpierre, Chattenneraies, Baddolphen*, [and] di-uers others dead in the place. There is of the *Wallons* past at *Amiens* 350. or 400. whereof 120. left in the Hospital being hurt. *De Maine* did send after them to *Amiens* to come to him by the *Signeur Belleanglise:* to whom they answered, they would not returne, calling *de Maine* Runne-away. The King commanded all the strangers to be slaine, and the *French* to be saued. There are few *Spaniards* or *Ital-ians* left aliue, except those which saued themselues by flight, for although they offered great sommes of money for their ransome, yet were they all slaine. The Pesants mocked *de Maine*, saying he caused them to come to kill the Kings men, but yet killed the others, and cryed, *God saue the King*. It is the most notable vic-torie that of late was heard of, and being throughly [**sig. B3/9**] considered, must be confessed to come of God.

The Tuesday night before the battaile, there was seene in this place two Armies in the Skie, the one greater than the other, and the lesse ouercame the greater. This fight was seene at the time of the preparing of the Battaile; [and] the like at the same time in the Camp; [and] now we vnderstand the issue there-of by the victorie. God hath shewed himselfe apparantlie to fauour the cause, in so much that they say in the Campe, that the praiers of the Hugonots are much auaileable[44] in the sight of God. *Vernone* yeelded on Friday after, and the King entred it on Saterday: *Maunte* yeelded vpon Monday, and the King entred it vpon Tuesday. There was found 3. great Cannons with powder and shot, and there the King refreshed himselfe well. The 18. day the King departed out of *Maunte* to go to *Corbell, Meus* [and] *Mullen*, where the Duke of *Longueuile*[45] hath 2500. horse, and 6000. footmen: which Townes are like to bee deliuered to the King, the which will bee a great helpe to aduance the parlie[46] of them of *Paris*, which they seeke.

Monsieur de Villeroy[47] hath bin at *Maunte*, [and] hath since twise spoken with the Marshall *Byron*. The King hath licensed the Gentlemen of base[48] *Normandie* to goe home to their houses to refresh themselues, hauing sufficient forces be-sides. *Monsieur de Tauannes*[49] fleeing from the Battell, hath retired himselfe to *Roan*, in shewe, to keepe them assured to *de Maine*. *Monsieur de Villiers* Gouer-nour of *Newha-* [10] *uen* comming thether, being called by the Countrie to take the gouernment and strong places, hath bin repulsed by *Monsieur de Tauannes* and *Milray*. And although they make great shewe to withstand the King, yet

---

[44] availeable (available)—efficacious, serviceable
[45] Henri d'Orleans (1568–1595), duke de Longueville, partisan of Henri IV.
[46] parlie (parley)—negotiation of terms of surrender
[47] Nicholas de Neufville (1543–1617), seigneur de Villeroy, later Secretary of State for Foreign Affairs from 1594 to 1617.
[48] base—lower
[49] Jean de Saulx-Tavannes (1555–1629), notable of the Catholic League.

haue they resolued in their priuate counsell to yeeld, the King comming by force, not expecting any rescue at all.

The Duke *de Aumale* is in *Picardie*, and the Duke *de Maine* hath withdrawne him, his wife and children out of *Paris*, and conueied his wife and children to *Per-one*. Himselfe is now at *Soissons* gathering what forces he can; but not likelie to gather any at this present, hauing no other hope, but the accustomed lyes of his preachers, and other his wonted practizes.[50] From *Deepe* the 20. of March. 1590.

FINIS.

---

[50] practizes (practices) — stratagems

The Trve Reporte of the seruice in Britanie (1591) ||
STC (2nd ed.) #18655

In 1591, Sir John Norreys was dispatched with about 2,400 English soldiers to Brittany, to help Henri IV's general, François de la Noue; ranged against them were the Duke de Mercoeur, leading the forces of the Catholic League in Brittany, and Don Juan del Aguila, with 3,000 Spanish soldiers. On 5 May, Norreys landed at Paimpol, then marched inland to join the Prince de Dombes, who was besieging a Leaguer garrison in Guingamp. Norreys and Dombes took Guingamp on 23 May, and Norreys then proceeded to conduct a somewhat toothless (since underfunded and undermanned) campaign in Brittany for the rest of the season.

This pamphlet is an interesting pendant to *A Discourse and true recitall of euerie particular of the victorie obtained by the French King, on Wednesday the fourth of March, being Ashwednesday* (1590); also concerned with the civil wars in France, it is written in English, about English soldiers, and is presumably taken from an English manuscript letter rather than from a printed French account. (Henri de Bourbon, duke de Montpensier [i.e., the Prince de Dombes mentioned in this pamphlet] is sometimes listed as its author, but the internal textual evidence argues that this is a mistaken attribution.) It is one a series of news pamphlets about Norreys' campaigns, which together form a semi-continuous narrative about his endeavors in Brittany from 1591 to 1594. It includes the articles of surrender for the town of Guingand; these provide significant amounts of political information, both for the contemporaneous reader and the modern historian, and also provide insight into how surrenders were negotiated in the late sixteenth century.

[TITLE PAGE]

THE TRVE | Reporte of the seruice in | *Britanie.* | Performed lately by the Honorable | Knight Sir Iohn Norreys[1] and other | Captaines and Gentlemen souldiers[2] | *before Guingand.* | Together with the Articles which the Prince | *D'ombes[3] accorded to the defendants | of the Towne.*

LONDON

Printed by Iohn VVolfe, and are to | be sold at his shop right ouer against | the great South-doore of | Paules. 1591.

[sig. A 2/1] The true report of the seruice in Britanie, performed lately by the Honourable *Knight Sir* IOHN NORREYS *and other Captaines and gentlemen souldiers before Guingand: together with the articles which the Prince D'ombes accorded to the defendants of the towne.*

A Marshall man principally deuoteth him selfe to hazard his lims and life in the seruice of his Prince [and] countrie for honour and crownes:[4] as it were shame to eclipse him the one, so it is iniurie to scant him the other: for the surest whetstone of valour and vertue is renowne and glorie: in defrauding the souldier of his pay, you cut his purse and rebate[5] his edge: in deprauing[6] his honour, you cut his throate and strike him stone deade: whereby I was induced to publish the renowned seruice done lately by that honourable knight S[IR]. IOHN NOR-REYS in Britainie: to the end that neither he, neither the rest of the braue Captaines, gentlemen and souldiers should want their due commendation, that both they may be encouraged to continew their braue [and] heroicall mindes, and others inclined to aduance themselues to the like honorable attempts [and] actions. I am the better able to performe this my promise by reason of a letter I receiued thence from a gentleman so well qualified, that neither he wanted skill or wit to record the seruice with the pen, neither valour [and] [2] courage to performe anie enterprise with the sword, being a principall actor in the execution thereof, the copie whereof I present to the reader, that he may be truely enformed of the seruice, and yeelde the actors their due commendation.

---

[1] Sir John Norreys (ca 1547–1597), notable English general.
[2] gentlemen souldiers (soldiers)—gentlemen serving in the ranks rather than as officers
[3] Henri de Bourbon (1573–1608), prince de Dombes, later duke de Montpensier, notable in service of Henri IV.
[4] crownes (crowns)—a particular sort of coin, usually stamped with a crown; coins in general, money
[5] rebate—dull, blunt
[6] depraving—defaming, disparaging

SIR, by my last letters I aduertised you of the safe ariuall of our armie in Britanie, the third of May, continewing about the Abbay of Beauport a weeke, for the arming of the souldiers, mounting the artillerie and marshaling our Campe. The tenth, we began our march, and lodged with our troupes before *Guingand* the 13. Since which time, through the wonderful paines and continuall trauel[7] of Sir IOHN NORREYS our L[ord]. Generall, the towne is rendered to the Prince D'OMBES, sonne to the Duke MOMPENSIER[8] of the house of *Burbon*, Gouernour of Britanie for the King.[9] The reporte whereof may seeme straunge to you, for we our selues do wonder at it, considering the strength of the place by arte and nature, and how greatly the conseruation[10] therof imported *Philibert Emanuel, Duke Mercurie*[11] of the house of *Vandemont* a collaterall branch of *Lorrayne*, Gouernour of Britanie for those rebellious Leaguers[12] who murthered his brother in law the late king[13] his owne sisters[14] husband: as well in regarde of his honour and reputation, as of his profit and peculiar interest, the towne being his proper inheritance, in the right of his wife *Marie*[15] daughter and heire to *Sebastian*[16] Duke of *Ponthieure*, whose father *Francis*[17] *Vicount* [sig. A 3/3] *Martigues* of the house of *Luxemburg* attained large territories in Britanie, marrying *Charlotte*[18] sister and heire of *Iohn de Brose*[19] who descended of the house of *Ponthieure* a collateral line of the Dukes of Britanie.[20] The duke *Mercurie* notwithstanding hee was thus particularly interested in the town of *Guingand* wanting neither sufficient garison, munition or victuals, hauing *Don Ioan de Lagula*[21] in a readinesse

---

[7] travel (travail)—labor

[8] François de Bourbon (1542–1592), duke de Montpensier, notable in service of Henri IV.

[9] Henri IV de Bourbon (1553–1610), king of France from 1589 to 1610.

[10] conservation—preservation

[11] Philippe Emmanuel (1558–1602), duke de Mercouer, notable of the Catholic League.

[12] Leaguers—members of the Catholic League, the hard-line Catholic faction that fought consistently against the Huguenots, and sometimes against the moderate Catholics when they were allied with (or conciliatory toward) the Huguenots.

[13] Henri III de Valois of France (1551–1589), king of France from 1574 to 1589. Henri III was murdered by the unhinged Dominican friar Jacques Clément, who acted with the encouragement of certain notable Catholic Leaguers.

[14] Louise de Lorraine-Vaudémont (1553–1601), wife of Henri III of France.

[15] Marie de Luxembourg (1562–1623), duchess de Penthièvre.

[16] Sebastian de Luxembourg (?–1569), duke de Penthièvre.

[17] François de Luxembourg (?–1553), viscount de Martigues.

[18] Charlotte de Brosse (ca. 1505–?).

[19] Jean III de Brosse (?–1566), duke de Penthièvre.

[20] This genealogy is correct in all particulars.

[21] Don Juan del Aguila (ca. 1546–ca. 1603), Spanish soldier, later commander of the Spanish expeditionary force to Kinsale, Ireland, in 1601–1602.

with foure thousand Spaniards at *Pontiguy* besides his owne troupes: yet suffered this defensible place to bee lost without blowes vpon dishonourable and base conditions, whereby we may see how God rebateth the edge of rebels harts, daunteth their courages and ranuerseth[22] their actions with his byblows[23] or vnlooked-for counterbusses.[24]

That the particularities of the matter may bee better knowne vnto you, you are to vnderstand that the town of *Guingand* is strongly waled round about in-uironed with a large ditch and a deepe counterscarfe,[25] extending it selfe in length from the South Southeast, to the North Norwest. Vpon the South end of the town where was sometimes an old castle, there is now a very strong bulwarke with three *Flankers*,[26] and in the middest thereof a *Cauallero*[27] which commandeth the whole towne. Not farre from it Eastwarde is the gate of the towne, of it selfe verie strong, and before it a verie great *Rauelin*[28] within the counterscarfe of the ditch: at the bottom whereof there is a most daintie[29] *Sallye*,[30] insomuch as a thousand men may issue out at the same, and not one bee dis- *[4]* couered vntill their heades appeare aboue the counterscarfe. And aboue them are two drawne briges for the Saliants,[31] the one for horse, the other for foote, [and] right before the *Raueling* is a pretie conceited[32] *Turnepike* or *Barricado* to checke the throng and multitude of pursuers. From this place Northwarde the wall is embowed[33] like a horne with three *Flankers* vpon it, and so ranforced[34] within with earth, as it is accounted a *Terra-pleyn*.[35] The West hath a very deepe ditch ful of water: neither could any aproch be made that way by reason of the marrishis. The North end of the towne hath manie *Flankers* and a deepe ditch, yet somewhat

---

[22]   ranverseth (reverses)—overthrows

[23]   byblows (by-blows)—side-blows or side-strokes

[24]   counterbusses—light, retaliatory blows

[25]   counterscarfe (counterscarp)—the outer wall or slope of the ditch, which supports the covered way; sometimes extended to include the covered way and glacis

[26]   flankers—fortifications projecting so as to flank or defend another part, or to command the flank of an assailing enemy

[27]   cavallero—a fortification raised ten or twelve feet higher than the rest of the works, so as to command the adjacent fortifications and the surrounding countryside

[28]   ravelin—an outwork consisting of two faces which form a salient angle, constructed beyond the main ditch and in front of the curtain

[29]   daintie (dainty)—excellent

[30]   sallye (sallyport)—an opening in a fortified place for the passage of troops when making a sally

[31]   saliants (salliers)—ones who take part in a sally

[32]   conceited—conceived, designed

[33]   embowed—bent, curved

[34]   ranforced—reinforced, strengthened, fortified

[35]   terra-pleyn (terreplein)—the surface of a rampart behind a parapet; often the level space where guns are mounted

drie [and] fast by[36] an Abbey of *Iacopins*[37] which the villaines them selues pulled
for the most part downe, lest it should anie way distresse[38] the towne, standing
within lesse then eightie paces of the towne wall. Notwithstanding this their
prouident[39] malice, the rebels left as much standing for vs as serued to cut their
owne throates. My Lord Generall hauing quickly found that this part of the
towne was fittest to receaue a breach,[40] made shew to the quite contrarie[41] parte
thereof, as at the South parte hee caused trenches to be cast,[42] and passages to
be made through the walles of old houses, euen to the verie counterscarfe of the
ditch, a long trench was likewise cast verie neare the walles of the East side of
the towne, and in the middest therof a platforme of earth to be erected to some
reasonable height, as if the canon should haue beene placed there: in the meane
time all trauel was vsed in making of a Mine[43] according to our Ge- [5] nerals
direction, neare to the entended breach, and the waies made for the bringing[44]
and dressing[45] of the places fit for the Canon to play vpon, which was performed
in so good sorte as that by the 20. day of this moneth our artillerie was brought
downe to the *Iacopines* cloister, and there placed within lesse then an hundreth
paces of the wall. And this was one of our greatest combats both in respect of
trauel [and] hazard, to both which how my L[ord]. did expose himselfe truely I
could not but wonder, and in my hart was angry to see it, and yet if he had not so
hazarded himselfe, I did partly perceiue that little woulde haue beene done.

On fryday the 21. we began our batterie, and notwithstanding it continued
all the day, yet by reason of the few peeces of artillerie, not able to make sufficient
batterie, the dayes worke brought forth no great effect other then the crushing of
two *Flankers*, and the beating of the *perrepet*,[46] so that the breach was very small
and the same so repaired continually by the souldiers and inhabitants within
the towne, maintaining the rampart with fetherbeds, horse dung and bags of
earth almost to the lowest part of their *perrepet*. The next day verie earely once
againe wee began our batterie, and continued it vntil two or three of the clocke
in the after noone, by what time the breach seemed verie faire. Whereupon the

---

[36] fast by — very near
[37] Jacopins (Jacobins) — Dominican friars
[38] distresse (distress) — to subject to pressure, to harass
[39] provident — thrifty
[40] breach — a gap in a fortification, made by artillery fire
[41] contrarie (contrary) — opposite
[42] cast — dug
[43] mine — a subterranean gallery in which gunpowder is placed, so as to blow up the enemy's fortifications above the gallery
[44] bringing — probably a shortened version of "bringing about"; that is to say, occasioning, accomplishing, effecting
[45] dressing — preparing, making ready
[46] perrepet — parapet

French humor[47] vrged verie hotely to an assault, and so importuned the Prince *D'ombes* that he consented thereunto. Our Generall although he was hardly[48] drawne to yeeld his consent, vnderstanding by a Sergeant [6] of a band whom he had sent to discouer[49] the breach, that the rentrenchment within was exceeding deepe, and the mounting vp the breach very steepe, sliding and difficult, but especially because the myne was not so forwarde to be answerable[50] to the breach: notwithstanding seeing the French men offering to attempt the place of them selues which had beene some disgrace vnto vs, yeelded to their humor, and most instantly demaunded the pointe[51] and honour of the assault for the English men, which being graunted conditionally that they shoulde bee seconded[52] by the French. Such was the emulation of our commanders and Captaines to winne honour, that all being willing to attempt the seruice, to auoide contention our Generall caused the dice to bee cast, so that it fell to Captaine IACKSON and Captaine HERON to leade the first two hundreth to the assault, which after their deuout prayers recommending them selues to God, they performed verie valiantly, scrambling vp with a notable resolution, standing a long halfe houre at the push of the pike[53] in the face of a whole storme of the small shot,[54] especially Captaine IACKSON who came to the point of the breach, but not being throughly seconded by the souldiers vnable to get vp by reason of the steepenes of the place, yet were they hardly[55] commanded to retire, performing their retraite with no lesse good order then their attempt to the assault, Captaine HERON receiued a shot in the throate, whereof he presently dyed, and not aboue twelue others slaine: Captaine IACKSON [sig. B/7] sore hurt. Captaine WOLFE in the top of the breach had three daungerous woundes in the head, and others in his body: Captaine CATESBYE a voluntarie[56] gentleman sore hurt in the arme. Also Captaine WHITTON and Maister *Paule Wingfeeld* with some other yonge gentlemen to the number of 30. Which losse can not be thought great in such a peece of seruice, considering the great strength within to defend the place. The second attempt was giuen by the Baron of *Molac* Collonel generall of the French infanterie in these partes, and very well answered by himselfe, and some few of

---

[47] humor—temperament, particular inclination, whim
[48] hardly—with difficulty
[49] discover—reconnoiter
[50] answerable—adequate, sufficient
[51] pointe (point)—the leading position, so as to be the first into the breach
[52] seconded—supported
[53] the push of the pike—the confrontation of pikemen (or soldiers generally) face-to-face, pushing and stabbing at each other with pikes until one side or the other breaks and runs. Actually and proverbially fierce and trying combat.
[54] small shot—musket balls
[55] hardly—probably "forcibly"
[56] voluntarie (voluntary)—a volunteer

the French gentlemen, but the common souldiers aduancing them selues coldly[57] to the breach, receiued the greater hurt, and by that occasion were slaine of them many more then of our nation. Some others straight presented themselues for a third assault, but the breach being found so difficult, and resistance within strong and well prepared, it was aduised to stay vntill the next day that the battery had made the breach more easie. During the time of the assault Captaine DENNIS a braue gentleman being sent with some forces to make offer of a *scalado*[58] to one other part of the towne, aduancing himselfe too farre, receiued a Musket shot in the bottome of his bellie, wherof he dyed about twelue of the clocke the same night. That night those within demanded a Parley,[59] which being accorded, certaine deputies out of the towne repaired the next morning to the Prince *Dombes*, and in the end grew to a capitulation,[60] the copie whereof [8] you shall receiue herein inclosed. Which in my iudgement would haue beene accorded with much more aduantage to the Prince, if he had pleased to haue insisted vpon it: but being glad to recouer the towne, which is saide to be the strongest in Britanie, except *Nantes* and *Dinant*: withall doubting least[61] the Duke *Mercury* with the helpe of *Don Iuan de Lagula* should come to the succour of the towne, (which it is likelye had beene performed, if the French had beene in so good readines as the Spaniardes) he woulde not treate anie long agreement.[62] But all thinges being accorded on both sides, on Whitsonday[63] the towne was surrendered into the handes of *Monsieur Cargomart* appointed gouernour for the Prince. And Captaine GARGANTON which before held the place for the Duke *Mercurie*, with one other named *Contary*, sent by the Duke *Mercurie* to assist the other, departed the towne the 24. of May, with an hundred and twentie horse, and about two hundreth and sixtie foot, in all mens iudgement able and strong enough to haue kept the place for a much longer time. We had in the towne foure Ensignes,[64] one Cornet,[65] one Cannon Perrier,[66] one Demy Culuering,[67] and sixe Sacres[68] and Minions,[69] two thousand waight of pouder, and great store of victuals. The hauing of this towne

---

[57] coldly—without enthusiasm
[58] *scalado* (escalade)—the action of scaling the walls of a fortified place by the use of ladders
[59] parley—negotiation of terms of surrender
[60] capitulation—terms of surrender
[61] doubting least (lest)—afraid that
[62] treate anie (treat any) long agreement—conduct prolonged negotiations
[63] Whitsonday (Whitsunday)—the seventh Sunday after Easter
[64] ensignes (ensigns)—troops
[65] cornet—company of cavalry
[66] perrier—a cannon for discharging stones
[67] demy culvering (demi-culverin)—a small cannon
[68] sacre (saker)—a small cannon
[69] minion—a small cannon

greatly importeth the King, for in a manner all base[70] Britaine doth depend vpon it. The Courtes of Parlement,[71] which was ordinarily held at Reynes were by the rebellious Leaguers transferred to *Guingand*, which argueth in what esti- **[sig. B 2/9]** mation they held the strength of the towne. Thus haue I plainly and truly reported the seruice of *Guingand*, and I perceiue our Generall meaneth to entertaine vs in action, for we are presently to march against *Morlays* a rebellious towne coasting[72] vpon the sea, whereby I am enforced to leaue my penne, and betake my selfe to the launce, for the trompet soundeth, *mont'a cauallo*.[73]

Articles accorded by the Prince Dombes to | the beseeged within the towne of *Guingand*, | *in Britanie*.

1   THe Gouernour, Captaines and Souldiers of *Guingand* shal render the towne into the Princes handes to morrowe the 23. of May, being Whitsonday, before noone.
2   The Prince will permit that the horsemen shall depart the towne with their horses and furniture, and the footemen with their Harquebuze[74] and swordes by their side.
3   The Cornets,[75] Ensignes,[76] and Drums which are in the towne, shall be deliuered to the Prince, and all their artillerie and munition of warre.
4   All Englishmen and Irishmen, if there be anie, shall be put into the hands of the Prince.
5   All Spaniards shall remaine prisoners.
6   The gentleme[n] who haue no charge of[77] souldiers, who retired themselues to the towne for refuge, shal pay 15000. crowns, and therby freed to enioy **[10]** their possessions and mouables.
7   The inhabitants of the towne shall pay 25000. crownes, and thereby shall be warranted from all pillage, enioying the kinges protection according to his late ordinances.
8   The prisoners the Kinges seruants, shall be set at libertie, and deliuered to the Prince.
9   For the assurance of this treatie, they shall presently giue hostages, two for the gentlemen, two for the souldiers, and two for the inhabitants.

FINIS.

---

[70] base — lower
[71] Parlement — the Parlement of Brittany
[72] coasting — bordering, adjacent
[73] *mont'a cauallo* — (I must) get on horseback
[74] harquebuze (arquebus) — an early gun
[75] cornets — standards, banners
[76] ensignes (ensigns) — standards, banners
[77] no charge of — not served as

I. E., *A Letter from a Souldier of good place in Ireland* (1602) || STC (2nd ed.) #7434

Much of Ireland rose in rebellion against the English crown in 1594, in what would become known as the Nine Years War. After several disastrous defeats, most notably the battle of the Yellow Ford in 1598, the English had finally begun to reassert control over Ireland in 1601. In October 1601, however, a Spanish army of about 3,400 men under the command of Don Juan del Aguila landed in Kinsale, near Cork. Lord Mountjoy, the Lord Deputy of Ireland, hastily assembled an English army to besiege Kinsale; rebel Irish armies under Hugh O'Neill and Hugh Roe O'Donnell also marched to Kinsale, to attempt to relieve the siege and join forces with the Spaniards. In December 1601 the Irish and Spanish attempted to launch a co-ordinated attack on the English, but miscommunications caused the Irish to launch an unsupported attack, and they were thoroughly defeated by the English. In January 1602 d'Aguila made terms for the surrender of Kinsale, and the Spanish withdrew from Ireland, never to return. After Kinsale, the mopping up of the Irish rebellion was only a matter of time, and it was completed in 1603.

This pamphlet describes the English victory at Kinsale. It is notable not only for describing a major English victory, but also for being one of the few English printed pamphlets describing the events of the Nine Years War. It is also notable for the extended rhetorics by which Mountjoy and d'Aguila both justified their decision to come to terms over the surrender of Kinsale—both of which deprecate the Irish, as a nation and as soldiers, as a way of salving both Spanish and English honor. The balance of military narration and political extenuation reveals sharply the culture of political backbiting prevalent in both England and Spain at that time.

The pamphlet is something like the official English account of Kinsale. It draws heavily from the English campaign journal, greatly flatters the English in general and Lord Mountjoy in particular, and may have been written by Mountjoy's secretary, Fynes Moryson.

[TITLE PAGE]

A | LETTER | from a Souldier of | good place in Ireland, to | his friend in London, touching the | *notable Victorie of her Maiesties*[1] *Forces* | there, against the Spaniards, and | Irish Rebels:

And of the yeelding vp of Kynsale, and other | places there held by the Spanyards.

LONDON

Imprinted for Symon Waterson.

1602.

[1] TO THE RIGHT Worshipfull my especiall good friend, Sir W. D. *Knight.*
SIr in my last of þe 19. of December I wrote to you at large of the arriuall of the newe supplie of Spaniards at Castel-haue[n], Baltemore, and Beerhauen, and of their intents and beginnings to fortifie, in all those three important places. Likewise that Sir *Richard Leuison*[2] towing out of *Kinsale* Hauen[3] against winde [and] weather, fought with them within Castle Hauen most valiantly, and of their ships being sixe, sunke and made vnseruiceable fiue: the men being most landed before hee could come to them, by reason of the weather, and beating[4] vpon him very dangerously from the land with their ordinance.[5] That they were said to be 2000. in number, with great store of ordinance and munition, [and] that as they reported, some thousands mo[r]e were comming after. That a great part of the Irishry of *Mu[n]ster* becommen Rebels of new, were reuolted to them, and re-ceiued into þe King of *Spaines*[6] pay. That *Odonell*[7] with good Forces of horse and foote out of the North, by [2] the benefit of the then extreame [and] sudden frost, gat passage almost vnlooked for by himselfe, and slipping by the Lord President of *Munster*[8] (who was sent to impeach[9] him) with such forces as could be spared

---

[1] Elizabeth I Tudor (1533–1603), queen of England from 1558 to 1603.
[2] Sir Richard Leveson (ca. 1570–1605), English soldier.
[3] hauen (haven) — harbor, anchorage, port
[4] beating — firing
[5] ordinance (ordnance) — artillery
[6] Philip III Hapsburg (1578–1621), king of Spain from 1598 to 1621.
[7] Hugh Roe O'Donnell (1571–1602), lord of Tyrconnel, second-most important Irish rebel in the Nine Years War (1594–1603).
[8] Sir George Carew (1555–1629), then Lord President of Munster, English soldier and official.
[9] impeach — impede, hinder

from the Army) was ioyned with them. That *Tyrone*, [10] with *O Rourck*, *Redman Bourck*, *Mac Guyre*, *Mac Mahone*, *Randal Mac Surley*, *Oconor*, *Slygoes* brother, *Tyrrel*, the Baron of *Lixenho*, and the rest of the old fugitiue Rebels of *Munster*, with the greatest and choisest force that was euer amassed in *Ireland*, were drawne nere our Camp. And that these all, together with sixe Ensignes [11] of those newly arriued Spaniards, in all to the number of 6000. foote, and 500 horse, by *Powle*, were on foote ready to march towardes *Kynsale* and our Campe, with intent and most assured confident hope with helpe of them in the Town, which should haue salyed out on the Campe, vpon the attempt of *Tyrone* and *Odonell*, and were aboue 2000. Spaniards, almost all old souldiers, aswell to releeue and rescue the Towne, as to remoue our siege, and vtterly to breake, dishonour, and defeate vs. And truely Sir, when I did then consider, on the one side this great strength, the newly ioyned men and horses to bee all fresh, vigorous, and strong, hauing all the Countrey ope[n] to them, abounding with victuals, forrages, armies, munition, and all furnitures: [12] those in the Towne, the most of them experienced souldiers, well armed, and in no such want as was supposed: On the other side, our men in numbers scant [13] equall to them, all almost tyred and wearied out with the miserie of a long Winters siege, our horses decayed, [14] leane and very weake, our best meanes of victuals and forrage likely to be cut from vs, with many other impediments whereof I speake not; When I say, I well wayed and pondred with my selfe these poynts, and layde together withall, this one of great importance, that when we should be forced (as it [3] was likely) to answere two forces at once, one from the Towne, another without, [15] a great part of our men were like enough to shrink, or at least not to stick firmely to vs (which by good coniectures I could make probable to you) Blame me not, if vpon these consideratio[n]s I wrote to you then somewhat distrustfully of our estate, as taking indeed our liues and honors, this seruice, and by consequence this whole Countrey likely to be put to an vnequall iumpe. [16] And so may I well say they were, although by the goodnesse of GOD especially, and by the most vigilant circumspection and valiant prowes of our worthy Generall, things out of these difficulties haue now sorted to so happy successe, as by that which followeth you shall sufficiently perceiue. To continue therefore my accustomed Relation to you, and to begin from that said day of the 19. of December, It may please you to knowe, that on Sunday the

---

[10] Hugh O'Neill (ca. 1540–1616), 3rd earl of Tyrone, leading Irish rebel in the Nine Years War (1594-1603).

[11] ensignes (ensigns) — troops

[12] furnitures — war materiel

[13] scant — barely amounting to

[14] decayed — physically wasted

[15] without — outside

[16] iumpe (jump) — venture, hazard, risk

20. wee still plying our attempts to the Towne, with face[17] and shew as though we nothing cared for *Tyrone* and his companie, at night certaine intelligence was brought vs, that he would bee the next night within a myle and a halfe of vs, with all the aboue recyted Forces. And accordingly vpon Munday the 21. towardes night, hee shewed himselfe with most part of his horse and foote, on a hill betweene our Campe and *Corke*, a myle off vs. At which time seeing two Regiments of our foote, and some horse drawne out of our Campe, and making a resolute march towardes him, hee fell backe to the other side of the hill, where hee encamped that night, strengthened with a fastnesse[18] of wood and water. Whereby though his retyre[19] might bee imputed to some touch of credite,[20] yet had hee this aduantage, that he might keepe from our Armie all passages and meanes for forrage: The other side ouer the Riuer of *Ownibuoye* beeing wholly at his disposition, by reason of the generall reuolt of those parte.

[4] On Tuesday the 22. some of *Tyrones* horse and foote made shewe againe in the place where they had done the day before, and that night were some of their horse, and 500. foote discouered, searching if they might finde fit way to the Towne.

On Wednesday the 23. aswell by intelligence otherwise, as by letters of *Don Iohn d'l Aquila*,[21] Generall of the Spaniards, and Captaine of the Towne, newly intercepted, we found that he had importuned *Tyrone* and his company very much, to giue an attempt vpon our Campe; intimating vnto them his owne necessitie, and likelyhood to bee shortly forced[22] within the Towne, their faithfull promises to succour him, the facilitie [and] vndoubted successe of the enterprise, he assuring them, that our numbers could not be but much lessened, and those that were remaining, greatly decayed and weakened with the long winter siege, so that it was not possible we should be able to maintaine so much ground as we had taken whe[n] our strength was full, if they on the one side, and he on the other put vs well too it: which he for his part promised them assuredly to doo very soundly from the Towne, whensoeuer they should thinke fit to doo the like from their Campe. And it seemeth that vpon this advise they tooke their determinate resolutio[n] for this course, and to put it in execution with all speed, either that night or the next at the furthest. Those of the Towne in the meane time gaue vs alarums, made Sallies, and did by all meanes what they could to keepe our men in continuall trauell,[23] that they might be the lesse able for resistance when

---

[17] face — external appearance
[18] fastnesse (fastness) — stronghold
[19] retyre (retire) — retreat
[20] imputed to some touch of credite (credit) — taken to damage his reputation
[21] Don Juan del Aguila (ca. 1546–ca. 1603), Spanish soldier, and leader of the 1601-1602 expedition to Kinsale, Ireland; he also served in Brittany during the early 1590s.
[22] forced — taken by force
[23] travell (travail) — labor

this attempt should come to be performed. The Lord Deputie[24] till now applied himselfe in show wholly towards the Towne, but indeed not meaning any force-able effectuall attempt vpon it, till he sawe what would become of *Tyrone* and his Forces, [5] and therefore hadde an especiall eye, by continuall espiall, vpon his moouings, and lest suddaine hurt should be taken from him, or the Towne, if both he without, and they within should inuade at once, he made Fortes and Bar-racadoes, heightned the ditches, deepened the Trenches, stopped and strength-ened all the Auenues to the Towne, hadde the whole Army in a readinesse vp-pon euery suddaine warning, and kept strong and watchfull guardes alwayes in all places. And now late in the night of this Wednesday, the three and twentieth day, being assuredly enfourmed of their intent of attempt vpon his Campe that night, or the morrow after, his Lo[rdship]. gaue order to strengthen the ordinary guards, and to put the rest of his Army in readines, but not as yet into Armes: commaunding that the Regiment volant,[25] which was a squadron of viii. Com-panies of foote, selected out of al the old Bands, conducted by Sir *Hen[ry]. Poore*, and appointed to be alwayes in a readines to answere all Alarames, and therefore exempted from all other duties, should draw out beyond the west parte of the Campe, and there stand in Armes, not farre from the maine guard of horse.[26]

A litle before the breake of day Sir *Ric[hard]. Greame*, who had[27] the guard of horse that night, sent the Lo[rd]. Deputie word, that the skowts had discouered the rebels matches[28] in great numbers, whervpon his Lo[rdship]. caused the Arm-ie presently to arme, and 300. cheife men to be drawne out of the quarter, where the Earle of *Thomond*[29] and 3. other Regiments lay, to make stand betweene that quarter, and the Fort vppon the west hill, himselfe with Sir *George Carow*, Lo[rd]. President of *Munster*, Sir *Richard Wingfield*,[30] marshall of *Ireland*, ad-uanced forward towards the skowt,[31] and hauing giuen order to *Sir Hen[ry]. Dau-ers*[32] Liuetennant generall of the horse, for the ordering of those troopes, sent the Marshall, to take view of [6] the Enemy, who sent word he was aduanced horse and foote neere the toppe of the hill, where the Erle of *Thomond* first quartered,

---

[24] Charles Blount (1563–1606), 8th Baron Mountjoy, Lord Deputy and Lord Lieu-tenant of Ireland from 1600 to 1604.

[25] regiment volant (flying regiment)—regiment designed and organized for rapid movement

[26] maine (main) guard of horse—main body of cavalry

[27] had—had command of

[28] matches—possibly small lamps; possibly the wick (and cord) used for firing early guns

[29] Donough O'Brien (ca. 1560–1624), 4th earl of Thomond; a Catholic Irish noble-man, he stayed loyal to England during the Nine Years War.

[30] Sir Richard Winfield (ca. 1560–1634), later Viscount Powerscourt.

[31] scowt (scout)—body of scouts

[32] Sir Henry Danvers (1573–1644), English soldier, later earl of Danby.

within lesse then 2. musket shotte of the towne. Whervpon the Lo[rd]: deputie calling to him sir *Oliuer Lambert*[33] Gouernor of *Connaught*, who beeing there without Charge,[34] was commaunded to attend his Lo[rdship]. that day, made choise of a peece of ground beetweene that and the towne, of good aduauntage, both to embattel,[35] and fight, as hauing on the backe a Trench drawne[36] from the Earle of *Thomonds* quarter, and so secured from the Towne: And on the front, a boggish glyn passable with horse only at one foord: The ground wheron the Enemy must haue drawn in grosse[37] to force the passage flancksered from the Earles quarter by the canon, and situate in the midst of all our Forces, and returned word to the Marshall, that in that place hee was resolued to giue the Enemy battel, if hee came forward: commaunding further, the Regiment of Sir *H. Folyat* and three old Companies of the Regiment of Sir *Oliuer Saint-Iohn* to bee brought thither, the rest of the Army being al ready in Armes, together with fiue hundred Sea-men, brought by Sir *Richard Leueson* to attend,[38] when, and what, he should command.

But *Tirone*, whose meaning ouer night, was, to haue beene with vs before daie, and as wee since learned, to haue put al the Spaniards into the Towne, with viii. hundred of the best Irish vnder *Tirrell* seeing it now faire day light, and discouering the Marshall and Sir *Hen[ry]: Dauers* to bee aduaunced with all the horse, and Sir *Hen[ry]. Poer* with his Regiment, stopt at the foote of the hill, and anon, thinking it to bee no day for him, retired the Troopes he had aduanced againe, to the bodie of his Armie beyond the Foord. Presently the Marshall sent the Lord Deputie word, that the Enemy retired [7] in some disorder, wherevpon his Lo[rdship]: commanding the forenamed troops to folow him with al speed, aduanced himselfe into the head of al, to see with his owne eie, the maner of the enemy, [and] in what sort thereupon he might determine to proceede. But before he could, either well view, or direct, a violent storme, during some quarter of an hower, gaue the enemy oportunitie, not yet perfectly discouered, to drawe off ouer a plaine in three great bodies of foote, all their horse in the Rere, and the wings with all their other loose[39] men fallen[40] vp into the head.[41] Which the L[ord]. Deputie, the day now clearing, perceiuing and discouering, by this their

---

[33] Sir Oliver Lambert (ca. 1560–1618), English soldier and official, later first Baron Lambert of Cavan.

[34] charge—particular responsibility; assigned military task and command

[35] embattel (embattle)—to fortify; to form in order of battle

[36] drawne (drawn)—dug

[37] grosse (gross)—a compact body

[38] attend—to wait, in readiness for service

[39] loose—unattached; separated from their assigned companies

[40] fallen—rushed

[41] head—front of the army

disorderly March, that they were in feare, being certified[42] also, that there was not before them any place of so good aduantage to make head[43] on, as those they had passed and quited, resolued to follow, and to see what profit might be made of an enemy thus troubledly[44] retiring. Whereupon dispatching presently Sir *Geo[rge]. Carew*, Lo[rd]. President of Munster with three cornets[45] of horse backe to the Campe, to attend there against the Towne, and whatsoeuer other attempt, because he was to be the fittest Commaunder in his Lo[rdship's]. absence, and because there had otherwise no horses bene left in the Campe, himselfe hauing with him, in al, betweene three and foure hundred horse, and vnder 1200. foot, made after the Enimy. And aduancing some mile further on, pressed him so hard, that he was forced to stand firme in three bodies vpon a foorde of a bogge (which bogge to assaile them, we must of necessity passe) and in all apparance, with a Resolution there to abide[46] vs and fight. They maintained a good skirmish[47] on our side the Bogge, with their loose wings, newly drawne out of their bodies, and hurt some of our men and horses, till with our wings they were at length beaten backe.

[8] The Marshall being somewhat aduaunced, espied a Foord, a musket shot off on the left hand, neglected by their foote, and onely guarded by their horse: whereof aduertising[48] the Lord Deputy, with desire of leaue[49] to force[50] them that way: the Lord Deputy approouing it, and commaunding to drawe vp the foote with all expedition,[51] the first wings of foote once arriued, seconded with[52] sir *Henry Poers* regiment, the Marshall, with the earle of *Clanricard*,[53] who neuer ceased vrging to fight, taking with them sir *Richard Greame*, and other companies of horse: with them, and those foote, forcing the enemies horse that kept the passage, passed ouer, and with that aduantage, finding themselues side by side with the enemies battell,[54] and further on then their rere, charged their battell in flanke, but finding them to stand firme, wheeled about. At which the enemies taking corage, drew on their horse, with a cry to a charge, who came on

---

[42] certified — informed
[43] make head — advance against opposition
[44] troubledly — in a disorderly way
[45] cornets — companies of cavalry
[46] abide — wait for, withstand
[47] maintained a good skirmish — kept a good-sized body of skirmishers
[48] advertising — informing
[49] leave — permission
[50] force — break through their defenses by force
[51] expedition — promptness
[52] seconded with — supported by
[53] Richard Burke (1572–1635), 4th earl of Clanrickard; an Irish nobleman who stayed loyal to England during the Nine Years War.
[54] battell (battle) — the main body of the army

brauely within fiftie or sixtie paces of our horse, and there after their country[55] fashion stopped, shaking their staues, and railingly vaunting,[56] but durst charge no further. Which the Lord Deputy seeing, sent presently ouer the Foorde to them his owne cornet of horse, vnder sir *William Godolphin*, and the Lord Presidents cornet vnder Captaine *Minshow*, (which twoo cornets he had appoynted before, to keepe stil a grosse in the Rere, to answer all accidents) together with twoo of our three bodies of foote vnder sir *Iohn Barkeley* Seriant maior of the Campe. Wherevpon the Marshall and Earle of *Clanrickard* seeing a second at hand, vniting themselues with Sir *Henrie Dauers*, hauing with him Captaine *Taffe*, Captaine *Flemming*, and other companies of horse, charged againe the Enemies horse, who not abiding the shocke, fledde. The the sight whereof, the battell dismaying, our menne thought [9] it better to charge againe vpon them, then to follow the horse, and so coragiously doing, vtterly brake them. The rerereward[57] of the Enemie, in which was *Tyrrell*, and all the Spaniards, stoode firme vpon the bogge on the right hand, vnto whom, within caliuer[58] shot, the Lorde Deputie had drawne vp our Rere, which was Sir *Oliuer Saint Iohns* 3. companies, commanded by Captaine *Roe*, in absence of Sir *Oliuer*, (dispatched few dayes before by the Lord Deputie, and Counsaile,[59] for speciall affaires to her Maiesty) charging him first, not to stir, till he receiued direction from him. But seeing *Tirrell*, and the Spaniards drawing betweene our horse, beeing on the execution, and the bodies of our foote, his Lo[rd]ship. hauing hitherto, by direction, set al other me[n]s swords on work, himselfe now in the head of our said Rere, where he had before resolued to fight, charged the Enemy in flancke, and put them to a disorderly retreite after their fellows to the toppe of the next hill, where they made stand a little while. But the Irish quiting the Spaniards, the Spaniardes in short time were broken by the Lord Deputies horse, commaunded by sir *William Godolphin*, and most of them slaine. The vantgarde of the Enemy, with all the loose wings, which were many, seeing what happened, threw away their armes (and all our men being otherwise busie) escaped. The chiefe Commaunder of the Spaniards, *Don Alonso d'Ocampo* was taken prisoner, with three Captaines, sixe Alferrez,[60] and fortie souldiers. *Tirone*, and *Odonell*, with the rest of the Irish Lords, ran apace, and saued themselues. Those of the battell were almost all slaine, and there were (of the Irish Rebelles onely) found dead in the place, about twelue hundred bodies, and about eight hundred were hurt, whereof many dyed that night: and the chace continuing almost two miles, was left off, our men

---

[55] country—national
[56] railingly vaunting—abusively boasting
[57] rereward—rearguard
[58] caliver—a kind of light musket or arquebus
[59] Counsaile—the Council of Ireland, which governed Ireland for England in co-operation with the Lord Deputy of Ireland
[60] alferrez (alférez)—Spanish for ensign, lieutenant

[10] being tyred with killing. The Enemy lost two thousand Armes brought to reckning,[61] besides great numbers imbezeled,[62] al their powder and drummes, and ix. ensigns,[63] whereof 6. Spanish. Those of the Irish that were taken prisoners, being brought to the Campe, though they offered ransome, were all hanged. On our side, onely one man was slaine, the Cornet of sir *Richard Greame.* Sir *Henry Dauers* was hurt with a sword slightly: sir *William Godolphin* a little raced[64] on the thigh with a holbert,[65] Captaine *Crofts* the Skowt-master with a shot in the back, [and] not aboue sixe mo[r]e common souldiers hurt. Many of our horses were killed, and mo[r]e hurt. And thus were they vtterly ouerthrowne, who but the very night before, were so braue and confident of their owne good successe, as that they reckoned vs already theirs, and as wee since haue vnderstoode, were in contention whose prisoner the Lord Deputy should be, whose the Lorde President, and so of the rest. The Earle of *Clanrickard* carried himselfe this day very valiantly, and after the retreite sounded, was Knighted by the Lorde Deputy, in the field amongst the dead bodies. So did all the rest of the Captaines, Officers, and Souldiers, named and vnnamed, and especially the Lo[rd]. Deputy himselfe, who brake, in person, vpon the floure[66] of the army the Spaniards, and omitted no duety of a wise diligent Conductor[67] and valiant souldier. Vpon the fight ended, he presently called together the Army, and with prayers, gaue God thankes for the victorie. A victorie indeede giuen by the God of Hostes, and maruellous in our eyes,[68] if all circumstances be duely considered, and of such consequence for the preseruation and assuraunce to her Maiestie, of this deeply endangered kingdome, as I leaue to wiser consideration, contenting my selfe with this, that I see the God of power and [11] might, disposed to protect the iust cause of his seruaunt, our gratious Queene *Elizabeth*, against the pride, malice, and powerful disdain of the greatest potentates, hir enemies. To him be the glorie.

After this glorious victorie thus valiantly atchieued, the Lord Deputy the same day hasted to his campe, lest any thing (in his absence) might happely[69] haue beene attempted there. But, not finding the Ennemy to haue made any sally, which indeede had beene but vaine for him, considering the small fruit he reaped by them heretofore, euery one that he made hitherto redounding stil to his owne

---

[61] reckning (reckoning) — official accounting
[62] imbezeled (embezzled) — carried off secretly or privately; here, probably means that individual English soldiers took guns for their own use
[63] ensigns — troops; standards, banners
[64] raced — scratched, cut, slashed
[65] holbert (halberd) — a combination of a spear and a battle-axe
[66] floure (flower) — best
[67] conductor — leader
[68] Allusion to Psalm 118:23; cf. Matthew 21:42, Mark 12:11.
[69] happely (haply) — by chance

detriment and losse, and euery place of our Camp, at this time, being so wel and sufficiently strengthened and prouided for against him as is sayd before.

The next day his Lordship commaunded Captayne *Bodlegh* Trench-maister generall of the Campe, who as well in the fight, as in the workes,[70] had deserued speciall commendation, to see the formerly begunne Forte and platforms, to be vndertaken againe, and neerer approches to be cast[71] out towardes the towne. But after fiue or sixe dayes labour *Don Iohn d'lAquila*, captaine of the Towne and Forces within, offered a parlee,[72] sending the Drumme *maior* of the Towne with a sealed letter to the Lord Deputy, by which he required,[73] that some gentleman of speciall trust and sufficiencie[74] might be sent into the towne from his Lordship, to conferre with him, whom he would acquaint with such conditions, as hee then stoode vpon. His Request being assented vnto by his Lordship, sir *William Godolphin* was imployed in the negotiation, which was carried in this sorte, word for word, as it is taken out of the originalls here, *viz.*

Don Iohn tolde sir *William*, that hauing found the Lord Deputy (whome he termed the Viceroy) although a sharpe and powerfull, yet an honorable Enemy, and [12] the Irish, not onely weake and barbarous, but (as hee feared) perfidious friendes, he was so farre in his affections reconciled to the one, and distasted[75] with the other, as did inuite him to make an ouerture of such a composition[76] as might be safe and profitable for the State of *England*, with least preiudice[77] to the Crowne of *Spaine*, by deliuering into the Viceroy his power,[78] the Towne of *Kynsale*, with all other places in *Ireland*, held by the Spanish, so as they might depart on honorable termes, fitting such men of warre, as are not (by necessity) inforced to receiue conditions, but willingly induced, for iust respects to dis-ingage themselues, and to relinquish a people, by whom their King and Master had bene so notoriously abused, (if not betrayed.) That if the Viceroy liked to entertaine further parley touching this point, he would first be pleased to vnderstand them rightly, [and] to make his propositions such as might be sutable, to men thorowly resolued, rather to bury themselues aliue, and to endure a thousand deaths, then to giue way to one Article of accord, that shuld taste of basenes or dishonour, being so confident of their present strength, and the royall Second of Spaine, that they should make no doubt of yeelding good accompt of themselues

---

[70] workes (works) — earthworks, fortifications
[71] cast — dug
[72] parlee (parley) — negotiation of terms of surrender
[73] required — requested
[74] sufficiencie (sufficiency) — ability, competency
[75] distasted — disgusted
[76] composition — terms of surrender
[77] prejudice — injury, damage
[78] power — (military) forces

and their Interest in this Kingdome, but that a iust disdaine, and spleene[79] conceiued against the nation, disswaded them from being further engaged[80] for
it, then of force they must, Sir *Wil[liam]*. *Godolphin* being commaunded by the
L[ord]. Deputie onely, to receiue *Don Iohns* propositions and demaunds. Hauing
made his L[ordship]. and Counsel this Relation, was by them returned with the
answere following. That howbeit the Lord Deputie hauing lately defeated their
succours, didde so well vnderstand his owne strength and their weakenesse as
made him nothing doubt of forcing them within a short time, [13] whom he
did know to be pressed with vnresistable difficulties, how much soeuer they laboured to couer and conceale the same, yet knowing that her sacred Maiestie out
of her gracious and mercifull disposition would esteeme the glory of her victory
to be blemished by a voluntary effusion, and an obstinate expence[81] of Christian
bloud, was content to entertaine this offer of agreement, so as it might be concluded, vnder such honorable articles for her highnes as the aduauntage she had
against them gaue reason to demaund: being the same which are sette downe
in the Articles of agreement following, signed by the Lord Deputie, and *Don
Iohn* [and] others: sauing that there was in them besides, the leauing of his treasure, munition, artillery, and the Queenes naturall Subiects to her disposicion,
all which points hee did peremptorely refuse, with co[n]stant asseueracion[82] that
both he and all his would rather indure the last of misery then be found guilty
of so foule a Treason against the honour of his Prince and the reputacio[n] of
his profession, though hee should find himselfe vnable to subsiste, much more
now, when hee might not onely hope to sustaine the burden of the warre for a
time, but with patience and constancie in the end to ouercome it. That he tooke
it so ill, to bee misunderstood in hauing Articles of that nature propounded vnto
him, as were they but once againe remembred in the Capitulacion,[83] the Viceroy
should from thencefoorth vse the aduantage of his sword and not the benefite
of his former offers: adding, that the Viceroy might rather thinke to haue made
a good and profitable purchase for the Crowne of England, [14] if with the expence of 200000 Duckats hee had procured *Don Iohn* to quite his interest and
footing but in Baltymore alone, to say nothing of Kynsale, Castell-hauen, and
Beerehauen: for (said he) suppose that all we with the rest of our places here had
perished, yet would that *Pen Insula* (beyng strong in it owne nature, bettered by
our arte and industrie, prouided as it is of victuals, munition, and good store of
Artillerie) preserue vnto the King of Spaine a safe and commodious[84] port for

---

[79] spleene (spleen)—ill-will
[80] engaged—entangled
[81] expence (expense)—loss
[82] asseueracion (asseveration)—emphatic assertion
[83] remembred (remembered) in the Capitulacion (capitulation)—mentioned during
the negotiations of surrender
[84] commodious—beneficial, serviceable

the arriuall of his Fleete, and be able to mayntaine it selfe against a land Armie of ten thousand, vntill Spaine (being so deepely engaged) did in honour releeue the[m]: which would drawe on a more powerfull inuasion then the first, being vndertaken vpon false groundes, at the instance of a base and barbarous people, who in discouering[85] their weakenes and want of power, haue armed the King my Master to relie vpon his owne strength, beyng tied in honour to releeue his people that are engaged, and to cancell the memory of our former disaster. But this was spoken (said he) in case the Viceroy were able to force this town, as I assure my selfe he cannot, hauing vpon mine Honour within these wals at this instant, aboue two thousand fighting men, that are strong and able, besides those, which hauing been sicke and hurt, recouer dayly: the greatest part of these, composed of old Souldiers, which fall not but by the sword, and those that were new, beyng now both trayned to their Armes [and] growne acquainted with[86] the Climate, are more able to endure then at the firste: our meanes as good as they haue beene any times these two monethes, such as **[15]** the Spaniardes can well away[87] withall, and therof to suffize vs for three moneths more. We lodge in good warme houses, haue store of munition, and (which is best of all) stand well assured that our succours wilbee shortly here. To bee playne, wee preserue our men, and reserue our strength the best wee may, hoping to front[88] you in a breach,[89] which if our harts fayle vs not, we haue hands and breasts enough to stop against treble your forces: though I will giue the Viceroy this right, That his men are passing good, but spent and tyred out with the misery of a Winter siege, which he hath obstinatly maintayned beyond my expectacion, but with such caution, and vpon so good guard, as hauing nicely watched all aduauntages, I could neuer fasten a Sallie yet vpon him, but with losse to my selfe: wherein I muste acknowledge my hopes deceaued, that grounding on some errour in his approches, promised my self the defeate of at least a thousand men at one blowe. But when wee meete on the breach, I am confident on good reason, to lay fiue hundred of your best men on the earth, and rest hopeful that the losse of those will make a great hole in an Armie that hath already suffred so much extremitie.

But to co[n]clude our businesse, the king my Master sent me to assist the Condees,[90] *Oneale* [and] *Odonnell*, presuming on their promise, that I should haue ioined with them within few daies of the arriuall of his forces. I expected[91]

---

[85] discouering (discovering)—revealing
[86] acquainted with—accustomed to
[87] away (await)—wait, remain in readiness, hold themselves in readiness
[88] front—to meet face to face, especially in definace or hostility
[89] breach (breech)—a gap in a fortification, made by artillery fire
[90] condees (condes)—Spanish for counts; here apparently "leading noblemen"
[91] expected—waited

long in vaine, sustained[92] the Viceroyes Armie, saw them drawne[93] to the great-est head[94] they could possibly make, lodged within two myles of Kynsale, re-enforced with certaine [16] companies of Spanyards, euery houre promising to releeue vs, and beeing ioyned together to force your campes, sawe them at last broken with a handfull of men, blowne asunder into diuers parts of the world, *O Donnell* into Spaine, *Oneale* to the furthest of the North, so as now I finde no such Condees *in rerum natura*[95] (for those were the very wordes hee vsed) as I came to ioyne withall, and therefore haue moued this accord the rather to dis-ingage the King my Maister from assisting a people so vnable in themselues, that the whole burden of the warre must lie vpon him, and so perfidious, as per-haps might bee induced in acquitall[96] of his fauour, at last to betray him. Vpon relation made by Sir *VVilliam Godolphin* to the Lord Deputie and Councell, of these offers of *Don Iohn*, which at seuerall conferences had beene brought to such heads,[97] as are spoken of before: it was thought good, for diuerse important rea-sons, to proceed roundly[98] to the agreement. For whereas in the propositions by him made; there was not any thing that admitted exceptions on our part, but onely, that he required to carrie with him his ordinance, munition, and trea-sure, that beeing no way preiudiciall to the maine scope or drift[99] of our Treatie, which cheefely respected the common good and safetie of the kingdome, de-serued not almost to be thought vpon. Besides that, the Treasure beeing at the first but a hundred thousand Duckats, with foure monethes payment of so many men, and other necessarie deductions, could not but bee very neere wasted; and that little remaynder, more fit for a prey to the poore souldiour, [17] after his te-dious trauell, than for a clause in the composition. Furthermore, how needfull it was to embrace this accord, may clearely bee seene by whosoeuer considereth the state of our Armie, almost vtterly tyred: how full of daunger and difficultie it was to attempt a breach defended by so many hands: how long time it might haue cost vs, if wee had lodged in the Breach, before wee could haue carried the Towne, it beeing full of strong castles: how her Maiesties ships and others lying in the harbour, should haue been forced speedily to forsake vs for want of vict-uals: how by a long contrarietie of winds, our selues were not prouided for aboue sixe daies, at the time of this parley, though within fewe dayes after good store[100]

---

[92] sustained—withstood
[93] drawne (drawn)—brought, led up
[94] head—advance, headway
[95] *in rerum natura*—in existence, in the nature of things. The phrase is often legal or philosophical.
[96] acquitall (acquital)—repayment, requital
[97] had beene (been) brought to such heads—had culminated in the enumerated terms
[98] roundly—promptly
[99] drift—design
[100] store—quantity, numbers; here, of victuals and other provisions

arriued: it being indeed worthy of obseruation, that by her Maiesties great care, [and] the dilligence of her ministers, so good prouidence[101] was vsed, as, though this descent of Spanyards drew into that quarter all the forces of the kingdome which could be spared, all which were onely to liue by prouision out of England; notwithstanding all the difficulties of transportation, in so vnseasonable a time, no notorious wants were found in the Armie, but that which is vnseparable from a Winter siege, in that Climate: that we had neyther munition nor Artillerie left but for one batterie in one place at once, fiue of our peeces being before crazed:[102] and finally, that if we had missed of our purpose, the whole countrey had been hazarded. Furthermore, that which seemeth of greatest consequence to induce his Lordship to this agreement, was: That the Spanyards in Baltymore Castle-hauen and Beere- [18] hauen, by vertue of this contract were likewise to surren-der those places, and depart the countrey, which would haue prooued a matter of more difficultie, and haue drawne on a long warre in a corrupted[103] kingdome, to root them out, beeing strongly fortified and well stored with victuals, munition, and artillerie, for that of necessitie the Armie for some space, must haue rested, and in the end haue beene constrained after a new supplie of al necessaries, to her Maiesties intollerable charge, to transport themselues thither by sea, the way by land being altogether vnpassable. In which time, their succours out of Spaine in all likelyhood, would haue beene come vnto them, the king being so farre in-gaged in his honour to second his enterprise, and we barred of that prosecution of the Rebels, which now by this Agreement we may wholly entend.

The Treatie therefore was thus concluded, as by the Articles ensuing, signed on both parts, appeareth.

Mountioye.

IN the town of Kynsale, in the kingdome of Ireland, the second day of the month of Ianuarie, 1601, between the noble Lords, the Lord *Mountioye*, Lord Deputie, and Generall in the kingdome of Ireland, for her Maiesty the Queen of England, and *Don Iohn d'L Aquila*, Captaine and Campe- [19] maister,[104] Gen-erall and Gouernour of the Armie of his Maiestie the king of Spaine, the said Lord Deputie being encamped, [and] besieging the said towne, and the said *Don Iohn* within it, for iust respects,[105] and to auoid shedding of blood, these condi-tions following were made betweene the said Lords Generals, and their campes, with the Articles which follow.

First, That the said *Don Iohn d'L Aquila* shall quit[106] the places which he holds in this kingdome, as well of the towne of Kynsale, as those which are

---

[101] providence—thrift
[102] crazed—damaged, broken
[103] corrupted—evil, treasonous
[104] campemaister (camp-master)—a staff officer
[105] for iust (just) respects—probably "because of their proper and mutual esteem"
[106] quit—give up, relinquish

held by the soldiers vnder his command in Castlehauen, Baltymore, and in the castle at Beerhauen, and other parts, to the said Lord Deputie, or to whome he shall appoint: giuing him safe transportation, and sufficient for the saide people, of Ships and victuals, with the which the sayd *Don Iohn* with them may go for Spain, if he can at one time, if not, in two shippings.

Item that the Souldiers at this present being vnder the commaunde of *Don Iohn*, in this Kingdome, shall not beare armes against her Maiestie the Queene of England, whersoeuer supplies shall come from Spaine, till the said souldiers be vnshipped in some of the Ports of Spaine, being dispatched as soone as may be by the Lord Deputie, as hee promiseth vpon his faith and honor.

For the accomplishing whereof the Lord Deputie offereth to give free passe-port to the said *Don Iohn* and his army, aswell Spaniards as other na- [20] tions whatsoeuer that are vnder his commaund, and that he may depart with all the things he hath, Armes, Municions, Money, Ensignes displaied, Artillery [and] other whatsoeuer prouisions of warre, and any kind of stuffe,[107] aswell that which is in Castlehauen, as Kynsale and other parts.

Item that they shal haue ships and victuals sufficient for their money, accord-ing and at the prices which here they vse to giue. That al the people and the said things may be shipped if it be possible at one time, if not, at two: and that to be within the time aboue named.

Item that if by contrary windes or by any other occasions there shal ariue at any Port of these kingdomes of Ireland or England, any shippes of these in which the said men goe, they be entreated as frendes, and may ride safely in the harbor, and be victualed for their mony, and haue moreouer things which they shall need to furnish the[m] to their voyage.

Item, during the time that they shall stay for shipping, victuals shalbe giuen to *Don Iohns* people, at iust and reasonable rates.

Ite[m], that of both parts[108] shalbe cessation of armes, and security that no wrong be offred any one.

Item, That the Ships in which they shall goe for Spayne may passe safely by any other Ships whatsoeuer of her Maiestie the Queene of [21] England: and so shall they of the sayd Queene and her Subiects by those that shall goe from hence: [and] the sayde Shippes being arriued in *Spaine*, shall returne assoone as they haue vnshipped their men without any impediment giuen them by his Maiestie, or any other person in his name, but rather they shall shewe them fa-uour, and helpe them if they neede any thinge, and for securitie of this, they shall giue into the Lorde Deputies handes Three Captaines such as hee shall choose.

For the securitie of the performance of these Articles, *Don Iohn* offereth that hee will confirme and sweare to accomplish this Agreement: and likewise

---

[107] stuffe (stuff) — provisions of food, munitions of war

[108] parts — parties (to the agreement)

some of the Captaines of his charge shall sweare and confirme the same in a seuerall[109] writing.

Item that hee in person shall abide in this Kingdome where the Lord Deputie shall appoint till the last shipping vpon his Lordshippes word: and if it happen that his people be shipped all at once, the sayde *Don Iohn* shall goe in the same Fleete without any Impediment giuen him. But rather the Lord Deputie shall giue a good Shippe in which he may goe, and if his sayd men be sent in twoo shippinges, then he shall goe in the last.

And in like sort the saide Lord Deputie shall sweare and confirme, and giue his word in the behalfe of her Maiestie the Queene and his owne, to keepe and accomplish this Agreement, and ioyntly the Lord President, the Lord Marshall of the [22] Campe, and thother of the Councell of State, and the Earles of *Thomond* [and] *Clanrykard* shall sweare and confirme the same in a seuerall writing.

George Carew.	*I* promise and sweare to accomplish and keepe these
Thomond.	Articles of Agreement, and promise the same
Clanrikard.	likewise on the behalfe of his Maiestie Catholique
R. Wingfeild.	the Kinge my Maister.
Ro. Gardemor.	
Geo. Bourcher.	
Rich. Liueson.	*Don Iohn d'l Aquila.*

And so is this troubled Cloud, of most likely perillous danger for this time dissolued, to her Maiesties most singuler renowme; Not so much for the glorie of the euent, as for her owne Magnanimitie and Princely resolution, to leaue nothing vndone which might preserue that Crowne, how deare so euer it cost her; to the great honour of our Generall, Leaders, and Souldiers by land and Sea Actors therein, who, if it be well considered, that after the Enemies arriuall xxviii. Septem- [23] ber, it was xxvi. October before they could get all things readie to sit downe nere the Towne: xxix. October before their Ordinance could play, And that by i. Nouember. they had gotte[n] *Ricorren* castle, And then vii. Nouember were driue[n] shrewdly to diminish their strength by sending the L[ord]. President from them with two Regiments of foote and 325 horses against *Odonell*, That hee returned not till xxv. Nouember, his Companies 26. And then that the Supplyes of *Spaine* were landed. That the most of our shipping that did vs speciall seruice were gone towardes them, That *Odonell* was alreadie come, *Tyron* shortly after, and xx. December all in sight: 24 beaten: That xxxi. December the Parley begunne, ii. Ianuarie the Articles were sworne: ix. the Towne yeelded. These thinges (I say) considered, it cannot bee thought they spent any idle time, as by the Iournals also which I sent you heretofore doth particulerly appeare. Nay, let it bee duely considered indeed, that the Towne though not regulerly fortified

---

[109] severall (several) — individually separate

after the moderne sort, yet was of strong scituation, well walled, and rampierd[110] of the old fashion, and apt to receiue fit fortification, which the Enemie by his skill and leasure had giuen it, both within the Towne and without, as being accounted of great knowledge in fortification, and hauing beene a Moneth in it before our men could come neere much to molest him. And it may rather bee maruailed, þ[a]t such an Enemie with such a Companie, so prouided, not beeing constrained by sickenesse, famine, or other defect of prouision, and expecting [24] shortly (as himselfe tearmeth it) a Royall supplie fro[m] *Spaine*, should so soone yeeld vp, not only it, but the other Castles, [and] that of *Baltymore* especially so important, so strong, so fournished to hould so long out, as by his owne acknowledgement appeareth before. Well, going they are with þe loane of ordinarie vessels which they also pay for: for whome yea and almost for any enemie of lesse qualitie than these, all auncient estate[111] wisedome would haue aduised to haue made and giuen them a goulden bridge to passe ouer, rather than they should haue stayed longer vppon any Condition, much lesse vpon doubtfull hope of a small contemptible pillage to haue beene gotten of them, which must needes also haue beene bought with much blood, and with what further Charge[112] and hazard to the mayne,[113] God knoweth. And howsoeuer any perticuler humour[114] may take it, I thinke *Don Iohn* (all Circumstances considered) did aduisedly for his King to leaue it: And for our part I take it a Seruice to haue beene most honourably perfourmed, with singuler euident profite, and all probabilitie of certaine future securitie to our Prince and Countrey, and that otherwise it cannot bee conceaued off, of any that will indifferently iudge. The proofe whereof by the fruite beginneth here presently to appeare, by the diminishing of her Maiesties Charge, daunting of the Rebels, quiet, comfort, and encouragement of the good, and before dismayed Subiect, and will (I doubt not) but be generally felt with you there, by sparing your men and monneys, and putting you out of feare hereafter, of your and our, and all [25] *Englands* potent Enemie for his further attempting this way. And this for this of the late victorie and yeelding of the Towne, which is my purposed taske vnto you at this time. As for that which was done from the first landing of the Spaniards till the fight, I referre you to the Iournals sent you before. And for the generall course of the noble Lord Deputies whole proceedinges in this Land, since his first arriuall heere, I leaue it to others to bee treated of more at large hereafter, onely this I will now say in generall, let it bee but without humour iudicially considered, in what estate he found this Land, and to what hee hath now brought it, and there is none so vnindifferently affected, but must

---

[110] rampierd (ramparted)—fortified with a rampart
[111] estate—state
[112] charge—expense
[113] mayne (main)—main purpose; here, the subduing of Ireland
[114] humour (humor)—temperament, partial affection

bee forced to confesse, *Quantum mutatus ab illo*![115] And heere I end my obiect[116] of the fight, and yeelding of the Towne, and whole quiting[117] of all the Inuadors, with *Salmacida Spolia*,[118] an vnbloudie victorie of our part, most befitting a Virgin Queene, and a Bacheler Generall. And so doe betake you to the Almightie. At *Corcke* this 13 of *Ianuarie*, 1601.

Your assured at com- | maund.   *I. E.*

---

[115] *Quantum mutatus ab illo!*—How changed from what he once was! Virgil, *Aeneid*, 2.274.

[116] obiect (object)—probably "presentation"

[117] quiting (quitting)—ridding, removal

[118] *Salmacida Spolia*—Salmacian spoils. The reference is to "Salmacida spolia sine sudore et sanguine" (Cicero, *De officiis*, 1.18)—Salmacian spoils, (gotten) without sweat or bloodshed.

Anthony Nixon, *Swethland and Poland Warres* (1610) ||
STC (2nd ed.) #18596

In 1609, Karl IX of Sweden intervened in the Russian civil wars ("The Time of Troubles"), agreeing to send an army to support Tsar Vasilii IV against the Second False Dmitri in return for the cession to Sweden of Russian territory in eastern Finland. Karl IX sent General Jacob de la Gardie from Sweden to Novgorod in the winter of 1609 with an army of ca. 15,000 men, including regiments of German, French, and British mercenaries. From there de la Gardie's army marched toward Moscow, together with a Russian army, and their combined forces evicted the soldiers of the Second False Dmitri from Tushino and Moscow. In the meantime, however, Sigismund III of Poland had also intervened in the Russian civil wars, in hopes either of seizing border territories or of putting a Polish candidate on the Russian throne, and had sent an army to besiege Smolensk. The Russo-Swedish forces marched to relieve Smolensk, but were routed on the way by a much smaller Polish army at the Battle of Klushino (Kłuszyn), 24 June/4 July 1610. De la Gardie's surviving mercenaries were given the option of entering Polish service, or of being paroled to their native lands, if they swore never to fight against Poland again.

Anthony Nixon (*fl.* 1592–1616) was apparently a blackmailer, a forger, a pamphleteer, a plagiarist, and generally a disreputable literary hack in late Elizabethan and early Jacobean England. He specialized in ghost-writing accounts of true-life English adventure (*The Three English Brothers* [1607], *The Travels of M. Bush* [1608]), and also specialized in accounts of Swedish affairs (*The Warres of Swethland* [1609]). His own sentiments seem to have been markedly anti-Catholic.

This pamphlet was most likely commissioned by the printer Nathaniel Butter, who would seem to have arranged to have Nixon act as ghost-writer for an English soldier who had gone as a mercenary in Swedish service and returned to tell the tale. Nixon's ghost-written account is unique in English military news pamphlets: it is written from the point of view of a common soldier rather than an officer; it narrates the everyday misery of a soldier's life; and it actually mentions the defeat of Protestant forces by Catholics—albeit in Swedish service, and fighting against distant Poland in the still-more distant expanses of Russia. It is also stylishly written, and full of anecdote—including fleeing from rough seas to the shores of Denmark (probably in Vendsyssel-Thy in North Jutland), near-massacre by the Danish peasantry, thievery and robbery by the soldiery in Denmark and Sweden, near-mutiny in Stockholm over lack of pay, starvation during a winter campaign from Finland to Russia, and final, catastrophic defeat in distant Klushino—and is, all in all, a picaresque tale comparable to *Lazarillo de Tormes* or Grimmelhausen's *Simplicissimus*. Nixon may have slightly exaggerated his protagonist's miseries and defeat, to fit the genre conventions of suffering autobiography, but it is, on the whole, a remarkably acute and vivid account of the sufferings endured and inflicted by early modern soldiers.

[TITLE PAGE]

SWETHLAND | and Poland Warres.

A Souldiers returne out of Sweden, and his | Newes from the Warres: | OR, | *Sweden and Poland vp in Armes.*

And the entertainement of English Souldiers there: | with the fortunes and successe of those 1200. | men that lately went thither.

At London printed for *Nathaniell Butter.*

1610.

[sig. A iii./*1*]   *To the Reader.*

COuntrymen, I haue for your sakes drawne a Picture, both of my owne, and other Englishmens miseries: You may in halfe an hower runne ouer these afflictions, which I and the rest (that smarted[1]*by them) were many months enduring. I know it shall be a pleasure to you, to reade what wee haue felt; and as great a happinesse to me (who haue published this:) if the Story of a poore Souldiers trauels, can bring you any content- ment, let me finde at your handes (I intreate you) the selfe same loue which Sicke-men receiue from their friendes, when they begin to recouer; And that is a kinde visitation and reioycing, to see a crazed*[2] *and weake body reduced*[3]*to his former strength: Mine (I thanke God) is now so, and shall grow [2] more and more into health, by how much the more you pittie my misfortunes: you cannot pittie them, vnlesse you know them, you cannot know them vnlesse you reade this ouer which I sende you; and I would not will- ingly haue you read, vnlesse you buy; because you should pay for the Warres somewhat as well as I: not doubting therefore of the one, because I hope you desire the other: I wish your owne wishes to you: and so farewell.*

[sig. B/*3*]   *A Souldiers Returne out of Sweden, and his Newes from the Warres.*

THe Oliue Tree of Peace (vpon which groweth the happinesse, wealth and prosperitie of euerie Kingdome) hath flourished (euen vp to his full height) so long in *England*, that other Countries and Kingdomes neighbouring by her, be- holding the blessings, benefits and contentation[4] which *England* hath gathered by tasting the fruites of Peace, haue gotten some braunches of that Tree, and (by our example) planted the same in their owne Dominions. In doing of which, the French haue filled their Coffers with Treasures, which before were opened by

---

[1] smarted—suffered
[2] crazed—broken, damaged
[3] reduced—restored
[4] contentation—contentment

violence, emptied by seditious Leagues,[5] and wasted[6] to nothing by the miseries of a tedious and intestine warre:[7] the Spanish haue likewise with the same streame safely returned from the Mines of both Indies, and richly vnladed their Argozies[8] of Indian golde, vpon their owne shoares, of which golde (before Peace inhabited amongst them) they were euer least saue when they approached nearest home,[9] as the bringers of it from thence hither, and the loosers of it there, did in those [sig. B 1/4] times (the one with ioy, the other with madnes and sorrow) openly testifie.

So that these fires (whether of Ambition, of Zeale, or of Rage, I knowe not) which for many late yeeres haue flamed in the Low Countries, had not bin kindled there, I thinke the very name of Warre had bin almost forgotten, and the right pronunciation of it vnknowne to these parts of christendome. The violent heate of which Belgicke fires was so lasting, and burned so high, that it serued as a Beacon on the top of a hill, to call vnto their help other forren nations (who before were but lookers on) and inticed them (through the thirst of glory, honour and fame which are gotten in the fires) to become partners and sharers in the variable fortunes of those Battelles of the Dutch and Spanish. Insomuch that the Drumme being vnbraced heere, and hung by the walls (as hauing no vse of such thunder amongst vs, vnlesse it were for pleasure,) and most of our men of Action and of the Sword hearing the sound of theirs, and being drawne thither, I thinke it was then, and is now stil possible to call together 20000. of our english nation into one place, and amongst them all not to find or picke out one Souldier, when in other forren realmes (vext continually with vproares) it hath bin, and to this day is hard to call together 100000. and to call out of them any other person but a Souldier.

The Schoole of Warre decaying, and being throwne downe in one kingdome, hath from time to time bin erected in another. And as men who professe other Arts and Sciences, will (if they loue them truely) trauell ouer the world to enrich their bosomes with the perfit knowledge of those things with which their soules are inflamed: So the militarie Scholler (whose best learning is Practise,) accounteth euery Land his owne country where this profession of Armes is held in honor: and no loue of parents, wife, children, kinred[10] or friends hath power to keepe him from those glorious paths of danger.

---

[5] Leagues—the Catholic League, which fought at various points the kings (Catholic and Protestant) of France during the sixteenth-century Wars of Religion

[6] wasted—reduced

[7] intestine warre (war)—internal war, civil war

[8] argozies (argosies)—a large, abundantly laden merchant ship, or a fleet of such ships

[9] they were euer (ever) least saue (save) when they approached nearest home—they kept the least amount save when they fought nearest home

[10] kinred—kindred

[sig. B 2/5]   By this meanes, many Englishmen that were borne obscurely, and might (otherwise) haue died forgotten, haue by their noble aduentures and seruices in forren realmes (farre hence remoted)[11] not onely won eternall honours to their owne names, but also crowned their nation and natiue country with neuer dying glories: And in despite of Enuy [and] Obliuion (sworne enemies to virtue) who would beat downe the memorie of such high spirits, by throwing them into base and vnknowne graues, Fame does euermore build vp tombs for them in her immortal chronicles.

Whilest all men here at home sate playing with the Sun-beames of Quietnes, and that all the low Country[12] storms began likewise to be laid downe calme, so that the English souldier had no place to retire to, but to come and lie idlely on the bosome of his own country; behold, a fresh Allarum awakes and calls him from hence into *Sweden*. In the warres of which kingdome what hath bin done lately, I meane only, forsomuch as I, who was a seruitor in them, and am now the trumpet to proclaime mine own fortunes there, haue had triall, you shall now (deere countrimen) receiue a faithfull and honest relation.

Wherein I vow by the honor of a souldier, and by the loue, obedience and loyaltie which I owe to no other than my owne natiue countrey, I will set downe nothing but that of which (for the most part) I haue bin *Oculatus testis* (an eie-witnes.) And albeit in this relation the truth must compell me to deliuer such matter, as happily may terrifie those that neuer bare Armes, nor followed the fortunes of a Souldier, from euer going into *Sweden* and to serue in those warres: farre are my thoughts (God beares record of them) from any such disswasion, sithence[13] all men that know what belongs to the field, can tell, that he who vndertakes the life and condition of a Souldier, must endure worse and greater miseries, than I or any Englishman sent thither can vndergo in *Sweden*. Omitting therfore the ground of their quarrell, and not so much as once [6] touching the fire that hath now so sately[14] kindled warres betweene the kings of *Sweden* and *Poland*, because the heartburnings of kingdomes one against an other are diseases of State, and not fit to be medled with by me, being beyond my cure, I will write a Storie of my owne fortunes there only, which begins as followeth.

About a fortnight before Midsomer, which was 1609. a company of Voluntaries[15] to the number of 1200. souldiers, were at seuerall times shipped from *England* to passe into *Sweden*, to aide the King[16] of that Countrey in his warres

---

[11]   remoted—removed
[12]   low Country (Low Countries)—the Netherlands
[13]   sithence—since
[14]   sately—probably "fully" or "greatly"
[15]   voluntaries—volunteers
[16]   Karl IX Vasa (1550–1611), king of Sweden from 1604 to 1611.

against the king of *Poland*.[17] To which aid, diuers other nations did likewise resort, as *Frensh*,[18] *High Dutch*,[19] [et]c of all whom (as occasion ministreth) mention shalbe made in their due places. Of the English companies that went thither, the first was commaunded by one *Caluine* a Scot; who by appointment was made lieutenant Colonell and chiefe of the other Captaines ouer the footmen. The names of which Captaines are in this following Discourse set downe.

After the first company was gone, a second number of 300. men (of which I the relater of this, was one) were put into one shippe belonging to *Sweden*, and came from thence for vs. We being thus aboord, sailes were presently hoisted, anchors weighed, and by the assistance of God, wherewith the dexteritie of the mariners was furthered, in a short time had we gotten into the maine[20] sea, and with a prosperous gale[21] went forward on our voiage. But mans security oft-times changeth Gods fauors into sodaine indignation;[22] for when euery one at the parting from his owne country had a mery and fearelesse heart to runne to the certaine dangers that stood ready to meet him in another forren region: Behold (to put vs all in minde, that God was the God of Hostes, and that whether we went foorth to fight, or laied vs downe to sleepe, whether we were on the seas, or on the land, our safeties and dangers lay all in his disposing) behold, I say, in the height of all [sig. B 3/7] our iolity, seeing so prowd a saile swelling with the winds to carry vs the heauens on a sodaine altered their lookes, stormes fell vpon the waters, the waters threatned destruction to our ship, and we that were in her, stood wauering betweene the hopes of an vncertaine life, [and] the dreadfull terrors of a most iminent death. In this horror of the seas, were we tossed so long that all our victualles were almost spent: the misery of which, threw vs into more desperate feares: now were we assaulted by double deaths (Famine or Shipwracke) what course to take for our reliefe no man presently knew. Continue without foode it was impossible, and as impossible was it for vs to recouer[23] the land in any short time, without the assured destruction of vs all. At this season, our commanders were these.

	Lieutenant Benson.
viz	*Lieutenant Walston*, who was Prouost Martiall[24] of the field.
	And an Ancient[25] of the Colonels company.

---

[17] Sigismund III Vasa (1566–1632), king of Sweden from 1592 to 1599, king of Poland from 1587 to 1632.

[18] Frensh — emended from "Frenill"

[19] High Dutch — Germans

[20] maine (main) — open

[21] prosperous gale — favorable strong wind

[22] indignation — punishment

[23] recover — return to

[24] Provost Martiall (Martial) — the officer in charge of military discipline

[25] ancient (ensign) — standard bearer

These our Commanders were by our rashnesse droue into worse feares than those were that laid hold vpon our selues; for whereas they were resolued (blow the winds how they could) to continue still at sea, and not to land, till they set footing at their appointed shores, the common Souldiers had on the contrary part vowed and resolued to compell the mariners (seeing the present miseries, and no hopes promising better) to set vs all on shore vpon the first land that could be discouered. Our Commaunders did what they could by disswasion to alter this general resolution, because they feared it would be the losse of the greatest part of our Companies, if they came once to be scattered: and besides, they knew that it would redound[26] to their dishonour and shame, if they should not discharge[27] the trust imposed vpon them by our Captaines, which trust was to conduct vs [and] land vs before, whilst our [8] Chieftaines remained a while behind in *England*, to take vp the rest of our Companies. Yet all this notwithstanding, Land being discouerd, there was no eloquence in the world able to keep vs aboord our ship, but euery man swore if the master of the ship would not set vs on the shore, the sailes should be taken into our own hands; and what was resolued vpon (touching present landing) should in despite of danger be effected. Vpon this, the master of the ship and the mariners told vs, that if we put to land in that place, we should all either perish for want of victualles, which were not to be had in that country, or else should haue our throates cut by the people. But the dangers in which we were, and which we felt, being more certaine (as we imagined) than any other could be, of which we had yet no sence or feeling, [and] our hopes perswading vs that we could not fall into worse, than those we tasted already: besides, all of vs construing the words of the mariners, as not spoken by them, but as if they had bin set on to do so by our commanders in the ship, who by all means fauored to keep vs all aboorde: At the last we resolued rather to try our bad fortunes on the land, and to famish[28] there (if that kind of death must needes attend vpon vs) than to perish on the seas, which we knew could affoord vs no such mercie as the land was likely to lend vs. So that in the end, we got so neare the shore side, as the sailes durst venter without danger to the ship: and there casting anchor our small boat was hoisted out, [and] on shore we went, as fast as possibly we could. When our Officers sawe, that there was no remedy, nor force to detaine vs aboord, they then disheartned vs no longer, but to our great comforts told it, that the master of the ship (which thing he himselfe likewise openly confessed) knew both the Land and the Gouernour thereof (as indeed we proued afterwards he did:) and therefore desired they all our companies not to missebehaue themselues toward the people, for that it was an Iland called *Iuthland*, vnder the dominion of the king of [9] *Denmarke*, but subiect to the command of a Lord, who vnder the king (as his substitute) was the gouernor.

---

[26] redound—have an advantageous or disadvantageous effect

[27] discharge—perform a duty

[28] famish—starve

And that we might be the better drawne to a ciuill behauiour towards thinhabitants, our officers further told vs, that they would repaire to the Lord Gouernour of the country, and acquaint him with the cause of our vnexpected landing
there; vpon which we all promised to offer no violence to the people; neither was
that promise violated, because we found the inhabitants tractable, and as quiet towards vs, as we to them: yet the greater numbers of them ran away with feare, at
the first sight of vs, because (as afterward they reported) it could not be remembred
by any of them, that they euer either beheld themselues, or euer heard any of their
ancestors report, that any stra[n]ge people had landed in those places and partes of
the Iland: for they thought it impossible (as they told vs) þ[a]t any ship should ride
so neere the shore, as ours did, by reason of the dangerous Sands.

Our officers so soone as they were at land, went to the gouernor of the Iland,
whilst the souldiers (who staid behind them) ran to the houses of the Ilanders, of
purpose to talke with the people, and at their hands to buy victualls for a present
reliefe: but when we came among them, they could neither vnderstand vs, nor we
them; so that the market was spoiled, and we could get nothing for our money:
yet by such signes as we could make, they vnderstood our wants, pittied them,
and bestowed vpon vs (freely) a little of such things as they had. Yet in the end,
a happie means of our reliefe was found out by a souldier amonst vs, who was a
Dane by birth, but his educatio[n] hauing bin in *Engl[and]*. no man knew him to
be other than an englishma[n].

This *Dane* made vse of his owne natiue language, to the good both of himselfe, and vs, certifying[29] the people (who the rather beleeued him because he
spake in their knowne tongue) of the cause that compelld vs to land vpon their
coast, and that we intended no mischiefe, violence, *[10]* or mony:[30] to which report of his they giuing credit, stood in lesse feare of vs than before, and thereupon
furnished vs with all such necessaries, as the countrey affoorded to sustaine our
wants. The food which we bought of them was only fish, and a kind of course
bread, exceeding cheap. Of which food there was such plentie, that for the value
of 3. d. we had as much fish as xx. men could eate at a meale, and yet none of
the worst sorts of fish, but euen of the very best and daintiest, as Mackrels and
Lobsters, and such like. In which our trading with the poore simple people, we
found them so ignorant, that many, yea most of them regarded not whether you
gaue them a counter, or a shilling; for the bigger the peece was, the more fish
they would giue for it: but besides fish wee could get no other sustenance from
them, or at least, could not vnderstand that they had any other. But obserue what
happened in the meane time that we were thus in trafficke[31] with the Ilanders for
victualls, our Officers (as before is said) being gone to the lord Gouernor, who
lay about xii. english miles from the sea side, the maister of our ship on a sudden

---

[29] certifying—assuring
[30] or mony (money)—probably "or to take any of their money"
[31] trafficke (traffic)—commerce, trade

hoised vp sailes, and away he went, leauing one of his owne men at shore, who accompanied our Officers as their guide, through the Iland. The cause of the ships departure, did so much the more amaze vs, by reason it was so vnexpected, [and] the reason thereof vnknowne to vs: But we imagind the master of the ship and mariners feared to receiue vs into the vessel again, because some of our men at their being at sea, threatned the sailers, and offred the[m] abuses before they could be brought to set vs on land.

On the next day following the Lord Gouernor of the Iland came to vs, bringing our Officers along with him, yet not being so confident of vs, but that (for auoiding of any dangers that might happen) he came strongly guarded with a troope of Horsemen well armed. And (vpon his first approach) demaunding where our Ship was, it was tolde him in what strange manner it stole away and for- [sig. C/11] sooke vs: he then asked what wee intended to doe, to which wee all answered that we would bee ruled by our Officers: hereupon hee inquired of them what they would haue him to doe in their behalfes, they requested nothing else at his handes, but onely his fauorable Passe through the Country, and a Ship to cary vs forward into *Sweden*: to which request hee made answer, that he could grant no such licence vntil he had made the king of *Denmarke* acquainted with our being there, for the Iland belongd to the King he sayd, and he was no more but an Officer or Substitute vnder him. Yet in consideration that our Ship had so left vs in a strange land, hee promised to do all that lay in his power to effect our good: but withal told vs that the people had inward feares and were possest with suspitions, that our intents of landing vpon such a coast were not as wee our selues affirmed, onely to get foode, but rather to make spoyle of the poore inhabitants. And therefore to remoue all such feares and Ielosies out of the peoples hearts, he held it most conuenient for the generall safeties of both parties, to seperat our numbers and to spread vs abroad in the Country, one and one in a house, where it was agreede that we should receiue both a lodging, and meate, and drinke, vntill he had sent to the King of *Denmarke*, some of his owne men with our Officers, to vnderstand his Maiesties pleasure and what should become of vs.

To this we all agreed, and accordingly for that purpose, were by the Lord Gouernor, safely by this Armed horsemen which were his guard, conducted to his owne house. To that place were all the people of the Iland summond together, they came at the appointed day to the number of fiue or sixe hundred, circling vs rownd with Bills[32] Holberds[33] two-hand swords and diuers other weapons: And at the first sight of vs grew into such rage, that presently they would haue cutt all our throates, and hewed vs to pieces but that the Authority, of the gouernor kept them [12] from offring violence, yet was he fayne to vse the fayrest meanes of perswation to allay their fury. For they would not belieue but that our ariuall

---

[32] bills — concave axes with spikes at the back and shafts ending in spear-heads
[33] holberds (halberds) — a combination of a spear and a battle-axe

there was to destroy them, their wiues and children and make a conquest at last of their Iland. Yet the Gouernor shewed vnto them all our number, which was but 300. men, and those all vnweaponed, and so consequently, neither likely, nor able to vndertake any mischiefe against them.

Then stoode vp some bolder than the rest, and teaching the rest to be more cruell by swearing to haue our blouds[34] ere they stirred from thence, because (as they alleadged) our yeelding to be disarmed, was done but in policy to beguile them, with securenesse, whereas they rather doubted that some second supplies[35] were not farre behinde vs, that would likewise land on their coasts, and ioyne in the same conquest. But the Gouernor looking vpon the condition of men so miserable as we appeared, with an eie of clearer iudgement and pitty, than the common people could, who were euen blinded with their owne fury, insolence and madnesse, shewed the true nature of a wise magistrate, by mingling threats with milde speaches, charging the vnruely multitude, vpon paine of death, not to touch the least finger of vs, but to diuide vs equally into seuerall villages, as it should seeme best vnto them, and to bestow kind and louing entertainment vpon vs til they heard farder from him, which command of his they accordingly performed.

Immediatly vpon this setling of them and vs in quietnesse, one of our officers with two of the Gouernors men, were sent away to the king of *Denmarke*, to vnderstand his Highnesse pleasure, which Messengers were no sooner dispatched about the busines, but the Ilanders growing more and more suspitious, came againe to the Gouernor, and neuer would cease or giue ouer troubling him, vntill they had gotten him to make proclamation (in hearing of vs all) That if any of vs would freely discouer the true [**sig. C 2/13**] cause of our landing vpon that coast, and reueale the plots of any daungerous enterprise intended against them, he should not onely be rewarded with great store of money, and haue new apparell to his backe, but also should without tortures, imprisonment, or death be set free, and sent backe againe into his owne countrey. This proclamation strucke vs all with feare and astonishment, because albeit we to our selues were not guiltie of any plot, or villanie intended to the place or people, yet we knew this might be a meanes to endanger all our liues, how innocent soeuer. Our suspition of daunger fell out according to our feares, for one *Thomas Griffyn* a Welch man, one of our owne company, but a person as it appeared, of a base and diuellish condition, being tempted with the baite of gold, resolued to enrich h[i]mselfe, albeit it were by the sheding of innocent bloud: And thereupon like a false traitor to all the rest of his fellowes, he went and kneeled before the Gouernor, and with a face counterfeiting a guiltines and fearefull[36] destruction, told him, that if he might

---

[34] blouds (bloods)—lives
[35] supplies—reinforcements
[36] fearefull (fearful)—probably, "fear of"

be forgiuen for his part, and haue his life warranted,[37] he would discouer[38] such a secret, that the opening[39] of the same should be good to all the Country, and the concealing thereof the Ilands vtter ruine, with the confusion of the people. The Gouernor being glad of this discouery so promised, assured *Griffyn* both of his life, and of the reward, willing him not to feare any danger, but boldly, and with a constant[40] bosome to lay open what he knew: vpon which wordes, the traiterous *Iudas*[41] told him for certaine, that we came thither onely and for no other purpose than to surprise the Iland, kill the inhabitants, make spoile of their wiues and goodes and hauing set fire of their townes and villages to flie to sea againe. Yet for all this would not the Gouernor beleeue him, telling him it was a matter very vnlikely, that so small a number, so distressed for want of food, so weather-beaten and so disarmed, should venture vpon an enterprise so full of dangerous euents, but the villaine re- *[14]* plied, that all those complaints of want, were but songs to beguile the people, for that vpon the least Allarum giuen, other shippes that lay houering at sea, and furnished both with men and armor, would on the sodaine,[42] and that very shortly land for the same desire of spoile, as these their fellows had done, and therefore councelled the Gouernor to preuent such imminent mischiefes betimes.[43]

The Gouernour being thus farre vrged, presently called before him lieutenant *Walton*, whose lodging was appointed in his house, and hauing related to him all that *Griffin* had discouered, and withall, demaunding of lieutenant *Walton* what he could say to this matter of treason and conspiracy: the lieutenant at the first stood amazed, and vtterly denied any such intended villany, protesting by the faith of a Souldier, that this report of the Welch man proceeded f[r]om the rancour of a vile traitors heart, and therefore on his knees intreated the Gouernor, not to giue credite to so base a villaine (who for the greedinesse of a little money, went about to sell all their liues) and to make all thinhabitants of the Iland become murderers:) adding further, that if the Gouernor would but giue him leaue, he would make the treacherous slaue before his face there presently confesse that he had belyed his fellowes, and that there was no such Conspiracie amongst them. The Gouernor gaue him authority to vse his best meanes to trie a traytor, because it was not to be said, his desire to haue the bloud of any Christians shead wrongfully: but if he should find the Welch mans words to be true, he could do no otherwise than apprehend vs as traitors to his King and the

---

[37] warranted—guaranteed
[38] discover—reveal
[39] opening—revealing
[40] constant—confident
[41] Judas—Judas Iscariot; according to the New Testament, he betrayed Jesus in return for thirty pieces of silver
[42] on the sodaine (sudden)—suddenly, without warning
[43] betimes—speedily, before it is too late

Country and to lay such punishment vpon vs, as should be found due by their lawes. But lieutenant *Walton* earnestly intreating the Gouernor, that if he had any such ill thought of vs, he would be pleased to hold him in fetters as prisoner for vs all, till the trueth might be found out: And that traiterous villaine *Thomas Griffyn* being opposed face to face with the [sig. C 3/15] lieutenant still continuing in his first resolution, and most boldely perseuering in his accusations against his poore countrymen that lay scattred in seuerall houses about the Iland, not hearing of any such matters: Behold how all that *Griffyn* had discouered, were by a strange accident strongly confirmed to passe for currant, and whatsoeuer lieutenant *Walton* had vttered in opposition of *Griffyns* slaunders, were held as vntruths, and traps to betray the Country. For, iust as the traitor had told the Gouernor, that more ships were not farre off, but were ready to second[44] vs vpon our arriuall, it chanced that in the very heat of this businesse, and their feares of daunger where none was, two other ships full of armed souldiers came to the same place of the Iland where our ship put in: These two ships had brought souldiers out of the lowe Countries (a cessation of warres being there) and were going into *Swethland*, as we were, but by crosse windes and fowle weather, lay so long at sea, that wanting victualls, they were driuen in hither for succour. Whose sodaine approch and ariuall being signified to the L[ord]. Gouernor, the welch mans words were then thought true; all the Iland was presently vp in Armes to resist the strength and furie of a most dangerous supposed enemy: and so secretly did the Inhabitants put on Armes that we who were kept like prisoners amongst them knew nothing of these vproares. But night approaching, the Generall gaue speciall charge, that secret watch should be set and kept ouer euery souldier that lodged in any mans house, which by the common people was as narrowly[45] performed, for they did not only watch vs as the Gouernor commaunded, but amongst themselues a secret Conspiracie was made, that in the dead of night, when we should be fast asleepe, they should come and take vs in our beds, and there to binde vs with cords: it being an easie thing to do so, when our company were diuided one from another ouer the whole Iland. At the houre agreed vpon, the plot was put in force, for they [16] entred our Chambers, and bound euerie Souldier as he lay, making them all ready like so many sheepe, marked out for the slaughter. For mine owne part, I had fiue men and three women to binde me, who so cunningly tyed me fast with cordes, whilst I slept, and felt nothing, nor dreamt of any such matter, that with a twitch onely I was plucked starke naked out of my bed, and laide vpon the colde earth vnderneath a Table, with my armes bound behinde me, so extreamely hard, as foure men could drawe them together, my feete tied to the foote of the Table, and my necke bound to the vpper part or boord of the Table.

---

[44] second — support
[45] narrowly — painstakingly

In these miserable tortures lay I, and all the rest (in seuerall houses) all that night, and the most part of the next day, our armes and legges being pinched and wrung together in such pittilesse manner, that the verie bloud gushed out at the fingers ends of many.

The enduring of which torments was so much the more grieuous, because none knew what we had done that could incense them to this so strange and spitefull cruelty, neither could we, albeit we inquired, learne of our tormentors the cause, because we vnderstoode not their language. But to me whilst I stood thus vpon the racke, the old woman mine Hostesse came often running in and cryed in her language to me *Traue vp Iesus*, which was as much to say, Pray to Iesus: by which wordes of her I perceiued they meant to kill me: And still she mumbled out a storie, which I could not interpret, of one *William*, who lay at the next house I knew, so that I guessed her meaning was, that *William*, and all the rest of our company were in fetters too, like my selfe. Yet my priuate thoughts freed all the rest, because I was perswaded they had done nothing to deserue such tyrannous handling: Mary of my selfe, and my neighbour *William* I stoode somewhat in a perillous doubt, that they punished vs for a knauerie committed the very selfe same euening, after [17] which we were intangled in the net, and could by no strugling get out. And that was this.

I happened that night, when this coniuring was to binde vs like wicked spirites in such damnable circles,[46] to suppe with the said *William* at his lodging: and whilst we sate merrily at our meate, not mistrusting what Spiders were weauing ouer our heades, to catch vs like flies in their cob-webs, and then to kill vs, into our rowme comes stumbling a pedlar, with a packe and a boxe at his backe: We hauing so fit an Anuile to breake ieasts vpon, forgot our selues where we were, and beganne to growe merry in English with Seignior Mountebanke[47] our Pedlar, but he gabling in his language to vs, as fast as we did in ours to him, both laughed at one another, yet knew not for what. At last downe throws he his packe and box on the Table, and being a merry lad, and a customer to the house, went out of our rowme to visite the houshold. In the meane time my pew fellow *William* spying his opportunity opened the Pedlars box, which he thought had bin crammed with sweetemeates, but in stead of Sugar plummes he found nothing there but Sope, the purchase[48] of which scowring booty, made *Williams* heart leape for ioy, for (quoth he) my linnen thou seest is fowle, and this Sope shall make me tomorrow a cleane gentleman. And thereupon like a conscionable[49]

---

[46] According to traditional lore, one could keep a devil prisoner inside a circle, pentagram, or other geometrical shape.

[47] mountebanke (mountebank) — a wandering rogue

[48] purchase — spoil, plunder

[49] conscionable — conscientious, scrupulous, just

Chaundler[50] tooke out some halfe a pound and gaue great weight:[51] the one halfe of which prize I shared in, because I had as much neede as he to be washed, yet none of vs both had neede of the shaming which we mette withall anone afterwards. But note how iustly I was plagued: The selfe same Pedlar was one of the men that helped to binde me; the knaue was lesse mercifull in tying his knottes than a Beadle[52] or Hang-man, and more nimble to bind my hands behind me, than to binde vp his packe. I seeing what ware[53] the Pedlar made of my body, and how villainously the rest of his Consort[54] played vpon these hempen strings, that [*18*] were wownd vp about my armes, legges, and necke, thought verily that he and his crew had found me guilty for his Sope, and so condemning me behinde my backe, came likewise to punish me both behind my backe, and to my face. But crying out to them, because I saw they ieasted not with me, that the Soape was in my pocket, all the pittifull signes I could deuise were made, to shew I had thrust it there, but they for all the noise I made, plyed[55] their trussing[56] me vp in halters worse than fiue hangings, neither regarding the cries of the poore, imitating therein many worldly rich men, nor vnderstanding whether I cursed them to the pit of Hell, for so hard binding me, or whether I prayed them to vnloose me, neither did Monsieur Pedlar misse his halfe pound of Sope, so that I was worried by a sort of curres, I knew how, and where, but I knew not why.

Whilest thus the whole Iland was full of the cries of wretched men, and that euery house seemed a shambles,[57] ready to haue Innocents there butchered the next day, and that euery Ilander had the office of a common cutte-throate or executioner, Gods wonderfull working turned the streams of all their cruelty: For the two shippes that came out of the Lowe Countries, and whose arriuall draue so many miserable soules almost vpon the rockes of destruction, hauing in that dolefull and ruinous night, gotten some prouision aboord, weighed Anchor, and departed towards *Swethland*.

Which happy News being serued vp at breakefust to the Lord Gouernour betimes in the morning, and that the Shippes had offerd no violence to the Country, but had payd for what they tooke: About eleauen of the clocke the very same day at noone, wee were all like vnto so many dead men cutt downe, and bidden to stand vpon our legges, although very few had scarce legges that could stand.

---

50 chaundler (chandler) — retail dealer

51 gave great weight — provided more than the due amount

52 beadle — a minor official in church or town administrations

53 ware — watchful care; perhaps with punning reference to a "pedlar's wares", i.e., to a pedlar's merchandise

54 consort — companions; a group of instruments of the same family, such as viols, played in concert. Nixon, punning, here alludes to both definitions.

55 plyed (plied) — diligently continued

56 trussing — tieing

57 shambles — slaughterhouse

[sig. **D/*19*]** Of one accident more that befell, I thinke it not amisse to take note, which began merily, but ended tragically, and in bloud; and that was this: Foure of our company being lodged in one village, and they being bound to the peace, as you may perceiue the rest were; it happened that an hoast where one of them lay, had tippled hard,[58] and gotten a horses disease, called the *Staggers*.[59] In comes he stumbling to the roome where the poore Englishman was bound to the table, hand and foote: which thing the drunken Sot beholding, drew his Hatchet, which he wore at his girdle, according to the fashion of the country, and because he would be sure his prisoner should not escape; with his hatchet he cleft his head. And thin- [*20*] king in that drunken murderous humor, he had done a glorious act, away he reeles out of his owne house to that house where the other three Souldiers lay bound, where beating at the doores and windows, and the hoast asking what he meant to make such a damnable noyse, he told him so well as he could stammer it out, that the Lord Gouernour had sent him thither to put the three English [sig. **D 2/*21***] men to death. Vpon this the diuell and he (hand in hand) were let in, the one standing so close at the others elbow, that he neuer left him till he had cleft two of their heads, that lay bound: and being then weary (it should seeme) with playing the butcher, he neuer ceased swearing and staring, and flourishing with his bloudy axe about their heads, till the people of the house had hung the third man vpon a beame in þe roome. But they hauing lesse cunning in þe Hang-mans trade, then will to practise it, tyed not þe halter so fast about his neck, as to strangle him: so that after he had hung an houre, he was cut downe, reuiued, againe, was well, and afterwards was slaine in Russia.

This bloudy feast being thus ended, and all stormes as we well hoped, being now blowne ouer to our freedome, and sitting at liberty from our tormentors; on the necke of[60] these former miseries fell a mischiefe, more dangerous to vs then all the rest: for tidings were brought to the Gouernour, that our Ancient, who trauailed with the Gouernours two men to the King, had traiterously murdered those his guides, and then ran away himselfe: vpon this rumor, nothing but thundring and lightening flew from the common peoples mouthes: there was no way now with vs but one, and that one was, to haue all our throats cut, or our heads cleft with their axes. But the gouernour pittying our misfortunes, laboured both by his authority, and by faire speeches, to keepe that many-headed dogge (the multitude) from barking. And in the end, when he saw nothing but the bloud of vs poore Englishmen would satisfie their thirst, because they still held vs in suspition and feare, he most nobly, and like a vertuous Magistrate, pawned to the inhumane Rascals, (to my knowledge) his honour, all that euer he was worth, yea his very life vnto them, that within three dayes the messengers sent to

---

[58] tippled hard—drunk heavily

[59] staggers—equine encephalomyelitis, also called "Blind Staggers," a disease that affects horses' brains

[60] on the necke (neck) of—immediately after, on the heels of

the King, should returne home, and that during those three dayes we should bee
of good behauiour to the Islanders: and besides that[61] [22] they did not returne
in such a time, that then he would deliuer vs vp into their hands, to be vsed (or
rather misse-used) in what manner they best desired.

But God (whose helpe is most ready, when wretched man hath most need
of him) put foorth a hand of mercy, and preserued vs: for our Ancient with the
Gouernors two men, came home vpon the third day, to the Gouernours house,
and brought from the King of *Denmarke* his licence, to carry vs not onely through
the country, but commanding that we should be allowed shipping also, at conuenient place, to carry vs to *Sweueland*, whither we were to go: And according
to this lycence the Gouernour caused vs to be called all together the very next
day; at which time, *Thomas Griffin* the Welsh *Iudas*, who had all this while lyen
feasting in the house of the Lord Gouernour, began to tremble and to repent
him of his villany, begging most base forgiuenesse on his knees, both from the
Gouernour, and vs his countrimen and fellow Souldiers, protesting that what he
did came out of his feare to saue his owne life. But our Officers (vpon hearing
him speake thus) had much adoe to keepe the companies from pulling downe
the house where *Griffin* lay, because they would in that rage haue hewed the villaine in peeces.

But leauing him and all such betrayers of mens bloud to the hell of their
owne consciences, let vs set forward out of this infortunate Iland, [and] not stay
in any place else, till in small boates we come by water to *Elzinore* in *Denmarke*,
where wee ioyfully get aboard once more; and are hoysting vp sailes for *Sweueland*. Yet euen in this sun-shine day a storme falles vpon vs too: for our Officers
not hauing sufficient money to furnish vs with victuals, we were enforced to
pawne our Ancient and Lieftenant *Walton*, for the safe returne of the ship, with
condition that they should not be released vntill a sufficient summe of money was
sent to defray all [sig. D 3/23] charges.[62] So that we left our Officers behinde vs;
but the King of *Sweueland* did afterwards release them, and then they came to
vs. But before their comming, we hauing a good winde, landed at a place called
Newleas in *Sweue:* and from thence were carryed to *Stockholme*, (the Kings seate)
and there was the King at the same time: betweene which two places it was a
dayes march on horsebacke.

Vpon this our arriuall at *Stockholme*, we met with the rest that had gone before vs, and with diuers others of our countrymen, that came out of the *Low-
countries*, as before is related. In this place we lay so long, and had such poore
meanes, that wanting[63] money to buy foode, we wanted foode to maintaine life,
and so a number of vs were ready to sterue: till in the end, our miseries making vs

---

[61] besides that—if
[62] defray all charges—pay all expenses
[63] wanting—lacking

desperate, we fell together by the eares[64] with the *Burgers* of the towne: in which scambling[65] confusion and mutiny, euery man got one thing or other, of which he made present money[66] to relieue his body withall: yet lay we at the walles of the citty, crying out continually for money, money, till our throates grew hoarse with balling, but the stones of the walles gaue more comfort to vs, then the inhabitants. One day (aboue all the rest) we heard, that the King was to ride a hunting; and wee imagining that all the abuses, wrongs, and miseries, which we endured, proceeded from some vnder-hand hard dealing, and packing[67] of our Captaines and Officers, resolued to gather about the King at his comming forth, [and] to cry out for mony: but the King being angry (as we supposed) came riding amongst vs, drawing his pistoll from the saddle bow,[68] as if he purposed to haue shot some of vs: but seeing none of vs to shrinke from him, nor to be dismaied, he rode backe againe, we following him, [and] desiring; he would either giue vs money, or else to kill vs out-right; one amongst the rest (whose name was *William Attane*) spake to the King aloud, thus: *I hold it* [24] *honor to dye by the hands of a King, but basely to sterue to death, I will neuer suffer it.* Vpon these our clamors, the King looking better vpon our necessities, sent money the next day, and immediatly after gaue vs a moneths meanes[69] in mony, and two moneths meanes in cloath, to make vs apparrell.

Of the cloath we receiued some part, but the money being paid, was by our Captaines sent into England, to their wiues; no part of it euer comming to the poore common Souldiers hands: for presently vpon this, we were commanded aboord the ships, with promise that when we were aboord we should haue our money. But being in þe ships vnder hatches, away were we carryed with prouision onely of one moneths victuals, when by reason of the weather we were forced to lye eight weekes at sea: in all which time we had nothing but pickelled herrings, and salt stremlings,[70] with some small quantity of hard dryed meates: by which ill dyet, many of our men fell sicke and dyed. In the ship wherein I was, wee liued foureteene dayes without bread, all our best foode being salt herrings, which we were glad to eate raw; the best of vs all hauing no better sustenance.

At the last it pleased God to send vs to a place called *Vfrasound* in *Fynland*, where we landed, (*Fynland* being subiect to the King of *Sweueland*.) From *Vfrasound* we were to goe to *Weyborough*, a chiefe towne in the country of *Fynland*: where we no sooner arriued, but our Souldiers ran some one way, and some

---

[64] fell together by the eares (ears)—fought, quarreled
[65] scambling—clumsy, shambling
[66] present money—ready money
[67] packing—fraudulent dealing
[68] saddle bow—the arched front part of a saddle
[69] meanes (means)—resources needed for subsistence; sometimes "money"; here probably "wages"
[70] stremlings (streamlings)—small herrings found in the Baltic and in Swedish lakes

another, so long that the Captaines were left alone with the ships. This running away of them, being done onely to seeke foode, so great was their hunger.

By this carelesse dispersing themselues, they lost the command of the whole country, which they might easily haue had, if they had bene vnited together: and not onely were depriued of that benefite, but of horses also which were allowed by the King for them to ride vpon.

[25] So that, what by the reason of the tedious iourney, (which we were to trauell, being fourescore leagues) and what by reason of the extreme cold, being a moneth before Christmas, at which time the snow fell, and neuer went off the ground vntill Whitsontide[71] following, but all the raine and all the snow that fell, freezing continually, diuers of our men were sterued[72] to death with the frost.

Some lost their fingers, some their toes, some their noses, many their liues: insomuch that when wee all met at *Weyborough*, we could make no more but 1400. able[73] men; and yet when we were landed at [26] *Vfrasound* we were 2000. strong, the extremity of the cold country hauing killed so many of our Souldiers in so little time.

At our landing at *Weyborough* we had good hopes to receiue better comforts, both of money and victuals: for the inhabitants told vs, the King had allowed it vs, and in that report they spake truth: yet contrary to our expectation, we lay there about 14. dayes, and had nothing but a little Rice, of which we made bread, and a little butter, which was our best reliefe. Drinke had we none, nor money: our Captaines gaue vs certaine letherne pelches[74] onely made of sheeps skinnes, to keepe vs from the cold.

At this place we receiued Armes to defend vs against the enemy, and sixe companies that were allowed by the King for horsemen, receiued horses there. From thence we were to march into Russia, where our enemies continued. But the iourney was long and vncomfortable: for we marched from Newyeares day vntill Whitsontide, continually in snow, hauing no rest, but onely a little in the nights. So that the miseries and mis-fortunes which we endured vpon the borders of *Fyn-land*, were almost insufferable, by reason the number of them seemed infinite. For all the people had forsaken their houses long before wee came, because they were euermore oppressed by Souldiers: by which meanes wee could get neither meate nor drinke, but were glad to hunt cats, and to kill them, or any beast wee could lay hold on, and this we baked, and made them serue for dayly sustenance.

The greatest calamity of all was, we could get no water to drinke, it had bene so long frozen vp, and the snow so deepe, that it was hard to say, whether we

---

[71] Whitsontide (Whitsuntide) — the time of year around Whitsunday, which falls seven Sundays after Easter

[72] sterued (starved) — died lingeringly from cold

[73] able — healthy

[74] pelches (pilches) — coarse outer garments

marched ouer water, or vpon land. So that we were compelled to digge vp snow, and with stones red hot, to melt in tubs, and then to drinke it.

[sig. E/27] This affliction continued about 12. or 14. dayes, till we came into Russia. Vpon our very first entrance into which kingdome, we marched ouer an Arme of the Sea, that was 8. leagues ouer, many of vs steruing to death in that passage, by the cold freezing winds that blew the same day. In which frosty iourney, I saw so much bread as a man might buy for twelue pence, sold away in little bits for the value of forty shillings.

But this misery ended the next day, at our setting foot into Russia, where we found plenty both of corne and cattle; onely the people of the country ran away, leauing all their goods behinde them, but so cunningly hidden, that the best pollicy[75] of ours could hardly finde them out.

By this meanes of the peoples running away, wee were glad to play the Millers, and to grinde all our corne our selues, to bake our bread, and to dresse[76] our owne victuals. Then marched we vp to *Nouegrade*, (a chiefe citty in Russia) where we were to receiue all our meanes þ[a]t rested[77] behind vnpayed: but our Captains beguiled vs, and kept it for themselues: yet to stop our mouthes, they told vs we should go into *Muscouy*, and there all reckonings should be made euen.

Wee had scarce marched aboue three dayes towards *Muscouy*, but that newes came, how a certaine number of our enemies lay in a sconce[78] by the way; the strength of them was not perfectly knowne, but it was thought they were not aboue 700. And þ[a]t we must vse some strategem to expell them fro[m] thence: vpon which relation, our Captains drew forth to the number of 300. English horsmen, and 200. French horsemen: so that in all we were about 500. that were appointed to set vpon the supposed 700. Polanders (our enemies) that so lay insconced: vpon whom we went. Our chiefe Commander in that seruice was *Monsieur La Veile*, a French man, who so valiantly led vs on, that the enemy hearing of our comming, fled ouer a water that was by the sconce; yet not with such [28] speede, but that we slew to the number of 400. of their side, and lost onely three men of our owne: but we tooke the sconce.

About the sconce stood a faire towne called *Arioua*, with a riuer called the *Volga*, running through the middle, but no bridge ouer it: onely a few boates and floates,[79] (made [and] cut out of trees) were there, to carry the people ouer from the one halfe of the towne to the other.

This sconce furnished vs not only with great store of riches, but also with a number of Polish horses: and as many armes as serued to arme 500. men, our want of that commodity being as much as any thing besides: for of those fiue

---

[75] pollicy (policy) — cunning, stratagems
[76] dresse (dress) — prepare
[77] rested — remained
[78] sconce — a small fort or earthwork
[79] floates (floats) — rafts, flat-bottomed boats

hundred men that went vpon the seruice, there were not 300. fixed armes;[80] yet through the hand of him that deales victories, or ouerthrows, as it pleaseth him best, the day was ours.

Ouer this riuer *Volga* the enemies were neuer driuen before, either by the Emperour of *Russia*,[81] or by the King of *Sweueland*: for which cause (as afterward we heard) the next day when they departed from the other side of the riuer, they burnt that halfe of the town on which side they were themselues, and in most bloudy, barbarous, [and] cruell manner, made hauock both of men, women, [and] children, albeit (not aboue halfe a yeare before, þe inhabitants on that side had reuolted from their owne Emperour, [and] turned to the[m]. In which tyrannical vprore, their custome was, to fill a house full of people, [and] then (the doores being locked vpon them, that none might issue forth) the house was fired about their eares: and oftentimes were yong children taken by the heeles, and cast into the middest of þe flames. This inhumane tyrranny being practised not onely by the Poles, that were our enemies, but euen by those Russes that were traytors to their owne Emperour, [and] serued vnder the Poles, and were called *Cassakes*, whose cruelty farre exceeded the Polish.

The towne being thus burnt to þe earth, all the 6000. [sig. E 2/29] (which as I said before, fled ouer þe riuer, out of þe sconce, [and] were by vs supposed to be but 700.) came down in full battalion to þe riuers side with such fiercenesse, as if presently they and their horses would haue swom ouer, to fight with vs, which being perceiued, our poore 500. stood ready to resist them. But whether they feared our numbers to be greater then they were, and þ[a]t we had some other secret forces, I know not: but away they marched, þe selfe same day in which they came downe in that brauery not doing any thing; of which we for our parts, were not much sorry; because if the battailes[82] had ioyned, we knew our selues farre vnable to withstand them. And this was the seruice of the most note, that we went vpon.

Two or three other sconces [and] towns we tooke from our enemies, they not once daring to resist vs, because they knew nothing of our numbers [and] force. But the dishonest dealings of our Captaines, made the whole army discontent; insomuch þ[a]t our Souldiers would oftentimes deny[83] to go forth vpon seruice, because they had beene almost a yeare in the land, and had receiued no more but one *Ruble*, (amounting to the value of 10. s. English.) So that vpon these discontents, 50. of our men ran away to the enemy at one time, [and] discouered[84] to them our strength. After which we durst not be so bold as before we had beene.

---

[80] fixed armes (arms)—weapons ready for use
[81] Vasilii IV Shuiskii (1552–1612), emperor of Russia from 1606 to 1610.
[82] battailes (battles)—the main bodies of the two armies
[83] deny—refuse
[84] discouered—revealed

The fire of a new conspiracy was likewise kindling, but it was perceiued, and quenched with the bloud of þe conspirators, of which the chiefe were hanged. On therefore wee went: when wee came within 40. leagues of *Muscouy*, newes was brought that the enemy had beleaguerd[85] 7000. Russes that were our friends, and that vnlesse we forced the siege to breake vp, the 7000. Russes would euery man bee sterued where they lay. This sad report, (albeit wee had resolued neuer to go vpon any more seruice, vntill wee had our pay) so wrought in our hearts, that we much pittyed the miseries of others, because we our selues had tasted of the like.

[*30*] Our Generall (whose name was *Euerhorne*) was a Fynlander, and with a company of Fynland blades (as they tearme them,) well appointed on horse-backe, was by the King of *Sweueland*, sent after vs, as our Conuoy,[86] vntil we should come to *Pontus le Guard*,[87] who was chiefe Generall ouer the whole army of strangers that came into the land: so that according as he was sent and charged by the King, he ouertooke vs before we came to *Arioua*. By the intreaty therefore of this Fynlander, and the flattering promises of our owne Captaines, we were contented[88] to go vpon this seruice, and to deliuer[89] the Russes, or to dye our se-lues in the action. Yet with condition, that (as they promised to vs) wee should by the way, meete our chiefe Generall (*Pontus le Guard*) who with certaine numbers of English, French, [and] Dutch, (which the yeare before were come into the land) was vpon a march out of *Muscouy*, not onely to meete vs, but to ioyne with vs, and pay vs all our money which remained good to vs; prouided likewise, that so soone as euer we should release the 7000. Russes, our money should be payed downe. On these conditions (I say) we yeelded to go vpon the businesse.

At length *Pontus le Guard* met vs (according to the promise:) and with him was money brought to pay vs, and his word giuen that presently wee should receiue it. But the lamentable estate, in which the poore besieged Russes were (within the sconce) being at the point of death for want of food, required rather speedy execution, then deliberation: so that the necessities of their hard fortunes crau-ing haste, on we went, hauing about 19. or 20000. Russes, that were people of the same country, ioyned to our army, to aide them in this enterprize. But as we all were vpon a march, the enemy hauing receiued intelligence of our approaching, set forward to the number of 8000. Lanciers and more, to intercept vs by the way: and being within one dayes march of the place to [**sig. E 3/*31*]** which we were like-wise going, they set fire vpon three or foure villages hard by the place where we lay at grasse[90] with our horses, for a token that they were comming. And this was

---

[85] beleaguerd (beleaguered) — besieged

[86] convoy — escort

[87] Count Jacob Pontusson de la Gardie (1583–1652), Swedish soldier and statesman.

[88] contented — made content

[89] deliuer (deliver) — save from danger

[90] grasse — emended from "gcasse"

done vpon Midsommer day last in the morning, by breake of day. Then came they thundring with shouts and cryes to set vpon vs: but no sooner was the Alarum giuen, when the greatest part of those 19. or 20000. Russes, that were ioyned to vs as our aide, fled most basely, before any blow was giuen. This sodaine cowardize of theirs, somewhat amazed vs: but the houre being now come, wherein we were not to talke of dangers, but to go meete dangers, with our sixe companies of English horse, we brauely resisted the Polanders, and with great hurt to them, but with little losse vpon our part, charged them three seuerall times.

At last *Pontus le Guard* (our chiefe Generall) tooke his heeles and fled too, leauing vs vtterly destitute of all direction: which much astonished vs, as not well vnderstanding what to do: for our greatest strength (being by their flight) taken from vs, none but we strangers were left in the field, and of vs there was not in all, aboue two thousand, and of that number there were aboue sixe hundred French horsemen, who seeing both the Generall gone, and the Russes fled, turned their backes vpon vs, and ran away too most valiantly, yet not out of the field, but to the enemy.

Then were we not aboue twelue or foureteene hundred at the most, left to resist eight thousand at the least: vpon whom notwithstanding, our sixe companies of English horsemen, charged three seuerall[91] times, without any great losse, but with much honour: And at the fourth time, for want of powers to second them (which the French should haue done) all our sixe companies were scattered and ouerthrowne with the losse of few of our colours. The captaines ouer these sixe companies of horse were these.

[32]	Captaine *Crale*, of whose company I was.
	Captaine Kendricke.
	Captaine *Benson*.
Viz.	Captaine *Carre*.
	Captaine *Colbron*.
	Captaine *Creyton*.

Which sixe Captaines had not in all their companies, aboue 500. men. In this battaile, Captaine *Creyton* was slaine in the field; Captaine *Crale* was shot in the knee, and within a short time after, dyed of that wound; not aboue twelue of his company escaping. Captaine *Kendricke* was wounded in diuers places of the head, and dyed. Captaine *Benson* was shot in the hand, and wounded in the head, and yet escaped, and liued: onely Captaine *Carre* and his Cornet[92] escaped, but all his company scattered [and] lost. Diuers other Officers were slaine, whose names I cannot remember.

Thus were all our English horsemen dispersed and ouerthrowne, to the number of 500. and vpwards: Our Generall *Euerhorne* with his companies of *Fynland*, or *Fynsco* blades, were also put to retraite: so that there was not left in the field, aboue 6. or 700. which were footmen. And of these, one halfe was English, one

---

[91] severall (several)—separate

[92] cornet—company of cavalry

halfe Dutch, who kept onely a certaine place by a wood side, barricadoed about with Wagons, hauing with them foure field peeces,[93] with which they did great spoyle[94] to the enemy. But their number being but few, neither durst they venture on the enemy, nor durst the enemy enter vpon them, but kept them still (as it were besieged) in that place only, because they could no wayes escape. The inconuenience of which cooping vp in so narrow a roome, being looked into, and the dangers on euery side well considered, it was held fittest for safety, to summon the enemy to a parlee.[95] In which parley, the enemy offered, that if they would yeeld, and fall to their sides, they should [33] haue good quarter[96] kept. And if any man had desire to go for his owne country, he should haue liberty to go with a pasport, from the King of Poland. Or if any would serue the King of Poland, he should haue the allowance of very good meanes duly paid him. Vpon thiese compositions[97] they all yeelded, and went to the enemy; only Captaine *Yorke* [and] his Officers, with some few of their Souldiers, went backe into the country, and came not to the enemy; as the rest had done: who from thence marched vp to þe Polish Leaguer, being ten miles distant from the place, and there they continued. But such as desired to trauaile[98] to their owne countries, were sent to the King of Polands Leaguer, which lay at that time, at a place called *Smolensco*, and there accordingly had their Passe, to the number of 100. of which number I my selfe was one. What became of the rest, I know not: but I with fiue more, held together in trauaile, vntill we came to *Dantizicke*, a great towne in Prussia, being distant from *Smolensco*, one hundred leagues.

FINIS.

---

[93] peeces (pieces) — cannon
[94] spoyle (spoil) — plundering, damage
[95] parlee (parley) — negotiation of terms of surrender
[96] quarter — mercy, especially to an enemy
[97] compositions — terms of surrender
[98] travaile — travel

A Iovrnall or Daily Register of all those warlike Atchieuements which happened in the Siege of Berghen-vp-Zoome (1622) || STC (2nd ed.) #1898

In 1621, while the Thirty Years War was gathering steam in Germany, the Twelve-Years Truce between the Netherlands and Spain expired, and the two nations went to war again. The Spanish armies, under the command of the Marquis Spinola, went on the offensive, capturing Jülich early in 1622, and then besieging the strategic town of Bergen-op-Zoom in north Brabant. After a prolonged siege, the Spanish forces were forced to break camp and retreat from the town.

This pamphlet describes at length the day-to-day life of a garrison under slow and (in this case) ultimately ineffective siege. While best read in tandem with Henry Hexham's *A Historicall Relation of the Famous Siege of the Busse* (1630), a very long account of a successful siege, this provides a good introduction to the mechanics of siege warfare in the 1620s. Appended to it are two letters, putatively from a Catholic and a Protestant in the Spanish Netherlands, but probably propagandistic fictions designed to enhearten the citizenry of the United Provinces, both Protestant and Catholic, to resist the Spanish armies. At the end of the pamphlet is a list of the "Tragedies and Comedies of Bergen," noteworthy for illustrating aspects of daily life in a siege, events considered memorable, and the somewhat heavy and cruel sense of humor that appealed to the soldiery of the period.

[TITLE PAGE]

A | IOVRNALL OR | DAILY REGISTER OF | all those warlike Atchieue-
ments | which happened in the Siege of *Berghen-* | *vp-Zoome* in the Low-
countries,[1] betweene the | Armies of the Marquesse *Spinola*[2] Assay- | lants, and
the Prince of *Orange*,[3] Defen- | dants, of the said Towne; together | *with the*
raising of the | SIEGE.

IN THE END IS | added two Letters, which discouer[4] | the Errours fore-con-
ceiued of the successe of | that Siege, and the after-Designes of the *Spanish* |
Armies, if they had taken in *Bergen:* with | some particular accidents of warre, |
which were occasions of mirth | *to the beholders.*

All faithfully translated out of the | *originall Low-Dutch*[5] *Copie.*

LONDON, | Printed for Nathaniel Butter, Bartholomew | Downes, and
Thomas Archer. | 1622.

[1]   THE IOVRNALL OF THE SEIGE OF *Bergen-vp-zoome.*
TO omitte that which being besides our purpose, cannot bee expected of vs;
namely the antiquity[6] of this towne, [and] the siege of it by the Prince of *Parma*,[7]
1588. both which may bee seene in our *Dutch* Stories:[8] Wee will now come to the
late siege of the Marquesse *Spinola*; and set nothing downe, but what we haue
had from very good hands, or haue seene our selues.
The Marquesse *Spinola* and *Don Lewis de Valasco*, hauing gotten *Steenberghen*
by composition;[9] the conquered Prouinces of the Netherlands reioyced mightily,
by making of bone-fires vpon the rumor thereof; in such manner, as if the fish
which they thought to catch, had had the hooke alreadie in his jawes.
The *Spanish* Forces not resting here, went presently thereupon the eighteenth of *Iuly*, 1622. to assault *Berghen-vp-Zome*, and fell instantly vpon the

---

[1] Low-countries (Low Countries) — Netherlands
[2] Ambrosio Spinola (1569–1630), marquis de los Balbases, commander of the Spanish armies in the Netherlands in the 1620s.
[3] Maurice of Nassau (1567–1625), prince of Orange from 1584 to 1625; ruler of the
Netherlands, and foremost Dutch general of the age.
[4] discover — reveal
[5] *Low-Dutch* — Dutch
[6] antiquity — apparently, "history"
[7] Alessandro Farnese (1545–1592), duke of Parma, commander of the Spanish
armies in the Netherlands in the 1580s.
[8] stories — histories
[9] composition — terms of surrender

Horneworke,[10] which lyeth neere to the *Rayberg*; but they were brauely repulsed by the Citizens, and those few souldiers which were left within the same.

[2] The Prince hearing this newes, sent immediately out of his Campe neere the *Rhyne,* diuers Companies into this Citie.

The aforesaid eighteenth of *Iuly,* being holy Munday, the Enemie began (according to their custome) in stead of ringing the *Mary*-bell, to cry out ioyntly, *Iesu Maria,* three times together: but wee not vsed to such songs or tunes, wondred at it, and were partly afraid, not knowing what they meant by it.

The same night, some of our Garrison went to take possession of a high ground, without[11] the Gate towards *Steenberghen.*

The nineteenth of *Iuly,* sixtie of our horse[12] made a sally, intending to see wherefore they cryed out the last night behinde the *Raybergh.* The Enemie perceiuing them, thought to sound an Alarum with their Trumpets; but our horse without any long deliberation set vpon them, and tooke two Trumpetters, besides seuen or eight horse, and brought them into the Citie, none of the said sixtie horse being hurt at all. By this happie[13] attempt our courages increased: and when we espied off from our Steeple, the aide comming vnto vs, and the Enemie then ceasing with his Ordnance:[14] some of our Garrison cried out aloud to them, That they had caried their Ordnance to the Lombard.[15]

The twentieth and one and twentieth arriued here, these three following Regiments, *viz.* of the Lord of *Lockeren,* of Colonell *Hinderson,* and of Colonell *Fama*; so that our Garrison amounted at that time to fiue thousand men. There came like- [3] wise with them these Enginers, namely, Captaine *Ralfe Dexter* English-man, Mr. *Dauid* of *Orleans,* Mr. *Tretorain,* Mr. *Omkees,* Mr. *Klair,* Mr. *Byvordt,* and another English-man.

They went presently, hauing aduised[16] with *Mounsieur Rhynhouen,* Gouernour of the Citie, to fortifie the olde workes[17] and raise new, which were necessarie for

---

[10] horneworke (hornwork)—a single-fronted outwork, the head of which consists of two demi-bastions connected by a curtain and joined to the main body of the work by two parallel wings. It is thrown out to occupy advantageous ground which it would have been inconvenient to include in the original enceinte

[11] without—outside

[12] horse—cavalrymen

[13] happie (happy)—fortunate

[14] ordnance—artillery

[15] caried (carried) their ordnance to the Lombard—Lombardy was known for artillery manufacture, and a lombard was a sort of cannon; either way, the phrase seems to mean "a useless task," like "bringing coals to Newcastle."

[16] advised—consulted

[17] workes (works)—earthworks, fortifications

defence; the Rauelins[18] and Lines[19] being designed out; were in one night raised brest-high, and the next night perfected[20] and brought to their full height, the most part of those workes being made without the *Steenbergher* gate, for without the gate towards *Wowe*, there was an Horne-worke begunne foure or fiue yeare since, and left vnfinished. In the meane time, our Ordnance mounted vpon the North-sconse,[21] to *Boere Verdriet*, and the *Bosh*-gate, was night and day discharged vpon our Enemies, which endammaged them exceedingly, as not discerning as yet where our bullets[22] lighted: wherefore they made a defensiue worke of Bavins,[23] about a quarter and a halfe of a league distant from the Citie, vpon the way towards *Halteren*.

The two and twentieth on a Friday, being the day of S[aint]. *Mary Magdalen*, our Souldiers went with three thousand foote, and foure troopes of horse to wake the Enemies out of their sleepe. They marching without the gate towards *Wow*, left the Garden of Mr. *Verwels* on their left hand, and the *Raybergh* on their right; and entred by the back-side into the Quarter of *Don Lewis de Valasco*, being there intrenched. Our horse hauing giuen a signe of the passage found, both the *English* and *Scots* [4] came on very furiously: and the Enemies being already awakened, cried out *VienZ a, VienZ a*;[24] and ours crying out, Quickly, quickly, kill, kill; set valiantly vpon the Enemies, and slew many of them; and hauing spent their gunpowder, and perceiuing that a third thousand came not on to second[25] them, they sounded a retreate with the Drumme (being deepely entred into the Enemies Quarters) and taking their way behinde the hill to the Citie, they thanked their fellowes for the succour which they expected.[26]

We vnderstood afterwards, that sundrie Gentlemen with a Sergeant Maior, and two Captaines, besides fiue hundred of the Enemies souldiers, were slaine in the same skirmish: on our side Captaine *Seaton* was killed, and another Captaine hurt, besides fiue and twentie souldiers slaine; but our men brought a Cornet[27] with his men into the Citie.

---

[18] ravelins — outworks consisting of two faces which form a salient angle, constructed beyond the main ditch and in front of the curtain

[19] lines — trenches

[20] perfected — completed

[21] sconse (sconce) — a small fort or earthwork

[22] bullets — cannonballs

[23] bavins — a bundle of brushwood or light underwood

[24] *Vienz a, Vienz a* — Come to, come to

[25] second — support

[26] expected — had expected, but had not come

[27] cornet — standard-bearer

In the meane time wee laboured very hard on three small redoubts,[28] which in a right line lead to *Kick-inde-Pot:* the new Horne-worke without the gate towards *Wow*, was likewise taken in hand, and diuers other workes made higher and thicker.

Without the gate towards *Steenberghen*, they laboured likewise very hard on the Horne-worke, and in the Quarters of the Lord of *Lockeren* and *Mounsieur Fama*, there was made also a Line of an hundred and sixtie rods, (euery rod containes thirteene foot) because they conceiued the Enemie about to erect two batteries behinde the *Rosselbergh*, on this side of the *Rysbergh*.

In those daies, the enemies considering that the [5] Garrison discharged their Ordnance vpon them, and sallied forth at their crying of *Iesu Maria*, they left[29] the same. Whereupon our souldiers mocked them, saying that they had compelled the Enemies to forsake their redeemers: but I thinke they did it, because they were beaten vpon two of our *Ladies* daies before.

The three and twentieth of *Iuly*, the Enemie began to play with his Ordnance, without the gate towards *Steenberghen*, vpon the hauen,[30] he hit likewise sometimes the roofes of the houses within the city, the tops of the Ships, and the railes[31] of a Bridge: spending that day three and twentie shot, without doing any great hurt. The same night the city wrought hard[32] vpon all their workes; and principally on the North side, seeing the Spanish Campe erected diuers batteries vpon that side. This night our horse sallied forth both on the South and North side, and draue away his sentinels and watches, causing also an alarum in his Campe: They tooke certaine horse, and prisoners, and brought them into the city, so that they were in some trading.[33]

In these daies there came to vs, many bauins, baskets, boards, beames, and other such like prouision.

The foure and twentieth there was brought to vs, good store[34] of gunpowder, lead, matches, granades, fire bals,[35] and other munition: We shot the same day fiercely with our Muskets, seeing the Spanish forces began to approach. In the euening [6] about ten a clocke the enemie discharged eight cannon shot againe, so that certaine women which were not vsed to the roaring of the Ordnance,

---

[28] redoubts — small fortifications, often detached from the main system of fortifications

[29] left — stopped doing

[30] hauen (haven) — harbor, anchorage, port

[31] railes (rails) — railings

[32] wrought hard — wreaked severe damage

[33] in some trading — unclear, but possibly means that the prisoners were ransomed

[34] store — quantity, numbers

[35] fire bals (fire-balls) — balls filled with combustible or explosive materials, used as a projectile, either to damage the enemy by explosion or to set fire to their works

grew very heauy[36] and prepared themselues to die, but they were laught at. At the
same time also, some few left the city for feare.

From the fiue and twentieth vntill the eight and twentieth, there was done
nothing of any moment, but onely that our workes were fortified and strengthned daily; the trees without the citie were cut downe (the citizens lending their
hatchets to the said purpose) and conueied thither. There sallied now and then a
few at a time forth, and returned with prisoners and horses.

The enemie also hauing gotten more forces, began on the North side to approach, creeping and crinckling[37] on like a snake. The fiue and twentieth, they
threatned vs, that they would beat vs quite away, being *S[aint]. Iames* his day, for
the honor of that Saint: but we vnderstood by their owne souldiers, our prisoners,
that the same day one of our Cannon shot, slue 100. of the enemies.

The eight and twentieth and nine and twentieth, the Enemie beganne about
foure a clocke in the morning, to play with his Ordnance vpon the city, but he
did little hurt, but we mightily endammaged his new battery with our shot, and
spoiled one of his peeces.[38]

August.

The first of *August* 80. of our horse sallied forth, [7] behinde the high ground,
taking their way, and leauing the trenches of the enemies; they not contenting themselues by giuing an Alarum vnto the Camp, slue likewise diuers, and
brought sundrie prisoners and horse into the Citie; many being incited by their
good successe, sued daily for leaue to sally forth, but they were delayed till better opportunitie.

The second day our Ordnance shot cruelly vpon the *Spanish* Campe, thereupon about two a clocke in the night, our Garrison with fortie Musketiers sallied
forth to make the Enemies to rise out of their sleepe, and slue aboue an hundred
of them. Whereupon there arose likewise an Alarum in their Campe, and our
Garrison continued the skirmish with them, vntill the afternoone the next day,
at which time they returned victoriously to the Citie.

The third, fourth, fift, and sixt, there was nothing done but working vpon
the fortifications and shooting, and the old Maior of the Citie on the sixt day lost
both his legs by a Cannon-shot, and died vpon it.

The seuenth and eight day, there came diuers of the Enemies souldiers running to our Citie, being very neere two hundred.

The ninth day, some of our souldiers, both horse and foot, sallied forth behinde *Burghuliet*, and slue there diuers of the enemies, beside them which they
hurt, returning home; and although [8] they were not ouer-loaden with bootie,
they yet gaue God thankes, for that they escaped without the losse of any man,
which happens but seldome.

---

[36] heavy—despondent
[37] crinckling (crinkling)—twisting, winding
[38] peeces (pieces)—cannon

The tenth being vpon Saint *Laurence* day, there was an Alarum giuen in the North Quarter, but it was not knowne at the same time within the Citie: there came at the same instant a strong conuoy into the Enemies Campe, with all kinde of warlike prouision: this night they laboured hard on both sides at their fortifications. The Enemie gaue a token in the North, that hee would giue vs an assault; wherefore, we would not weaken any Quarter, to make it destitute of necessary defence, in case of necessitie.

The tenth and eleuenth we sallied forth vpon the Enemie, and skirmished with him: the Captaine *Fryers* Lieutenant behaued himselfe in the said skirmish as valiantly, as euer any souldier did in our time, and offered vp his soule with such a garland of Laurell for the Country: likewise *Mounsier de Preau*, Cornet of *Mounsieur de Mee*, jealous of his honour, went with him to the heauenly ioyes, leauing the rest in this vnhappie and miserable world.

From the eleuenth vntill the fourteenth, the Enemie shewed himselfe very ciuill and peaceable; but in the meane time our Cannon did not cease.

[9] The fifteenth, there was made a halfe-moone[39] neere vnto the corner of *Beckaff.*

The sixteenth came the Enemie in the night, about ten of the clocke, stealing vnto one of our Sentinels *Perdu*,[40] hee discharging his Musket, made an Alarum, and retired to the little halfe-moone, neere vnto the Horne-worke of *Beckaff*, being closely followed by the enemies; vpon his arriuall the Pitch was presently set ouer the fire, and they paid them home, as you shall heare.

Captaine *Cary*, Captaine *Ralfe Dexter*, and all other Captaines vnder the command of the valiant Colonell *Hinderson*, ranged themselues presently in battell-array,[41] to resist the *Spanish* forces with their valour: the Colonell aforesaid, sent likewise some to the little halfe-moone before mentioned, to aide them within it. The Enemie being very furious, would not let passe twelue a clocke, for the day before was the Assumption of our Lady, hoping, perhaps, thereby to haue the better successe.

We being yet hardly in order, the Enemie came, without making any noise, close vnto vs, but as soone as he perceiued our bullets, hee cried loude out, with a generall crie *fuera viliaco:*[42] The besieged cried likewise, Take the Roague, kill, kill, so that the skirmish grew very hotte: but the Enemies perceiuing that [10] they could doe no good with their furie, retired quietly by the side of the halfe-moone; and afterwards set presently vpon the Garrison againe, crying as they did before; but they were likewise beaten backe: and although they assaulted the

---

[39] halfe-moone (half moon, demilune) — an outwork resembling a bastion with a crescent-shaped gorge, constructed to protect a bastion or curtain

[40] sentinels perdu — soldiers placed on hazardous sentry duty, often in an advanced position; from the French, *sentinelle perdue*

[41] battell-array (battle array) — the order of troops arranged for battle

[42] *fuera viliaco* — "Away, villain!" — possibly with the implication of "Kill the villains!"

said halfe-moone eight times, and got twice vpon it, yet were they continually re-pulsed; at euery assault the Enemie had fresh men; but the *English* and the *Scots* withstood them, without being once so much as relieued, a great while, vntill they called for aide, and were presently thereupon seconded[43] by the Low-Country-men, whereupon they shot together so fiercely vpon the Enemies, that they gaue ouer the halfe-moone, after they had lost many hundreths vpon the place; and in-trenched themselues behinde the same worke. Whiles this fight lasted there were shot three thousand Cannon shot (namely, from the *Bosh* gate, the Horne-worke, and the Contrescarpe[44] at the *Wow*-gate) amongst the Enemies, and did for the most part light vpon the Enemies, because their matches[45] were seene.

In the said fight was the valiant and generous Collonell *Hinderson*, shot with a musket in the vpper part of his thigh, standing at the same time vpon the Rampeir,[46] being brauely at push of Pike[47] with the enemie, and being fallen from the same, in his heauy armour, he was carried to [11] the *Hage* where he died, Captaine *Carie* and the Enginer Captaine *Ralph Dexter*, went likewise the same way (after they had valiantly fought) besides one hundred twenty fiue of our souldiers. This fight lasted from ten in the euening vntill fiue a clocke in the morning. The enemie lost in this fight one Count, fiue Captaines, diuers Lieuten-ants and Ensigne[48]-bearers, besides eight hundred souldiers.

The same day there was a cessation of armes for the space of an houre agreed of, to burie the dead on both sides: In the meane time, the Enemie working very strong, contrary to the agreement, we discharged our Ordnance vpon them, and slue many, and the Enemie doing the like, the dead were for certaine daies left vnburied.

We perceiued about the same time, that the Enemie was verie sorie in regard of the misfortune happened vnto him, and would seeke meanes to reuenge himselfe.

In those daies came certaine Switsers besides other souldiers into the citie; Likewise the Italians which lay nere vnto the Quarter of the Lord of *Lockeren*, began to shoot diuers of our men with long Harquebuses[49] through the heads, vsing this deuise: they tied greene grasse about their owne heads, that they might not be perceiued, when they looked ouer the Rampeirs to shoot, for they seemed only like some greene earth cast into the aire.

---

[43] seconded — supported

[44] contrescarpe (counterscarp) — the outer wall or slope of the ditch, which supports the covered way; sometimes extended to include the covered way and glacis

[45] matches — possibly small lamps; possibly the wick (and cord) used for firing early guns

[46] rampeir — rampart

[47] push of pike — the confrontation of pikemen (or soldiers generally) face-to-face, pushing and stabbing at each other with pikes until one side or the other breaks and runs. Actually and proverbially fierce and trying combat.

[48] ensigne (ensign) — standard, banner

[49] harquebuses (arquebuses) — early guns

[12] But afterwards we perceiuing their deuise, discharged our shot vpon the grasse aforesaid, striking downe the safme many times, with the head, and whole body.

The twentieth being Saint *Laurence* day, after the Vespers were sung, the enemie came againe about ten a clocke, at one side of the halfe moone, and would by force leape ouer the Ramparts; the Swissers which were lately arriued perceiuing the same, began to curse and sweare, daring them to come ouer, they in the meane time thrust fiercely at them with their pikes; but the Swissers slashed them againe brauely in peeces with their curtle-axes.[50] This fight increasing, the whole quarter rose in armes, and discharged certaine thousands of Musket shot vpon the enemies, and flung granades likewise, and other fire workes amongst them, in such manner that the enemie lost againe aboue 500. men, and we had 20. slaine, and about 50. hurt.

The one and twentieth came six Companies into the City; and the enemie shooting very cruelly, we answered them with the like; It was the same day resolued in the citie, to build a halfe moone vpon the hauen, betwixt the North Sconse and the citie.

The two and twentieth, three and twentieth, and foure and twentieth, were two English Ensignes[51] slaine with Musket shot, the one being [13] hit by a Fryer, who was very skilfull in discharging of the long Harquebuse. The same day there went two troupes of horse hence towards *Breda,* 60. more got leaue to goe by land thither, and went in the night forth from the *Bosh* gate, riding behind *Burgvliet* and arriued the next day at *Breda,* with 18. prisoners; almost all our workes without the city were perfected at the same time, but yet euery day we laboured hard vpon the trauerses[52] or trauers lines and offcuttings and such like.

The six and twentieth and seuen and twentieth there came seuen companies into the Citie with Collonell *Morgan,*[53] the Landgraue *Philips* of *Hessen,* and the Yonker[54] *William* of *Nassaw,*[55] so that the Garrison was at the same time ten thousand strong; it seemed that at the same instant, the enemie would attempt something on the waters side; but we within prepared our selues to resist him.

In those daies there rose an Alarum in the city, for that a Corporall with 10. or 12. souldiers, fell about noone vpon the approaching enemies, sallying forth

---

[50] curtle-axes (curtal axes)—cutlasses; heavy, slashing swords

[51] ensignes (ensigns)—standard bearers

[52] traverse—a barrier or barricade thrown across an approach, the line of fire, etc. as a defense; parapets of earth raised at intervals across the terreplein of a rampart or the covered way of a fortress, to prevent its being enfiladed

[53] Sir Charles Morgan (1575/1576–1643), English soldier.

[54] yonker (younker)—a young nobleman or gentleman

[55] William of Nassau (1601–1627), natural son of Maurice of Nassau, prince of Orange.

out of the Quarter of the Lord of *Lockeren*; after they had slaine some few, they returned all safely backe, bringing away diuers Muskets and shouels.

Collonell *Morgan* in those daies with a Frenchman being Captaine of the Trunckes,[56] surueyed **[14]** all the workes and mines:[57] those Truncks were almost all made in two or three daies.

The nine and twentieth the Enemie made a worke of bauins opposite vnto the *Coninsbergh* and the furthermost halfe moone, neere vnto the new horne-worke aboue the Crabbe sconse: Whereupon we shot fiercely and cast granades and fireworkes vpon the Enemies, killing aboue an hundred of them, and burning the greater part of their bauins, before our retreat. The Enemie being desirous to reuenge this spite,[58] *Don Inigo de Brosgado* gaue an onset vpon a little halfe moone, lying at the quarter of *Monsieur Famaes* Quarter without the line: Our souldiers beat them off sundry times very valiantly, with musket shot and granades; hereupon the Enemie caused his horse to driue them on againe; so that with much adoe they intrenched themselues at last behinde the said little halfe moone: Our souldiers kept the Enemies backe, with granades and burning of straw, vntill their fellowes had pillaged the dead. The Enemies lost here 500. men, besides those which were hurt, *Don Ioan de Portugals* Corps (being slaine among the rest) was afterwards ransommed for 500. *Gilders*; which is 50. *li. Sterling*. On our side were killed the Lieutenant of the Lord of *Lockeren*, Captaine *Hans Van de Bosh*, besides twentie souldiers: Moreouer there were forty hurt.

[15] The last of *August*, and the first of *September*, the Enemy would approach with rowling Trenches[59] about the *Coninsbergh*, but hee was beaten backe.

The 2. of *September* there happened a Skirmish in the out-workes, and wee droue the Enemies with our Canon and Granades, out of some of their formost workes, taking afterwards with vs the Instruments[60] which they left behind them, with other such commodities. The Enemy lost there many; on our side there were 20. slaine, and 12. or 14. hurt. The same Euening the Enemie made Boone-fires (in regard of the Victory which hee pretended that *Don Cordua*[61] had

---

[56] trunckes (trunks) — probably "trenches"

[57] mine — a subterranean gallery in which gunpowder is placed, so as to blow up the enemy's fortifications above the gallery

[58] spite — outrage, injury, insult

[59] rowling (rolling) trenches — apparently a pre-built fortification that could be rolled into place and used as a trench

[60] instruments — tools

[61] Prince Gonzalo Fernández de Cordoba (1585–1635), Spanish general during the Thirty Years War.

gotten against *Count Mansfield*,[62] and the Duke of *Brunswicke*,[63] passing through *Brabant*) and discharged his Ordnance: in the meane time the Spanish retreated a little from their worke on the Northside, and our Forces getting notice thereof, went presently thither and pulled it downe, carrying the boards and other materialls into their Garrison.

The 3. wee had newes from *Breda*, of *Count Mansfields* arriuall there: in the euening was all our Cannon as well within as without the City, discharged to welcome *Count Mansfield*; the Enemy answered vs with 8. or 10. Shot. The same night our Garison inuaded againe the Enemies Workes, on the North side, and pulled a great part of the same downe to the ground, and tooke almost all the Bavins away, without any resistance or opposition of the Enemies.

[16] The 4. the Enemy assaulted our halfe moone on the North-side foure times in one night; but our Garison driuing them backe, assaulted them afterwards in their owne Campe, and tooke aboundance of Pikes from the Enemies, and burnt great store of their Bavins, (brought thither to fortifie withall) we saw 30. of the Spanish Campe lying dead vpon the ground, besides others which lay here and there dispersed; wee had two slaine, and three or foure hurt.

The 5. and 6. there happened certaine strange Accidents, which are rehearsed at the latter end of this Booke.

The 7. we blew vp one of our Mines on the North side, perceiuing that the Enemie had likewise one there, which also burst as well as ours; wee repair'd our Worke presently againe, and lost nothing by it.

Our Garison went the same euening betwixt ten and eleuen a clocke towards the Enemies Trenches, and made them to retire close to their Batteries. We tooke there aboundance of Bauins for the space of two howers together, and destroyed his Gabion-baskets,[64] with sundry other workes.

The 8. day in the afternoone, *Don Cordua* arriued in *Spinola's* Campe, being accompanied with 56. or 57. Companies, and certaine Ordnance to strengthen the Siedge. We heard this day that the Enemy [17] was raysing a Fort at *Saint-Vliedt*, a place lying betwixt *Lillo* and this City.

The 9. wee burnt on the North side great store of the Enemies Bauins, which hee had brought thither to aduance his approaches.

The 10. our Garison sallied forth againe on the North side, and tooke away all the Bagges of the Enemies by day light, which they had prepared to fill vp our ditches withall, and to assault our Workes afterwards, they are filled with stones, and so bigge, that a man hath much adoe to carry one of them.

---

[62] Count Ernst von Mansfeld (ca. 1580–1626), Protestant mercenary general during the Thirty Years War.

[63] Christian of Brunswick (1599–1626), Protestant military leader during the Thirty Years War.

[64] gabion—a wicker basket, of cylindrical form, usually open at both ends, intended to be filled with earth, for use in fortification and engineering

The eleuenth and 12. our Souldiers continued both in the North and South side of this City, to endamage the Enemies by their sallies: the Workes which hee made in the night, we spoyled in the day, beating him out of his Trenches, with the death of many of his Souldiers, burning some of his Bauins, and taking away the rest euen in our owne quarters.

In the same dayes, and the eight next following, there came 20. 30. or 40. of the Enemies dayly running vnto vs, for want of pay, as they told vs.

The 13. and 14. the Enemy shot very furiously vpon the City, and did much hurt to diuers Houses and Steeples; but God be praised few persons were hurt: This night hee approached with a Line from the Wood, towards the great Horne-worke, lying [18] South-west from the City; but wee stayed[65] him presently with a Counter-line.

The 14. our Soldiers beat the Enemies out of their Trench on the South-side, and slew all that they could meet withall, and finding there two Barrels of Beere, dranke them both quite vp, and so hauing gotten some booty of Apparell and Armes, they returned backe againe into our workes.

The 15 in the night, the English and Scots, vnder the Command of Col-lonel *Morgan*, assaulted the Enemies quarters; and hauing driuen them away, they tarried there till morning, and eat vp all their prouant,[66] and cast downe 50. Roddes of the Enemies Line, which hee had newly begunne; but the next night the enemies wrought on the same againe, resoluing to finish it fully. But it is a very memorable thing to tel; an English Grey-hound which followed his Mais-ter when hee sallyed forth, senting and snuffling about in the Enemies quarter, found there a Bagge of poysoned Bullets, (which are against the Law of Armes) and brought the same vnto his Maister. And I, getting some of them of the Ser-geant Mayor of the English, sent them to my friends for a raritie. The same day about 100. of our Horse of *Berghen*, rode forth from *Breda*, and tooke seuen or eight Horse of the Enemies, neere *Huys-berghen*, about a League and a halfe from hence, lying South-east from this City: and afterwards they sent sundry Troopes close to the *Raybergh*, and brought 75. Horse into *Breda*.

[19] The 16. the Enemy blew a Mine vp on the North [si]de, whereby two of ours were kild, and foure or fiue hurt: but wee set presently vpon the Enemies, and caused them to retire.

The 17. there were sent hither backe againe from *Breda*, 60. of our Horse, which lay within this City before.

The Enemy at this time threatned vs mightily; wherefore there was order giuen, that all the Companies should tarry for the space of eight daies without the Citty; whereas they in former time returned vsually the fourth day into the Towne.

About the same time wee got many Horses of the Enemies; but seeing wee wanted pasture for them, there were many times good Horses sold for the value

---

[65] stayed—checked
[66] provant—provender

of 1. 2. 3. or 4. shilling sterling money; yea, the English bartered them away sometimes for a little Tobacco.

The same day wee laboured on both sides, night and day without ceasing, and principally vnder and about the forsaken halfe moone, lying in the South part of the City, vpon the corner of the great horne-worke, neere vnto the Wood; both wee and the Enemies hauing vndermined the very same piece: but our Mine was eight foot deeper then theirs. About the euening wee blew vp a counterfeited or false Myne, which wee had made vpon purpose not farre from the other: the Enemy thereupon thinking, and vnderstanding likewise by the Runagates, that our Mine was blowne vp, without hauing taken any ef- [20] fect; they thought to make vse of theirs, and to draw our men thither by inticements: but the Foxe had inuited the Crane, as the Prouerbe saith.[67] Collonel *Morgan* hauing sent a little before 200. Musquettiers into a Ditch, with charge to make an Alarum into the very Trenches and Workes of the Enemies; which by them was so brauely per- formed, that they droue the Enemies close to the *Rayebergh*, and into their owne Quarter, where they were strongly seconded. Then began our Musquettiers softly to retire, and forsooke the ground which they had gotten, only in policy,[68] to leade the Enemies another manner of dance then the Spanish Pauin:[69] They followed our men hard, and came in great numbers into the compasse of the aforesaid for-saken halfe-moone, and further too, where they were saluted by our bright and well-oyled Musquets, and afterwards blowne vp into the ayre both by ours, and likewise by their own Mynes too, when they little suspected any such matter, as is aforesaid. They made a pittifull noyse and a lamentable cry, and our Garison setting vpon them, kild many (which were sunke into the sand by the blowing vp of the Mynes, some sunke therein vp to their middle, some vnto their brests, and some vnto their shoulders) knocking them downe with their pieces in such manner, that wee gat our purpose of them. Wee might likewise haue blowne vp the Enemies battery, neere vnto the aforesaid halfe-moone, and endamaged him mightily thereby, seeing wee had a Myne vnder the same, if our Commanders generally had consented thereunto; the Enemies had [21] 11. Pieces planted vpon the said battery, and annoyed vs mightily.

The 18. they were labouring hard on both sides, at their Trenches, Mynes, Lines and Trauerses, and had some small Skirmishes with vs, wherein sundry were hurt; so that the linnen which some Patriots or wel-willers of the Countrey had sent thither, was well imployed in the dressing of the wounds: there were

---

[67] One of Aesop's Fables is about the Fox and the Crane. First the Fox invites the Crane to dinner, and serves soup from a flat bowl, from which the long-billed Crane can't drink; then the Crane invites Fox to dinner, and sets out a long- and narrow-necked flagon, from which the Fox can't drink. The moral is of apt return for unpleasant hospitality.

[68] in policy—as a stratagem

[69] pavin—pavane

likewise made 1500. Cushions for the breast, and aboundance of head pillowes for the sicke or hurt Souldiers.

The 19. wee perceiuing that the Enemies would blow vp one of their Mynes, (in the Quarter of the Collonel *Fama*, and the Lord of *Loqueren*, neere vnto the forsaken halfe-moone) wee went all out of our Myne, which was hard by the same) except a Frenchman and two other, which after the Enemy had blowne vp his Myne, were yet found aliue and drawne out: hereupon the Enemy came fiercely on, thinking that hee had paid vs home, with a purpose to settle himselfe vpon the forsaken halfe-moone; for a while wee resisted them, and they following vs afterwards at our Retreate, were blowne vp by our Myne; and buried aliue, this happened betwixt 11: [and] 4. a Clocke in the afternoone.

The 20. the Enemy began from all sides to shoot very fiercely vpon the City, endamaging mightily the Church and Steeple of the same, in such manner, [78/22] that the ordinary waiter nor no body else durst abide therein: Wee supposed that the Enemy did this because *Mounsieur de Greue*, Gouernour of *Isendycke*, was burning and ransacking *Flaunders* with 2000. Souldiers and 200. Marriners. This same day *Don Garcia Piementelli*, a braue Souldier, was kild by one of our Mynes, so that *Spinola* was very sory for his death.

The 21. wee blew two Mynes vp without the Bosh-gate, and saw the Enemies flying vp into the Ayre like Storkes. At *Antwerpe* they call now our City, *Berghen bring on*, in stead of *Berghen vp Zoom*, seeing there haue beene so many brought and sent thither from sundry places. But they dare no more assault vs so freely as they did in the beginning. We haue our hands dayly full of worke: but it is no matter; for whereas wee lose one man, the Enemy loseth tenne.

We thought that they would haue broken vp the Siedge vpon our fasting or prayer day, seeing the approaches were forsaken by them, about the Quarter of Collonel *Fama*, and the Lord of *Lockeren*.

It is remarkable to consider, that of so many iron Bullets which both high and low are dayly shot into the City, but few hurt or kill any, there is such store of them that are daily sent to the Store-house with Wheele-barrowes, and the Children play with the Musquet bullets which fall vpon the streets, vsing [23] them in stead of earthen Bullets (with which the Children in the Low-countries are vsed to play: for Custome being another nature as it were, both Men, Women and Children haue beene so vsed to the thundering of the Shot, that it causeth no astonishment or alteration in them any longer.)

The same day wee sallied forth on the North Quarter, and hauing driuen the Enemies out of their Trenches, wee burnt their Bavins and Faggots,[70] pulled downe their Lines, and slew many of them.

The 22. wee blew vp 3. Mines with good successe neere vnto the English Quarter, endamaging mightily both the Souldiers and Workes of the Enemies.

---

[70] faggots—bundles of sticks

But the fourth Myne which wee blew vp likewise thereabouts, towards the euening, did exceeding great hurt, burying the Enemies aliue in the Mynes, wherevpon there rose an Alarum in their Quarter, and almost all night long sixe of our batteries, and three of the Enemies played with their Ordnance incessantly.

The 23. and 24. wee were busie about blowing vp of our Mynes round about the City, and to surprise our Enemies: wee made likewise Counter-workes against his Workes, or new ap- [24] proaches, in such manner, that wee saw the same day about all our Quarter, great store of our Enemies slaine and swallowed vp by our Mynes: and it being very hot in those places, in regard of our Musquet shot, the Enemies durst not come to fetch them away; so that they became food for the Crowes and Wormes, and all this was effected with small losse of ours.

The 25. 26. and 27. the Enemies blew their Mynes vp, first in the North-west, and afterwards two Mynes in the South-east of the City, but did no hurt to vs nor our Workes: it is true that an Englishman and a Swisser were swallowed vp by the Sands vnto their knees, but they were presently drawne out by their feete; and against all expectation brought off aliue.

The 28. the Enemy was drawing a Trench East, South-east, toward the way of *Wowe*: but ours blew vp a Myne about foure a Clocke in the afternoone, through the Command of the two Collonels *Fama* and *Lockeren*, lying Northwest from the Citty, close to the forsaken halfe-moone, which tooke very good effect.

There was order giuen before by the said Collonels, that certaine Pioners[71] should bee in readinesse with their Mattocks[72] and Spades, and certaine Souldiers with halfe-Pikes,[73] to sally forth [25] when the Myne should bee blowne vp, to leuell the ground euen and plaine againe, so that our Souldiers might passe ouer it and set vpon the Enemies.

All this was very happily by the ayd of God performed, without any damage of ours, pulling besides a great deale of the Enemies Worke to the ground, and being afterwards seconded by 220. men, vnder the Command of Captaine *William Van Fama*, Brother of the Collonel, they filled vp the Enemies rowling Trenches, which are very narrow but deepe, and killed there a hundred and fifty of the Enemies, with Rapiers, Courtleaxes, Mattocks, Hatchets, Spades, and such like

---

[71] pioners (pioneers) — soldiers who dig entrenchments, build roads, and perform other construction work

[72] mattocks — agricultural tools used for loosening hard ground, grubbing up trees, etc.

[73] halfe-pikes (half-pikes) — short pikes, with shafts about half the length of full-sized pikes

tooles, taking also seuenteene Prisoners which were brought afterwards into the City, as likewise the booties gotten, of mony, Ierkins,[74] Cassocks,[75] [et]c.

I must not forget here to relate how that Youncker *William of Nassau*, base or naturall Sonne[76] to the Prince of *Orange*, was not onely a Spectator, but likewise an Actor in this Fray, running with a Sword in his hand amongst the thickest of them, and hauing afterwards gotten one of the Enemies halfe Pikes, did braue Seruice with it, and was none of the first that came off,[77] hee was onely hurt in the little finger.

[26] The same night the English did likewise an admirable Exploit in their Quarter, Captaine *Clerke* being the inuenter of it. They digged a concauity[78] vnder the Trenches of the Enemies, which lay vpon a high ground: The Spanish Souldiers perceiuing the noyse and rumbling vnder ground, ranne partly away (as being afraid to bee blowne vp) those which tarried, were afterwards when ours had broken through the ground, likewise driuen away, or slaine: This was such an inuention, as was yet neuer heard of before, by digging vnder the Enemies, to take from them their aduantages, and keepe them.

Collonel *Morgan* likewise deceiued the Enemies very cunningly: hee commanded certaine Hattes to be set vpon stickes behind the Baskets in our new halfe-moone, to make the Enemies beleeue our Souldiers were lying there, and so it fell out indeed, for the Enemy supposing the very same, came and cast therein diuers Granades, but few of them tooke fire kindly, although they could not haue done any great hurt amongst the Hats and stickes: in the meane time our Souldiers came stealing and creeping vpon them, and made themselues maisters of the halfe-moone, before which they had shed so much blood in former time, getting now the same againe by a deuice without losse of blood: before 10. of the Clocke, all things were mended and [27] repayred in the same, and the Gabions placed the English shooting from betwixt them vpon the Enemie. At the same time the English got in the South-east 60. paces of ground from the Enemies. And in the North-west Quarter, the Garison got likewise 50. paces from them.

The 29. we assaulted againe the enemies rowling or dry trenches, and slue some of them, so that they trebled their Watches to preuent more mischiefe. We blew vp a Mine in the afternoone, and after set vpon the Enemy, but lost 9. or 10. [and] among them a French Ensigne. We slue a Captaine of the Enemies, and a great number of soldiers, and tooke diuers prisoners.

The 30. day before six a clocke in the morning, there were threescore of the Enemies fledde vnto our Citie, being for the most part *Italians*.

---

[74] ierkins (jerkins)—short, close-fitting, often sleveless coats or jackets, usually of leather

[75] cassocks—cloaks or long coats

[76] naturall (natural)—bastard. Cf. n. 47, above.

[77] came off—probably "retreated"

[78] concauity (concavity)—pit, tunnel

The same day our Burgomaster receiued a Letter from *Breda*, sent by his brother, the Contents were this: That Count *Henry of Nassaw*[79] towards the euening would come with his Horse to *Rossendale* to lodge there, and that the *Prince of Orange* was following him, with sixe and twenty thousand Foote, and eyght thousand Horse, being all fully resolued to adventure their liues and bloods, for the honour of God, the welfare of these Lands in generall, and our rescuing.

[28] The 1. of *October*, wee perceiued that the Enemy had remoued almost all his Cannon, which were planted on the North side: wee thought hee would haue welcomed the *Prince of Orange* therewith, but yet they were not so courteous.

The same day there came diuers of the Enemies Souldiers running vnto vs, saying that all the Baggage[80] and Ordnance was remoued, except onely some fewe Field-Peeces, or Colverings.[81]

The same time, there arriued many Troopes of Horse in the South Quarter of the Enemies, little thinking to come to the remouing of the Siege. In the meane time they shot fiercely with their Musquets, and gaue vs certaine false Alarums; thinking to draw our Forces of both Quarters vpon their Mynes. But wee suspecting that they would depart with a stinke or a smell, would not come to them, but saluted them with our Cannon and Musquet shot. They blew vp afterwards their Mynes which were ready, although they could not annoy vs any way with them.

The 2. day there came an hundred and fiue and twenty of the Enemies to vs, telling vs, that *Spinola* was breaking vp.[82] Wee in the meane time played with our Ordnance vpon them. A- [29] bout noone they fired *Spinolaes* Quarter, and planted themselues in Battle-aray, as if they had beene afraid that wee would take the prize or booty from them: marching partly in the afternoone, and partly in the night following to their South Quarter, which likewise was almost all fired. They stood all night in order of battle, and sent the baggage away towards *Antwerpe:* the Foote followed the same, the Horse keeping in the meane time the Arriere-gard.[83] But our Ordnance spared neyther Gun-powder no[r] Lead, but gaue them their Farewell as well as they had before giuen them their wellcome. Our Souldiers visiting *Spinolaes* Campe in the meane time, found there Armes enough for fiue and twenty hundred men, and diuers Instruments, materials, and waggons, besides their vnburyed dead bodies, and great store of sicke and hurt men, complaining and lamenting against their owne Commanders. We brought them into the Citie for charities sake, and cured them as fitting.

---

[79] Frederick Henry of Nassau (1584–1647), prince of Orange and ruler of the Netherlands from 1625 to 1647.

[80] baggage—portable military equipment

[81] colverings (culverins)—a sort of cannon

[82] breaking vp (up)—breaking camp; therefore, packing up their equipment and leaving, abandoning the siege

[83] arriere-gard—rearguard

The Enemy departing hence with dishonor, had lost since the Siege 11000. men which were slaine, besides those which were runne away hither and thither, there being in this one Citie full two thousand of them.

Wee haue lost in this Siege sixe hundred braue men, besides those which are wounded, [30] whereof there are a great number.

God bee praysed for our Deliuery,[84] and the Prince and the Souldiers commended for their good endeuours.

There haue beene discharged since the first ariuall of the Enemy 200000 Cannon shot, both within and without the Citie.

[31] The Copies of two Letters written | from *Antwerpe*, the first by a good Protestant, | dated the 24. of *September*, and the other by | a Romish Catholike, dated before | *the 13. of September.*

DEarely beloued Brother in the Lord, it is now long agoe, since I receiued any Letters from you: It is true that I vnderstood by a Messenger, that you were well before the siege, hoping now the like. For asmuch as concerneth vs, we are in health, God be praised. Furthermore, we heare here daily of nothing else but heauy[85] newes. First, in regard of the great store of wounded and hurt men, which are daily brought hither, with twenty, thirty, yea, sometime forty Waggons at a time, lamenting and complayning pittifully, they dye also many times desperately[86] vpon the Waggons, cursing the houre of their birth. Secondly because wee heare daily such ill newes of *Bergen vp Zome*, for it is here reported, that the *Spanish* forces are gotten into your Walles, and sweepe the streets cleere with their Ordnance, in such manner that none dare walke the same by day light: The say here likewise, that the Towne is vndermined vnto the Steeple of the Church too, that the enemies deferre onely the blowing vp; vntill such time as they shall be sure, that the Church is full of Hereticks; relating moreouer that no Shippes can any more goe forth, or come into your Hauen, so that the Citie is not able to hold out aboue eight or tenne [32] dayes, adding thereunto, that the best Ordnance, besides the Horse, and all what was of any value, was sent thence already, and that whatsoeuer is left within it, is like to fall into their hands very shortly; and here are many which lay great wagers vpon the surrendring vp of the said City: Therefore I pray you to send me word by word of mouth, or by writing (as you shall thinke it most conuenient) how all stands.

Vale.[87] *Antwerpe, the 24. of Septem[ber]. Anno[88] 1622.*

---

[84] deliuery (delivery)—deliverance
[85] heavy—distressing
[86] desperately—wretchedly
[87] *vale*—farewell
[88] *anno*—year

The second Letter.

COsen, I haue written to you in former times, that *Holland* was in great danger, and I hope that you perceiue now, that I informed you of the truth, and therefore will resolue to come ouer vnto vs, if you please, I shall send you a Pasport to preuent all suspicion of your absolute departure. For it will not be long ere *Holland* will fall into vtter confusion and miserie. I doubt how you can escape in such a case, though you be a Catholique: for our *Iesuites* say, that the greatest part of the *Hollandish* Catholiques are poysoned by the potions of the Heretickes, making this comparison, that an Iron which hath once taken the ayre of the Loadstone,[89] participates[90] presently of the same nature, in such manner, that it cannot be taken away, or driuen out by fire.

Wherefore I am afraid that you will speed no better then the Catholiques haue done, which were in *Prague*, or *Heydelberg*, or those sometimes did, when [33] this City was sackt, where the Souldiers answered them which desired to be spared for their Romish religions sake, that there was no mercy to be found at their hands, but if they were Catholiques, it should be the better for their soules.

Can you looke now for any thing else, than a surprisal, and generall ouerthrow, seeing the Emperour and all Kings are on our side? You haue relyed and trusted vpon a bulrush,[91] therefore I pray you to come speedily away, for our forces intend suddenly to make an end of the siege before *Bergen*. And haue therefore appointed a Clergie for the diuine seruice, and a Gouernour to command in the Citie. Afterwards, Marquesse *Spinola* is set vpon *Tertolen*, and all the Islands of *Sealand*. *Don Lewis de Valasco* shall besiege *Sluys*, *Don Gonsales de Cordua*, shall with his forces, keepe the Campe of the Prince of *Orange*, in awe. Count *Henry Van den Bergh*, with the Baron of *Anholt*, and the *Bauarian* forces shall inuade *Friesland*. Therefore I pray you come presently hither, and deliuer me from my feare; seeing that at euery Canon shot I am doubtfull of your life, suspecting you to be slaine therewith: Doe likewise your best endeauour to draw all other good Catholiques out of that cursed *Sodome*, *Antwerpe* the 13. of *September, Anno 1622*.

[34]   *Tragedies and Commedies of* | BERGEN.

The Bullet must haue a lighting place.

A Souldier being shot through the hand, after hee was dressed, went to the Well vpon the market place to wash himselfe: in the meane time, there comes another

---

[89] load-stone — magnet
[90] participates — partakes
[91] bulrush — a reed; metaphorically, something fragile, with a delusive appearance of strength

dead[92] Bullet, [and] pierced his cheeke, without doing any other hurt: this vnfortunate Souldier, takes the Bullet out of his mouth, and returnes to the Surgeon to be dressed againe. The Surgeon espying him, was very angry; for that hee had so carelesly spoyled his late dressing; but when he perceiued how the case stood, he said vnto him, ryming in Low-dutch, *Misfortune runnes round, some it hits vpon the head, and you in the mouth.*

He is well kept, whom God keepes.

Three Children playing in the streete, there fell a Bullet down vpon a corner stone about the *Bosh-gate*, and rebounding, stroke the three Children downe, so that they all cryed out for feare; but before any came to helpe them, they had got vp of themselues, and played againe as before, without any other amazement: for vse takes away feare.

Whom God hath ioyned, shall no man put asunder.[93]

A Bullet vnderstanding this Prouerbe, strooke in [35] betwixt a Suter and his Loue, and cast *Iohn* vpon *Margaret*. *Fortune, and misfortune stand one next another.*
The more knaue, the better lucke.

Three *Spaniards* playing at Dice vpon the head of a Drumme, a courteous Bullet shot by the Garrison, with a great noyse tooke the Drumme quite away, so that they altogether strucken with amazement, fell to the ground; their fellowes thinking that they had been strooke dead, couered them ouer with Straw; but within a while, they crept all vp againe, not being hurt any manner of wayes.

One mans fortune, is another mans misfortune.

This Bullet hauing not yet left grazing, tooke afterwards, seauen legges of seauen sundry Wallounes[94] quite off; which was a pittifull sight to behold: this iron Bullet was cast at *Luycke*, therefore I say, ill payeth his owne Master.

A good bit spared, is for the most part eaten by the Catte.

A Corporall, with those Souldiers vnder his command, hauing gotten in a night halfe a Barrell of Beere, with great paines, and danger of their liues, and sitting round about it, a drye Bullet tooke the Can out of one of their hands, and flew afterwards into the Barrell, in such manner, that the Hoopes hit them on

---

[92] dead—probably, "whose force was already largely spent"
[93] Alludes to Matthew 19:6, and therefore to the Christian marriage ceremony.
[94] Wallounes (Walloons)—French-speaking Netherlanders

the heads, and one amongst the rest, said, if I had not knowne the like before, I would haue sworne it had beene Witchcraft, and complayning of this mischance said: The mouth thought the throat [36] cut; *Multa cadunt inter calicem supremaque labra.*[95] There fals much to the ground betwixt the cup and the lip.

Scholiers goods pay no Custome,[96] *in the Empyre.*

But it seemeth that the Bullets take no notice thereof; seeing they pursued the learned *N.N.* in his house, yea, in his priuate studie, yet our Bullet respected his learning so much, that it suffered him to rise from his seate to reach for a Booke, before it would take possession of his place; doing according to the Childrens saying; who rises from his seate, loseth his place, he hearing the Bullet with a great noyse to take his roome,[97] said, *There is nothing more vncertaine then life, and nothing more certaine then death.*

Wish and haue.

A fellow standing with his long necke, looking ouer a Rampire, heard the Bullets whizzing, with great feare, and said to his fellow, I wish I might haue a phillip[98] with a glancing Bullet, to shew that I had beene in the warres. A Souldier hard by, ouer-hearing him, very nimbly tooke a Musket bullet, and threw it at him as he went downe from the worke, hitting him in such manner vpon the head, that he sunke downe, and cryed out, I am dead, I am dead; the Souldier running to him to make him rise, takes the Bullet vp; he who thought himselfe shot, desiring to haue the Bullet, asked for it, but the Souldier refused to giue it him, alleadging, great miracles might be done with a Bullet wherewith a man was shot; but at last he agreed thereunto, though vpon this condition; that he should giue him a peece of money, and a Bottle of Wine, which [37] we dranke very merrily; and then suffered him to goe away with his Bullet. *Children are well pleased, when they haue their desire.*

Nothing venture, nothing haue.

An *Englishman* desiring to get a *Spaniards* cloathes, which lay dead without the Pallisadoes, neere to a halfe Moone; imboldened himselfe to leape ouer the Pallisadoes; and hauing tyed two Matches[99] together, he fastened them about the

---

[95] *Multa cadunt inter calicem supremaque labra.* — There's many a slip between cup and lip. Erasmus, *Adagia*, 1.5.1.

[96] custome (custom) — duties, taxes

[97] roome (room) — a place where one is seated

[98] phillip (filip) — a smart blow

[99] matches — the cords set on fire so as to set off early guns

Spaniards necke, and being leapt ouer the ditch againe, he beginnes to draw the dead bodie to him: but the match breaking, hee scratcht his head, and taking a new courage, went to him againe, and cast him into the ditch, and hauing stript him, put on his cloathes, his fellowes in the meane time shooting very fiercely with their Muskets vpon the *Spaniards*; aimed at him likewise not knowing any thing else, but that he was a *Spanyard*, hee thinking to climbe ouer the Pallisa-does, hung fast by the breeches, and crying for helpe, his fellowes tooke him off, so that he came safe backe againe (and is a Felt-maker now in London) saying, *Hauing is sure, getting is chance.*

Two curst dogs bite not one another.

A Marriner drawing downe with a Boat-hooke, the Gabion-baskets of one of the enemies Rampires, a bolde *Spaniard* takes hold on the hooke, to pull it out of his hand; but at last, after great haling and pulling, the *Spanyard* letting it goe, being not so well experienced in that weapon, the Marriner cryed out for helpe, intending to draw the *Spanyard* ouer, but [38] he crying out very fearefully, his fellowes pulled him backe in such manner, that his Gloue rending where it had catcht hold, they fell both to the ground, with great laughter of the Spectators, which saide, *In an equall match, there is no hurt done.*

Take heede what you catch at.

An English Gray-Hound running vpon the Wals of the Citie, it happened that a Bullet was shot thorough the Rampire, which the dogge perceiuing, snapt at, thinking to get a good mouthfull, but hee was by the same throwne downe the Walles, wherewith his chaps[100] being hurt and bloody, hee sung out his doggish Musicke.

There are diuers other Iests happened, but this Paper is not able to hold them all.

FINIS.

---

[100] chaps—cheeks, jaws

Hugh Peters, *Digitvs Dei, or Good Newes from Holland* (1631) || STC (2nd ed.) #19798.3

Since 1621, the war between Spain and the Netherlands had continued as a slow and grinding see-saw; the Spanish achieved an advantage when they captured Breda in 1625, but the Netherlanders more than recouped that loss with the conquest of s' Hertogenbosch in 1629. In 1631, Stadholder Frederik Hendrik began an invasion of Flanders, but was forced to retreat when he discovered that the Spaniards had launched a naval invasion of Zeeland, behind his lines. Meteorological and administrative foul-ups stymied the Spanish invasion, and the year ended with little progress made on either side.

Hugh Peters (1598–1660) was a Puritan preacher who served as regimental chaplain for English soldiers in the Netherlands in the early 1630s, minister in New England in the later 1630s, and regimental chaplain and Independent preacher during the British Civil Wars and the interregnum; he became (in)famous both for his preachings and his writings. He was a notable promoter of Parliament, regicide, and the Commonwealth.

This early work by him, describing the Spanish naval invasion of Zeeland in 1631, is a fascinating glimpse of a fighting Puritan in the making, whose narration reveals the sort of religious psychology that would later forge a revolution in the British Civil Wars. Peters's providentialism is particularly strong, and we can see in great detail how he interpreted worldly military incidents as signs of divine intervention.

[TITLE PAGE]

DIGITVS DEI.[1] | OR | GOOD NEWES FROM HOLLAND. | Sent to
the wor[shipfu].ll | IOHN TREFFRY. | AND | IOHN TREFVSIS. | ES-
QUIRES: | As allso to all that haue shot arrows agaynst Babels | Brats,[2] and
wish well to Sion[3] wheresouer.

NON NOBIS DOMINE[4]

Printed By Abraham Neringh, Printer in Rotterdam, by the ould Head. |
ANNO. 1631.

[1] S[I]RS

SInce my condition[5] [and] lot fell in these parts of the world which for a
long time haue beene Sedes belli:[6] I haue not bin altogether negligent in taking
up such observations as might either draw mee to a more serious consideration
of Gods prouidence, dispensing it selfe into many particulars, some more secret,
[and] some open to euery eye: or such as might by their presentment unto mee
of the worlds vanity [and] turnings, make mee see the glassie brittlenesse [and]
shiftlesnesse of the creature,[7] [and] so perswade to a stronger dependance uppon the creator, a Being that hath happinesse in it selfe. Nor hath it bin the least
of my care to cast an especiall eye upon the seuerall victories, [and] vnparaleld
deliuerances (if wee take up all circumstances) which this state hath bin honored
with. In the compasse of three yeares or there about, I haue seene strange turnings [and] returnings of prouidence, ebbs of State that left vs (at least the wise-
hearted) hopelesse of a flood: and then agayne high waters, that haue left many
thoughte[le]sse yea carelesse, of an ebb: heere haue I seene an enemy slighted at a
great distance, [and] too much feared neerer hand, many mountainous designes
which haue prooued molehills in execution, heere haue wee seene men looking one way [and] the Lord bringing the thing about another, sometimes God
destraining[8] for his glory where men would not giue it him other wayes: In a word

---

[1] DIGITUS DEI—the finger of God. Alludes to Exodus 8:19. Cf. Exodus 31:18,
Deuteronomy 9:10, Luke 11:20.
[2] Babels Brats—literally, "the children of Babel," but variously signifying Baby-
lonians, the giants descended from Nimrod, or evil-doing men of various sorts; here,
Catholics.
[3] Sion (Zion)—the Christian church; here, the Reformed (Calvinist) chruch
[4] NON NOBIS DOMINE—Not unto us, O Lord. Alludes to Psalm 115:1: "Not
unto us, O Lord, not unto us, but unto thy name give glory."
[5] condition—circumstances, social position
[6] *sedes belli*—the seat of war
[7] creature—anything created, whether animate or inanimate
[8] destraining (distraining)—constraining, compelling

heere hath bin imploiments for all kinds of spirits, all kinds of men, heere the sad
heart hath had matter to feed those black vapors that cherish melancholy, [and]
heere the freer spirit might haue a time to lauish it selfe out in warrant[a]ble[9]
ioyes [and] refreshments, heere the magistrate hath had worke enough to aduise,
[and] the people to bring in their assistances, the souldier hath had enough how
to deuise [and] how to execute to his greater advantage, and those that waite vppon the tabernacle[10] haue had no reason to bee idle, where dayes of attonement,
as well as the dayly sacrifice were to bee attended on: sometime wee haue bin slipping with Dauid[11] beside our selves and our comforts, while wee fretted at the
foolish, and saw the prosperity of the wicked,[12] sometimes with the same good-
man wee were as those that dreamed,[13] to see the downe-fall of the vngodly,
[and] what chaff they were before the wind.[14] Truly (S[i]rs) wee haue seene much
of Gods faythfulnesse [and] sufficiency,[15] [and] wee ar to bee blamed if wee have
not also seene our owne inability [and] nothingnesse.

But whiles I haue let my meditations travel from one place to another they
haue lodged longer in these two, viz: first in the consideration of our selues [sec-
ond]ly of the enemy: in the former whereof wee may take up matter of wonder, that the Lord continues[16] vs instruments of his glory, [and] the subiect of
his good- [2] nesse [and] bounty, who may iustly take shame to our selues that
wee ar no more sanctified in our drawing neare vnto him, or doe sanctifie him
soe little: alas (S[i]rs) strangers that looke uppon us may thinke that wee are his
onely iewell, since wee are kept so safely: but the truth is our beauty is but black-
nesse, our deformities are the speech of neighbor nations, [and] by the openesse
of our folly wee make the daughters of the Philistins reioyce.[17] Nor haue wee
lesse worke in the contemplation of the enimy, being the center to which subtilty,
cruelty, dilligence in euell, with many other the like, as so many lines haue their

---

[9] warrantable—justifiable

[10] those that wait upon the tabernacle—those who attend the Christian church;
here with probable reference to strict Reformed congregations. Cf. Numbers 8:24.

[11] "But as for me, my feet were almost gone; my steps had well nigh slipped" (Psalm
73:2).

[12] "For I was envious at the foolish, when I saw the prosperity of the wicked" (Psalm
73:3).

[13] "When the Lord turned again the captivity of Zion, we were like them that
dream" (Psalm 126:1).

[14] "Let them be as chaff before the wind: and let the angel of the Lord chase them"
(Psalm 35:5).

[15] sufficiency—sufficient capacity to perform needed tasks

[16] continues—retains

[17] David didn't want news of the death of Saul and Jonathan noised abroad: "Tell *it*
not in Gath, publish *it* not in the streets of Askelon; lest the daughters of the Philistines
rejoice, lest the daughters of the uncircumcised triumph" (2 Samuel 1:20).

confluxe.[18] What great cost haue they byn at in the not yet subduing a handfull of people nay (which is admirable) that which hath bin the co[m]mon breake-back to other states [and] countryes, hath bin the supplying of their treasures heere, [and] filling of their Magazins,[19] I meane their Army. They haue had heere many plowers plowing uppon their back,[20] [and] yet there remaines noe signe of a fur-row, I wish wee saw noe steps[21] of their sin. I will not heere discusse in what coyne the Lord hath bin paid for his kindnesse, nor what proceede they haue re-turned of their talents[22] concredited[23] to them. I haue inioyed this common ayre with them, and haue had my share in their particular mercies, I cannot bee silent. What a hand wee saw out of heauen by the surprize of Wesel, and the Bosch[24] following that, as if the former mercie had not bin enough for the[m]? Heere I will not treate,[25] I haue formerly advertisd[26] about them: what mercie the Lord hath sent them from the sea, [and] what siluer trophees from the enimy hath bin brought, is not now my purpose to speake: But since the Lord by an especiall hand led me to looke vppon the beginning [and] end of this late deliuerance, I shall aduertise therein according to truth, in which I may not seeme (it may bee) soe particular as some may expect, because I dare not call Opinion Fayth: nor so exact in tearmes, because a stranger to the Language though a freind to Souldiery: but this I shall doe, I wil labor to shew truth in her nakednesse, or at least in her owne apparell; and the order I shall propose will bee this; First I shall present the bare history, [second]ly some obseruations from it, [third]ly I shall add some vses wee may make of it: and first for the history.

Whilst the Illustrious Prince of Orange[27] after a triple victory, viz: Groll,[28] Wesell, and the Bosch, had sate downe the last summer to refresh him-selfe euen laden with honnor; Sanballat and Tobiah,[29] I meane they of Spayne and

---

[18] confluxe (conflux)—meeting place

[19] magazins (magazines)—the contents of a storehouse, expecially a stock of am-munition

[20] "The plowers plowed upon my back: they made long their furrows" (Psalm 129:3).

[21] steps—footsteps; therefore, traces or effects

[22] talents—riches, natural abilities. Alludes to the Parable of the Talents; see Mat-thew 25:14–30.

[23] concredited—entrusted

[24] Wesel and s'Hertogenbosch were taken by the Nertherlanders in 1629.

[25] treate (treat)—write about (these matters)

[26] advertisd (advertised)—informed (his correspondent)

[27] Frederick Henry of Nassau (1584–1647), prince of Orange and leader of the Netherlands from 1625 to 1647.

[28] The Netherlanders took Groll in 1627.

[29] Sanballat the Samaritan and Tobiah the Ammonite plotted an attack against the Jews of Jerusalem: Nehemiah 4:1–8.

Flaunders rose early, [and] went to bed late, eating the bread of carefulnesse,[30] in co[m]plotting[31] the raising their honnor out of the dust,[32] where Hee had buried it, as an instrument in Gods hand the yeares before: and surely if strength had answered their reuengefull spirits, the mischeife had had wings, before wee should haue knowne it was hatchd; For heerein they far outstrip their enimies, that their waters run deepely and silently. Now that you may vnderstand what [3] they had in their eye, that should exhaust so much of their treasure this yeare, and perswade with[33] their cleargie like the neighboring channels soe freely to emptie themselues into the common sea; I shall acquaint you with Marques Spinolaes[34] last will and testament left in the hands of the Infanta[35] at his departur out of these wars. Two things hee aduised out of his lo[n]g experience [and] best observations, that might infest[36] the States, whereof the first was, that the current of their commerce with forreine parts might be stoppd, or at least lessened, [and] therfore would that from Dunkerk, Osten, [and] other parts ships should bee set forth for the intercepting them in the narrow seas, which counsaile the world obserues hath bin taken, [and] that with noe ordinary successe: that to this day Dunkerk a meane Dunghill hauen,[37] dare write her selfe a M[ist]r[es]s. The [secon]d was this, that they should not spend themselues thus yeare after yeare, in the beseiging, beleaguring, [and] taking in of any one towne, which did spend them much treasure, [and] could not much disaduantage the enimy: but that they should (though with double cost) attempt the diuiding of the Provinces, especially Holland [and] Zeeland, which hee demonstrated to bee feasable. And for the better understanding the way, may it please you to take notice that about two or three houres sailing from Dort, there lies a village calld the Plate, with a conuenient hauen able to receiue many smal vessels: this village with the whole Iland uppon which it stands is alltogether vnfortified, [and] soe are all places about it: this hauen lookes right against Princeland a place of the same strength with the Plate, betwixt these two passe all our shipps to Zeland, Bergen, Ter Goose, Tertoll, Zeerikzea: etc.

---

[30] "And say unto the people of the land, Thus saith the Lord GOD of the inhabitants of Jerusalem, and of the land of Israel; They shall eat their bread with carefulness, and drink their water with astonishment, that her land may be desolate from all that is therein, because of the violence of all them that dwell therein" (Ezekiel 12:19).

[31] complotting—combining in a plot

[32] "Let the enemy persecute my soul, and take it; yea, let him tread down my life upon the earth, and lay mine honour in the dust. Selah" (Psalm 7:5).

[33] perswade (persuade) with—expostulate with, prevail upon, convince

[34] Ambrosio Spinola (1569–1630), marquis de los Balbases, commander of the Spanish armies in the Netherlands in the 1620s.

[35] Isabella Clara Eugenia (1566–1633), infanta of Spain, archduchess of Austria, and ruler, co-ruler, and governor of the Spanish Netherlands from 1598 to 1633.

[36] infest—annoy, molest, harass

[37] hauen (haven)—harbor, anchorage, port

This yeare about the time of this attempt their army entred Princeland, nothing remained but that they might make themselves M[aste]r of the Plate, [and] soo at once cut of the passage to Zeland, [and] the parts aboue said, [and] soone put Dort [and] Roterdam the Hart of the land in feare, from whence likewise they might haue an easie way to Dunkerk, [and] they recourse to them agayne. This with the consequences being vnderstood. I shall labor to show yow what faythfull ouerseers the Marquese had to his wil, and how tender they are on the other side to follow the mind of the dead. After the Prince of Orange had retreated out of fflaunders, [and] (whether through the foreflowing[38] of time, or too many loope holes made in their counsails or unfaithfulnesse in men betrusted, or correspondence by any false heart with the enimy) he had lost his designe, [and] inquartered himselfe at Drunen, neare Huisden, little other tidings came to vs, but the constant and extraordinary prouisions of the enimy by land [and] water, especially concerning certaine sloopes, [and] flat bottomed boates, [and] an engeneering Preist, who should haue spent much oyle [and] candle in the advancing of a strange designe. The tidings whereof comming thicker, [and] the child being neere the birth the towne of Bergen petition the Princes [4] ayde, who with that part of his army that lay at Drunen, being about 12 or 14000. foot beside horse, set forward for Bergen the 25. of August, and within 3. or 4. dayes was inquartered on the North-side of the towne. Sargeant Maior Cary being sent before with diuers companies for a safegard to those parts by which these shalloopes[39] might passe, as also 16. or 17. men of war, that vsually waite vppon the In-land waters.

Vppon the 11. of Septem[ber]: being thursday at 4. or 5e of the clock at night wee heard shooting from Falconesse, and the Doel, and there-abou[t]s, and saw shipping, but did generally conceiue that the enemy had made an attempt to come forth and was beaten back by our men, when as it appeared otherwise the next day, for the next morning being friday wee discerned vppon the wals of Bergen a fleete of 80. sayle or more comming towards the towne, and farther off some greater shipps in an other fleete: It is strange to see [and] heare how hardly[40] men were drawne to beleeue that the enemy was so neare, nor was there much credit giuen to it till they were before the very towne of Bergen: where my-selfe being a spectator amongst the rest, could tell[41] above 80. sayle, who as it seemes came the day before from Antwerpe, [and] soe past by our shipping (as wee saw over night) [and] onely changd[42] a few shot without farther Danger. Sargeant Maior Cary carefully attending vppon the chardge[43] committed to

---

[38] foreflowing—apparently, "passage"
[39] shalloopes (shallops)—boats used in shallow waters
[40] hardly—difficultly
[41] tell—count
[42] changd (changed)—exchanged
[43] chardge (charge)—duty

him, they bent their course toward Tertoll land, [and] about 8. or 9. in morning 22. saile of their Reregard comming on ground, the rest stayed for them betwixt Rommers-wall [and] Tertoll, till the returning of the next tide, which was at 3. in the afternoone: and thus they lay this whole day in the sight not onely, of Berghen, but of the Princes whole army: mee thought this time was alotted us from heaven, as if a voice had cried and bid vs yet try what prayer will doe: and if I should bee playner with you, [and] open you a window into my owne heart, mee thought this stopp[44] was the time wherein Iustice [and] Mercy compeered[45] before the great God of heaven [and] earth (as indeed it was a time for our saddest thoughts) Take Vengeance cries Iustice Oh spare sayes Mercy: Kill cries the one, Saue the other: There are no sins like theirs, cries Iustice: No God like theirs sayes Mercy: Giue successe to this designe cries the One, Lord they are Thy enemies sayes the Other: Holland is proud [and] secure sayes Iustice, But they may amend by this diliuerance: They haue not improoued[46] former kindnesses, But they may bee tried[47] by one more: Reuenge thy Sabbaths [and] let them haue noe rest that neglect this day of rest, heere Mercye paused, at length charging their teachers with this [and] excusing the poore people that knew noe better. You shall see what followed, and which preuayled.

The Prince perceiuing that it was now no time to aske, what shall we doe, but to bee doing, vnder command of Generall Morgan sent 3. Regements to Tertoll to guard those parts from the incursion, [and] landing of the enemy, who went to their worke with no ordinary resolution, [and] came close by [5] those partes where the enemy lay, [and] onely gave them notice by some shot that they there attended them, with which troopes the Prince went in person: In the meane time Count Ernest[48] advised for the cutting off the Reregard, that lay on ground, [and] to that purpose commanded such warlike shipping as lay at Bergen to be made ready, [and] 12 musketteres out of every companie of the army, to bee imployed in the designe, which came to 1200 or there abouts, the commander in cheife of our nation, was the noble [and] valiant Earle of Oxford[49] Lieutenant Collonel to my Lord Generall Vere,[50] to who[m]e were added Sergeant Maior

---

[44] stopp (stop)—halt, pause, lull

[45] compeered—rivaled; probably here "appeared together in rivalry." Alludes to Psalm 85:10: "Mercy and truth are met together; righteousness and peace have kissed each other."

[46] improoued (improved)—taken advantage of

[47] tried—tested and proved to be good or trustworthy

[48] Ernst Casimir (1573–1632), count of Nassau-Diez, Netherlandish nobleman and soldier.

[49] Robert de Vere (1575–1632), 19th earl of Oxford, English nobleman.

[50] Sir Horatio (or Horace) Vere (1565–1635), later Baron Vere of Tilbury, English general, generally in Dutch service.

Hollis, Captaine Dudly, Captaine Skippon,[51] S[i]r Thomas Colpeper, Captaine Iackson, with some other officers: and this I must say, my hart wittnesseth I flatter not I never saw men hugg an enterprise so, the common souldier even beseeching their captaines with teares that they might bee preferred to it, nor were they without the company of diuers Noble volunteers amongst whom that Noble Gentle-man my Lord Crauen,[52] (who hath much honored his nation abroad) must not be forgotten, who with the first presented him-selfe with his musket, ready to share in the common condition, whether good or bad. But as great bodyes mooue slowely, so these, for they set not forth till the enemie floated, who with the comming of the tide were soone at worke, [and] as before hauing a small boate with them, sounding the way ouer the many sands they were to passe, made toward Zerickzea hauing gotten their whole fleete together; about 4. of the clock ours followd them, [and] had the Princes owne ship to leade them the way, about 4, came some of our fleet that lay by Falconesse, [and] followed them [and] made in all about 25. saile, they passed betweene Tertol [and] Tergoose, on the one side whereof a godly minister before General Morgan came had wi[t]h much [and] earnest persuasions drawne his neighbors into a reasonable order for their owne defence, on the other side not only 20. companies of the Princes awaited them, but also the Boores or country people were in great readinesse being generally men of very good abilities in point of souldierie.

But it seemes that was not the white[53] they shot at, wherefore they past on beyond Zereikzea, before our ships could come neere shot of them: about 9 of the clock at night the friday aforesaid, the Princes ship shot by a village called Ould Kerke, [and] in short time brought her peeces[54] to beare vppo[n] them, in so much as wee haue it by credible testtimony, that with one broade side shee killd 23. men, other ships of ours came vp with them likewise, [and] gaue [and] received such rough intertainement as passeth among men at such times: a ship of Zeland had by one shot from the enimy 4 men slayne, [and] 4. hurt: our musketeres came not up to doe much seruice, for these reasons, 1 in such a hurry of businesse, [and] vppon the water command could not so easily passe, [and] besides that command they had, was to seconde[55] the ships that were prouided to fight at length; [and] moreouer the worke continued not so long as to make vse of all our men: The Princes ship receiued shot: 2. in the sayles [and] 1, in the midship, [and] quitted herselfe well, some 5. or 6. more did the like: but it playnely appeared the enemy seemed not much to regarde fighting, rather longing [and] striuing to bee M[aste]r of his designe, [and] therfore continually steered on their

---

51 Philip Skippon (ca. 1600–1660), later Parliamentary general during the British Civil Wars, and made Lord Skippon during the Protectorate.

52 Probably William Craven (1608–1697), Baron Craven, later 1st earl of Craven.

53 white — target

54 peeces (pieces) — cannon

55 seconde (second) — support

course, till towards morning the whole night being exceeding fayre [6] for one houres space [and] noe more the Lord cast a mist uppon them, by which (they themselues confessing it) they were much distracted,[56] lost their way, diuers of them came on ground, and the most of them at Muschle-creeke not far from Steenbergen, the vangard being at this time, within one houres time, or two at the most, of the place they aimed at: diuers of them blame Fortune and their pilots, but in truth (as some of them accknowledgd to myselfe) the blow was from heauen. and to proceede, this confusion taught vs who was their Generall, viz: Count Iohn of Nassau,[57] who would rather venture the Infantaes displeasure, then pay soe deare for his entertainment heere againe, as hee had lately done at Wesell: Insomuch that hee with Prince Brabenson and some other cheifes left the fleete, and heere I must remember a complement was put vppon Count Iohn at his departure from Antwerp, and embarquing, after many benedictions from the Infanta, and (questionlesse) much water sprinckled uppon him and his company, to praeserue him from the displesure of S[i]r Neptune etc. The Liuetenant Generall of the horse had a cringe[58] with him to this purpose, S[i]r (quoth hee) the designe you are ingaged in, is weightie, the cost hath bin great for the aduancing of it, and it will require a whole man, but I must tell you I conceiue not Count Iohn to bee That Man, and so they parted. And since wee haue spoken of Muschle-creeke, I must tell you of a passage that concernes the said Generall of theirs, where by I may put you in mind how fooles oracles may prooue wise-mens truths: not long before this attempt Count Iohn sending a Trumpet to our army, wished him if the Prince should aske what became of their shallopes, to answer that they meant shortly to come eate some Muscles: hee came to þe place indead, but I suppose hee had not time to fill his belly, or if hee tasted them I thinke hee hath not yet disgested them, that he cannot much reioyce at his banquet. Some other sloopes followed their Generall to Prince-land, and fired them at landing, so that betwene Willemstadt and Musclecreeke I saw diuers of the hulls of them lying by the shore; the rest quitted their boates with what speede they could, feare giuing them wings, and confusion and distraction taking away their wits: the reason they giue for making this great haste to the land is, because on these in-land waters they could expect noe quarter, and euery worme will reade us a lecture of the sweetenesse of life, 1400. seing a horse-man vppon a dike gaue themselues to him: a great conquest for one man! Divers in landing were drowned, many stript themselves to swim and so came naked to our army, most of their ships by the morning light were found in new Fosse-mere where they lay that day with our ships by them. Wee shall not neede to write what they returned

---

[56] distracted — confused, bewildered

[57] Count John VIII of Nassau-Siegen (1583–1638). Originally an officer in the Netherlandish army, he converted to Catholicism in 1613, and served as a general in the Spanish army in the 1620s and 1630s.

[58] cringe — a deferential, servile, or fawning obeisance

the Preists for their benedictions, but certainely many Tuns of diuels, and especially to the Preist who had the cheife hand in the plot, and did boaste great
matter [7] of carriing shipps under water and promising to bring their souldiers
into Berghen, which hee did truly performe: You must conceiue what a suddayne
change heere was, when our men came to take possession of their vessels, [and]
they scrambled away in the mud, which mynds me of a merry answere of the
Prince to one that told him the Preist would bring their men vnder the water, hee
sayd he then must send to Zeland for some fishermen to prick them vp[59] vpon
their Eel-speares. By 8. in the morning newes came to the Prince of their forsak-
ing their boates, whereupon he commanded diuers companies to march towards
Steen-berghen to enconter them supposing they might make head,[60] but before
our men were vpon their march, tidings came that most of them had giuen them
selues prisoners; [and] by 11. of the clock the first sight of them wee saw was 4.
or 5. Captaynes with 2. Capuchins[61] presented to the Prince, with whome hee
enter[t]ayned neere an houres talke, who all blamed Count Iohn for his starting[62] at a pinch:[63] The Capucians were presently begd by the Duke of vensdome,
into whose tuition[64] and fauor they were soone returned: the next sight that was
presented to vs was a fat trumpetter of Count Iohns in a carr[65] there followed
him the Captaine of the Princes ship on horsebacke behinde a Gentleman, with
the colours of the Admirall of their fleete, being a Burgoignian crosse which hee
presented to the Prince; after him followed in two diuisions the prisoners, garded
by a troope of the Duke of Bullen, which were betweene 2. and 3000. before the
last diuision was a wagon laden with their Officers; and this was obseruable, that
among all these, and 900. more wich lay at Steen-bergen there was no English at
all, but they were all Dutch, and Wallons; these were sent to such places, as the
towne of Berghen had to entertaine them in, especially an old peice of a Church
receiued most. Thus the saterday was cheerefully spent in veiwing these liuely
tokens of Gods fauor, on the day following command was giuen that publike
thanksgiuing should bee rendred both in the towne and army in which (I blesse
God) I had a share: and on Munday-night (with 3. volleyes af[t]er the manner
heere) it was made knowne very cleerely to Antwerpe, and the enemies army
(some of our cannon hauing very wide mouthes) vppon the sabbath was brought
in Dulken the once Gouernour of Grol, [and] a Iesuite with him [and] so dayly
diuers prisoners who had come on shore on diuers parts. Nor did wee at this time
thinke our labor ill bestowed to ride from place to place to looke on either their

---

[59] prick them up—impale, fasten, and pull them up
[60] head—headway
[61] Capuchins—Capuchin friars
[62] starting—swerving, flinching, recoiling
[63] pinch—a critical juncture
[64] tuition—custody
[65] carr (car)—cart, wagon

Punts [and] sloopes, or our men bringing in the spoyle,[66] som telling their freinds how hardly they had escaped, and shewing their chayne[67] [and] gnawne[68] bullets, som with rapiers, som scarfes, one with Count Iohns leading staffe,[69] another with a buffcoate,[70] [and] most laden with Antwerpes beere: Amongst diuers other things there came to my hande a knife of the keurlings[71] who are som of their company about Bridges,[72] that ne[it]her giue nor take [*8*] quarter, vpon which was engraven in Dutch Rithme.

Make hast from Bridges Prince of Aurania:[73]
Honnor your M[aste]r the king of Hispania:
Let our flaunders alone, come not heere to pillage:
For wee haue for you, nor citty, nor village.

vnder which was pictured the towne of Bridges, [and] the Prince running from it on horse-back, — Surely as the deliuerance was great, so the purchace[74] especially of amunition was not a little, as wee shall shew by the particulars following: And now mee thinkes by this time I saw the mother of Sisera looking out of a window, [and] crying through the lattesse, why stay his chariot-wheeles so long? Iudg[es]: 5. 28. etc. surely shee is much deceiued if she thinke they are deuiding the spoyle:[75] Thus the Lord ouerthrew Pharow [and] his host in the red sea,[76] for his mercy indureth for ever.[77] The weeke following the Prince commanded most of the prisoners to bee set vppon ships without sayle or rudder, by the head[78] at Berghen, till order should bee taken for ransome: the poore women at Antwerpe who had their husbands in the Service, with their heauy complaynts at Bergen gates made vs know how welcome those tidings were at Antwerpe: the last weeke the Drossart of Breda treated for their deliuery, and so they are departing home,

---

[66] spoyle (spoil) — plunder
[67] chayne — this could be "chain," but I think is "chawn" — fissured, reft assunder
[68] gnawne (gnawn) — corroded
[69] leading staffe (staff) — a staff borne by a commanding officer; a truncheon
[70] buffcoate (buffcoat) — a coat of buff leather
[71] keurlings (carlines) — (old) women; often implying contempt or disparagement
[72] Bridges — the town of Bruges
[73] Aurania — Orange
[74] purchase — spoil, plunder
[75] After the general Sisera was killed, "The mother of Sisera looked out at a window, and cried through the lattice, Why is his chariot *so* long in coming? why tarry the wheels of his chariots? Her wise ladies answered her, yea, she returned answer to herself, Have they not sped? have they *not* divided the prey, to every man a damsel *or* two; to Sisera a prey of divers colours": Judges 5:28-30.
[76] Exodus 14:27–28.
[77] Refrain of Psalm 136.
[78] head — probably, the inner part of the harbor

you may iudge with what ioy they shall bee intertained; and presently vppon the miscarriage of the enterprise their army marcheth both from Prince-land, and Rosendale, whereof 32. companies of foote are gone for Breda, and 10. of horse.

Vpon Thurs-day wee had generall thanksgiuing in our churches [and] expressing our ioy by fires, guns etc.

The sum of the officers taken by vs.

Colonels, Lieuten[ant]: Col[onels]: Sargeant Maiors, [and] men of great note.	19.
Captaines.	26.
Lieutenants.	10.
Ensignes. [79]	28.
Sargeants.	23.
Officers about the Canon.	6.
Som other officers, [and] Church men.	11.
Land souldiers.	3151.

Sea men.

Captaines.	12.
Lieutenants.	15.
Quarter Masters.	7.
Shippers.	1.
Sailors.	820.
Coming out of Antwerpe in all they were mustered aboue.	6000.

The number of the shipping come to our hands.

Shalloopes whose provision generally was 6. brasse Peeces, 8. Murtherers,[80] 4. Dunderbusses,[81] besides Lether Peeces.   36.

[9] Punts with one halfe Canon and two three quarter Canon.   10.

Pleyts[82] whose lading[83] was Lope-staues,[84] Nayls, Ice-spurs. 10 Horses, Hardles,[85] Beef-bridges etc.   [x]   [x]   9.

---

[79] ensignes (ensigns) — standard-bearers

[80] murtherers (murderers) — small cannon

[81] dunderbusses (blunderbusses) — short guns with large bores, firing many balls or slugs

[82] pleyts — river boats

[83] lading — cargo, freight

[84] lope-staues (loop-staves) — probably the curved strips of wood (staves) used to make barrels; or perhaps the loops used to tie the staves together in barrel-shape

[85] hardles (hurdles) — a frame placed on marshy ground or a ditch, to provide a firm passage

Other Amunition ships whose lading was Powder, Beere, Deales[86]   7.

That which I offer by way of observation cannot bee much: | Time wyll not af-
ford it: Yet these things | briefly take notice of.

1   That Reuenge is no Sluggard, Malice is vnwearyed: For wee vnderstand this
      worke [and] practise haue bin vnder hand these 6 yeares.
2.   Reuolters from Religion prooue her sharpest enemyes: witnes (besides
      Iulian)[87] Count Iohn, who will bee the Ring-leader in any designe that may
      make nothing of what hee formerly profest.
3   To expect better then Stratagems tending to ruine from a popish enemy,
      doth argue either ignorance of their courses, or groundles Confidence.
4   Security (hauing lost the vse of reason) will deny the Conclusion, rather then
      beleeue the danger. As wee saw when our people could hardly beleeue the
      enemy to be the enemy, though he lay before the Ports.
5.   High men are Vanity, [and] Low men are a Lye: which was playne when wee
      saw neither the great Commander, nor the comon souldier could helpe vs,
      the enemy out-brauing[88] vs the whole day.
6.   The Creature cannot bee sufficient for our succor, for he is not allwayes a
      present helpe in trouble:[89] wee could neither command wind nor tide, where
      as either of them might haue done vs much good.
7.   The Lord often layes the reine on the neck of his enemyes, they goe long vn-
      controld: these went all day in the face of our Army vntouched.
8.   Sudden Prosperity is no signe of lasting Happynesse: These Spiders had no
      sooner framed their web, but it was swept downe.
9.   The Lord brings his greatest workes about by Accident, the tide not serv[i]ng,
      which wee longd for, our ships could not come vp with them by day, [and]
      so escapt a scowring. Their Admirall putting out a light when he was on
      ground, brought the rest into the same net: they seeking a neerer way by the
      Fosse-mere, lost their way, with many such like.
10.   A poore creature is many times made the Lords great host, as Pharaohs Lice
      agaynst him,[90] and a hand full of mist throwne amongst these.
11.   Feare vnfits a man to know what hee should doe, [and] disinables him to doe
      what hee knowes: otherwise they might haue made head vpon the water or
      the shore, [and] gotten good quarter,[91] for ought wee perceiue.

---

[86] deales (deals)—planks; or possibly bottles of Deal wine
[87] Julian the Apostate, emperor of Rome (331–363, reigned from 361 to 363).
[88] outbraving—facing with a show of defiance
[89] "God is our refuge and strength, a very present help in trouble" (Psalm 46:1).
[90] The plague of lice is mentioned in Exodus 8:16–19.
[91] gotten good quarter—gotten into good order

12. Cruell men haue often their punishments giuen them out in proportion they devising new boates, they shall perish in their boates, they will bring hal- [*10*] tars for others which may serue themselues, the gallowes set up for Mordecay serues Haman. [92]

13. The Lord answers his servants some times in the very thing they aske, in our fast before the Prince went into the field wee made vse of that text [and] that petition of Dauids Psal[m]: 83.15. So persecute them with thy tempest [and] make them afrayd with thy storme: [and] behold wee haue our answere.

14. Outward strength [and] humane policyes are no sufficient Bulwarks agaynst Battryes [93] from heauen: it was easily seene here was no want of skill in this designe the preparations were not ordinary, but what are Tifney-walls [94] to a Canon-shot? or their plots to Gods mist?

15. Feare is an ill guide though a quick post, [95] many hundreds of them leauing their owne strength [and] betaking them selues to the mercy of an enemy.

16. God like an Indulgent Father striues to reforme by shewing a rod: Dauid had the same measure when hee Confesseth, Lord thou hast shewn me af-fliction. we saw what might haue bin our portion; wee felt not what the en-emy intended, [and] wee deserued. [96]

17. Diuine Providence (which fooles call Fortune) will serve it selfe vpon Let us sleepe [and] the enemy wake, let them attempt, [and] let vs study to prevent, let them bee strong [and] many, wee weake [and] few, let them goe on, [and] wee looke on, let them deuide the spoyle to euery one a damosell, [97] an office before they come where they are; yet Prouidence will serue it selfe vpon all this.

18. It is remarkable that the Lord doth sadly make the servants of Idolls to know that ther Maisters or Gods are nothing. In this attempt they will set forth vpon Saint Crosses day (it being by their Almanack the eleuation of the holy Crosse) [98] their Generall of all their Army being called by that name, and Count Iohn the Leader of the Nauall troopes being free of that Company, Such Crosses let the enemyes of God euer carry with them. hee had one he

---

[92] "And Harbonah, one of the chamberlains, said before the king, Behold also, the gallows fifty cubits high, which Haman had made for Mordecai, who had spoken good for the king, standeth in the house of Haman. Then the king said, Hang him thereon. So they hanged Haman on the gallows that he had prepared for Mordecai": Esther 7:9–10.

[93] battryes (batteries)—bombardments

[94] tifney (tiffany)—a thin silk; something flimsy

[95] post—rider, carrier of news

[96] This may allude to Psalm 25, where David sings of affliction, and deliverance from his enemies, beyond his deserts.

[97] Alludes to Judges 5:30.

[98] The Elevation of the Holy Cross is celebrated annually on 14 September.

wore on his brest before, he hath now another for his back: I wish it may doe him good at his hart.

19. The Lord doth not bind himselfe to any particular meanes that wee many times vse [and] to often trust vnto, either for our deliuerance, or the confusion of our enemies: wee iudged of one meane, he vsed another in this great work, as was playne to be seene.

20. It is admirable to see what a man or people may receiue in poynt of Honor [and] doe likewise in matter of Action, if the Lord goe out with them; as this is notable, this Prince of Orange neuer yet (since hee had the command) went out, but hee returned triumphing, the Lord euer make him triumphing [and] victorious in his cause.

[*11*]　　　　　The Vses wee may make in a word are these

1. Let vs euer heereafter learne to know the creature by their owne names, [and] not to call a horse or a man a God, or a water or fort a Sauiour: wee may take vp the words of the repenting church Hos[ea] 14.[99] The more fatherles the more mercy,[100] or the lesse wee Idolize vpon our selves the greater succor we may looke for from heauen.

2. Since the Lord can rule [and] guide, dispatch [and] ouercome workes of this nature so well; since hee hath thus graciously appeared in 31. as formerly in 88.[101] let both England [and] Holland bee willing to giue him the helme into his owne hands for euer. I wish his quarrell agaynst vs all bee not that wee haue vsed him too much like a Comon-man. wee see (though wee had never receiued his word) that his place is at the sterne, let not Religion lackquey[102] to Policy: Kisse the sonne least hee bee angry. Psal[m] 2.[103]

3. Giue him (who hath done all, [and] deserueth all) all the glory: Ioseph may haue any thing in Potiphars house but his wife,[104] [and] in Pharaohs but his throne:[105] as tender is the Lord of his honor [and] glory as they of either.

---

[99] "Neither will we say any more to the work of our hands, *Ye are* our gods: for in thee the fatherless findeth mercy": Hosea 14:3.

[100] mercy—emended from "merry"

[101] The Spanish Armada was defeated in 1588.

[102] lackquey (lackey)—serve, dance attendance upon

[103] "Kiss the son, lest he be angry, and ye perish *from* the way, when his wrath is kindled but a little. Blessed *are* all they that put their trust in him": Psalm 2:12.

[104] "*There is* none greater in this house than I; neither hath he kept back any thing from me but thee, because thou *art* his wife": Genesis 39:9.

[105] "And Pharaoh said unto Joseph, Forasmuch as God hath shewed thee all this, *there is* none so discreet and wise as thou *art:* Thou shalt be over my house, and according unto thy word shall all my people be ruled: only in the throne will I be greater than thou": Genesis 41:39–40.

Shall wee euen greiue his good spirit more, shall wee euer slight his sabbaths? can it bee?

4. See that prosperity stay not our foolish harts: the skill will bee how to im-
prooue the mercy. Sisera is then vndone when hee is careles in Iaels tent,[106]
who was a Neutrall: [and] such is outward prosperity, good [and] bad may
share in it, the wisdome is how to vse it; hee need walke warily that goes
on a glassy sea with iron shooes. But the wind is fayre, the sea-men call, the
Dutch printer is weary hee craues pardon for his faults, I must end before I
am halfe way the mayne.[107] This at least may saue the writing many letters;
You may trust the Intelligence[108] for the Truth: [and] to the God of Truth I
commend You.

In whome I am your lo[ving]. kinsman, | H. P.

---

[106] Jael slew the sleeping general Sisera while he slept in her tent: Judges 4:17–22.
[107] halfe (half) way the mayne (main) — half-way through the chief matter at hand
[108] the intelligence — this information, this news

Philip Vincent, *A True Relation of the Late Battel fought in New England* (1637) || STC (2nd ed.) #24758

Beginning in 1634, a series of violent incidents raised tensions between the ever-increasing number of English colonists in Connecticut, Rhode Island, and Massachusetts, and the Pequod nation, concentrated in western Rhode Island and eastern and central Connecticut. Misunderstandings played a role in this sequence, but it stemmed very largely from the desire of the English colonists to eliminate a powerful people from a strategic area of New England. In 1637, expeditionary forces of English colonists of Connecticut and Massachusetts, in alliance with the Mohegans and Narragansetts, fought and nearly exterminated the Pequods. About 1,500 Pequods were killed, and many of the remainder became slaves or servants among the English colonies and the Indian nations of New England and New York.

Philip Vincent (1600?–?) may have been a minister in England during the 1620s. He wrote two known works, *The lamentations of Germany* (1638), and this account of the Pequod War. He traveled to Germany from 1633 to 1635, and may have traveled to Guyana and New England; his interest in New England, and promotion of colonization in New England, indicates a Puritan affinity. Little more is known of him.

This pamphlet describes one segment of that annhilating war, from the English raid in the summer of 1636 that provoked the Pequod siege of Fort Saybrook, Connecticut, to the May 1637 destruction of the main Pequod fort in the Mystic river valley of Connecticut, and the accompanying slaughter of the inhabitants. It is notable as a transition between the military news pamphlet of England and the Indian war pamphlet of colonial North America, and allows us to see some of the first accounts of colonial wars within their European context. The pamphlet itself varies oddly, starting out with a glowing and positive description of the Indians, human like the Europeans, before veering into a brooding meditation on their all-too-human savagery that justified a merciless war against them. The conclusion dwells lyrically on the joys of New England as a site of settlement, particularly now that the Pequods have been wiped out. This pamphlet purports to be military news, but is essentially a real-estate brochure.

[TITLE PAGE]

A |True Relation of | the Late Battell fought | in *New England,* between | the English, and the | *Salvages:*

VVith the present state of | things there.

LONDON.

Printed by *M. P.* for *Nathanael Butter,* | and *Iohn Bellamie.* 1637.

[*1*]   *Ad Lectorem*

Authoris carmen εὐχαρίστικον de Victoria hac Nov'-Anglica, 1637.

DVcit in Americam varios gens Angla Colonos:
  et bene conveniunt sydera, terra, solum.
Ast ferus hoc prohibet, solis vagabundus in arvis,
  insolitoq[ue]; aliquos, incola, Marte necat.
Quod simul invstas crimen pervenit ad aures
  Angligenum, ira o murmure cuncta fremunt.
Tunc laesi justa arma movent,[1] *hostemq[ue] sequuntur,*
  struxerat, haud vanis, qui munimenta locis.
Invadunt vallum, palis sudibusq[ue] munitum:
  (pax erit: hoc uno solvitur ira modo.)
Vndiq[ue] concidunt omnes, pars una crematur:
  post, caesi, aut capti caetera turba luit.
Vtraq[ue] laetatur Pequetanis Anglia victis,
  et novus aeternum, hic, figimur hospes ait.
Virginia exultat, vicina Novonia gaudet,
  Signaq[ue] securae certa quietis habent.
Plaudite qui colitis Mavortia sacra nepotes,
  et serat incultos tutus arator agros.
Qua novus orbis erat, spiranti numine, (Lector)
  Anglia nascetur, quae novus orbis erit.
                         P. Vincentius.[2]

---

[1] *Tunc laesi justa arma movent* (Then the wronged wage righteous war)—alludes to Ovid, *Ars Amatoria,* 2.397, "*laesa Venus iusta arma movet*" (wronged Venus wages righteous war).

[2] To the Reader: | The author's song of thanksgiving for this victory in New England, 1637. | The English nation sends diverse colonists into America: | The stars, the country, the soil all prove favorable. | But a savage inhabitant, a wanderer in lonely fields,

[2] A true Relation of the late Battell fought in *New England*, between the *English* and *Salvages*, with the present state of things there.

NEw England, a name now every day more famous, is so called, because the English were the first Discoverers, [and] are now the Planters[3] thereof. It is the Easterne Coast of the North part of *America*, upon the Southwest adjoyning to *Virginia*, and part of that Continent, large and capable of[4] innumerable people. It is in the same height with the North of *Spaine*, and South part of *France*, and the temper[5] not much unlike, as pleasant, as temperate and as fertile as either, if managed by industrious hands.

[3] This is the Stage. Let us in a word see the Actors. The yeare 1620, a Company of English part out of the *Low Countries*,[6] and some out of *London* and other parts, were sent for *Virginia*.[7] But being cut short by want of wind, and hardnesse of the Winter, they landed themselves in this Countrey, enduring, with great hope and patience, all the misery that Desart[8] could put upon them, and imployed their wits to make their best use of that then Snow-covered land for their necessities. After two yeares experience of the nature of the soyle, commodities,[9] and natives, they returned such intelligence[10] to their Masters, that others tooke notice of their endevours, and the place. Then some Westerne Merchants collected a stocke,[11] and employed it that way. But they discouraged through losses, and want of present gaine, some Londoners, and others (men of worth) undertooke it, with more resolution, building upon the old foundation.

| Prevents this; and he kills some with unaccustomed strife. | As soon as the crime reaches the burning ears of | Englishmen, their wrath — oh! all things roar with a rumble. | Then the wronged wage righteous war, they harry the foe, | Who has built defenses in well-chosen spots. | They storm the rampart, fortified with poles and stakes: | (There will be peace: by this one method anger will be appeased.) | On every side, all are cut down; one group is consumed by fire: | Afterwards, slain or captured, the rest of the horde atones. | Both Englands are gladdened by the defeat of the Pequods | And the newcomer says, "Here we are established forever." | Virginia exults, neighboring Novonia [Nova Scotia] rejoices, | And they hold secure tokens of certain peace. | Applaud, you future generations who observe the martial rites, | Let the farmer sow in safety the untilled fields. | Where once was the New World, Reader, | England will be born with living spirit: she will *be* the New World. | P[hilip]. Vincent.

   [3] planters—settlers
   [4] capable of—capable of containing
   [5] temper—climate
   [6] Low Countries—Netherlands
   [7] The Plymouth Colony, on the *Mayflower*.
   [8] desart (desert)—wilderness
   [9] commodities—natural resources
   [10] intelligence—information, news
   [11] stocke (stock)—capital, sum of money

Hence a second plantation[12] adjoyned to the other, but supported [sig. B/4] with
better pillars, and greater meanes. All beginnings are ever difficult. The halfe,
saith the Proverbe, is more then the whole. Some errours were committed, and
many miseries were endured. No man is wise enough to shunne all evils that may
happen; but patience and painefulnesse[13] overcame all. The successe proved answerable even to ambitious expectations, notwithstanding the impediments in-
evitable to such undertakings.

There is scarce any part of the world but habitable, though more commodiously[14] by humane culture.[15] This part (though in it's Naturals)[16] nourished many
natives, distinguished into divers petty nations and factions. It were needlesse
curiosity to dispute their originall,[17] or how they came hither. Their outsides
say they are men, their actions say they are reasonable. As the thing is, so it op-
erateth. Their correspondency[18] of disposition with us, argueth all to be of the
same constitution,[19] [and] the sons of *Adam*, and that we had the same Maker,
the same matter, the same [5] mould. Only *Art* and *Grace* have given us that
perfection,[20] which yet they want,[21] but may perhaps be as capable thereof as we.
They are of person straight and tall, of limbes big and strong, seldome seene violent, or extreme in any passion. Naked they go except a skin about their waste,
and sometimes a Mantle about their shoulders. Armed they are with Bowes and
Arrowes, Clubs, Iavelins, [et]c. But as soyle, aire, diet; [and] custome make oft-
times a memorable difference in mens natures, so is it among these Nations,
whose countries there are like so many Shires here, of which every one hath their
Sagamore, or King, who as occasion urgeth, commandeth them in Warre, and
ruleth them in Peace. Those where the *English* pitched,[22] have shewed themselves
very loving and friendly, and done courtesies beyond expectation for these new-
come Inmates.[23] So that much hath beene written of their civilitie and peacefull
conversation,[24] untill this yeare.

But Nature, heavens daughter, and the [sig. B 2/6] immediate character of
that divine power, as by her light she hath taught us wisedome, for our owne

---

[12] plantation—colony. Here, the Massachusetts Bay Colony, founded 1629.
[13] painefulnesse (painfulness)—diligence
[14] commodiously—advantageously, profitably
[15] culture—cultivation
[16] naturals—unimproved, natural condition
[17] originall (original)—origin
[18] correspondency—similarity
[19] constitution—nature, character
[20] perfection—comparative excellence
[21] want—lack
[22] pitched—settled
[23] inmates—strangers; inhabitants
[24] conversation—social interaction

defence, so by her fire she hath made us fierce, injurious, revengefull, and inge-
nious in the device of meanes for the offence[25] of those we take to be our enemies. This is seene in creatures voide of reason, much more in mankind. We have
in us a mixture of all the Elements, and fire is predominant when the humours
are exagitated.[26] All motion causeth heat. All provocation mooveth choller, and
choller inflamed, becometh a phrensie, a fury, especially in barbarous and cruell natures.[27] These things are conspicuous in the Inhabitants of *New England.*
In whose Southermost part are the *Pequets,* or *Pequants,* a stately warlike people,
which have been terrible to their neighbours, and troublesome to the *English.*

In *February* last they killed some *English* at *Sea-brooke,* a Southerly Plantation beyond *Cape Cod,* at the mouth of the River of *Connectacutt.* Since that
the [7] Lievtenant of the Fort there, with tenne men armed, went out to fire the
Meddowes, and to fit them for mowing. Arriving there he started[28] three *Indians,* which he pursued a little way, thinking to cut them off. But presently they
perceived themselves incompassed with hundreds of them, who let flie their arrowes furiously, and came desperately upon the musles of their Muskets, though
the *English* discharged upon them, with all the speed they could. Three *English* men were slaine, others wounded. The eight that remained, made their way
through the *Salvages* with their swords, and so got under the command of the
Canon of the Fort, (otherwise they had been all slaine, or taken prisoners) one
of the wounded falling downe dead at the Forts Gate. The *Indians* thus fleshed[29]
and encouraged, besieged the Fort as neere as they durst approach. The besieged
presently dispatched a messenger to the Governour at the *Bay,* to acquaint him
with these sad tidings, who with all speed lent [sig. B3/8] unto their aide, Captaine *Vnderhill,*[30] with twenty souldiers. Not long after these *Salvages* went to
Water-Towne, now called *Wetherfield,* and there fell upon some that were sawing,
and slew nine more, whereof one was a woman, the other a childe, and tooke two
yong Maids prisoners, killing some of their cattell, and driving some away. Mans
nature insulteth[31] in victory and prosperity, and by good successe is animated

---

[25] offence—injury

[26] exagitated—stirred up

[27] According to the theory of the humors, inherited by early modern Europeans
from the Greeks, human beings contained four elements — blood, phlegm, black bile,
and yellow bile (choler). A person was healthy when he contained a balanced amount of
each humor, unhealthy when he contained an excessive or insufficient amount of one or
more humors. The theory of the temperaments linked a preponderance of each humor to a
different, characteristic psychology — respectively, the sanguine (blood), the phlegmatic
(phlegm), the melancholic (black bile), and the choleric (yellow bile, choler).

[28] started—made a sudden attack upon

[29] fleshed—hardened, eager for battle, animated by hatred

[30] Captain John Underhill (1609–1672), New England settler.

[31] insulteth—behaves with pride and arrogance

even in the worst of wicked actions. These *Barbarians* triumphed and proceeded, drawing into their Confederacy other *Indians*, as the *Nyantecets*, and part of the *Mohigens*; of whom about fifty chose rather to joyne with the *English*, and sat downe at *New-Towne*, at *Connectacut* (now called *Hereford*, as the other Towne that went from *Dorchester* thither is called *Windsore*.) Fame encreaseth by flying. The former sad newes w[a]s augmented by the report of sixtie men slaine at Master *Pinch[le]y* Plantation, [et]c. which proved false. The *Narragansets* neighbours to the *Pequets*, sent word to [9] the *English* that the *Pequets* had sollicited them to joyne their forces with them. Hereupon the Councell ordered that none should go to worke, nor travell, no not so much as to Church, without Arms. A Corps of Guard[32] of 14. or 15 souldiers was appointed to watch every night, and Centinels were set in convenient places about the Plantations, the Drumme beating when they went to the Watch, and every man commanded to be in readinesse upon an Alarme, upon paine[33] of five pound. A day of fast and prayers was also kept. Fourty more were sent to strengthen the former twenty that went to the Fort, and 50 under the command of Captain *Mason*,[34] which being conjoyned, were about 100. Two hundred more were to be sent after them with all expedition.[35]

The 50. *Mohigins* that joyned with the *English*, scouring about, espied 7 *Pequets*, killed five of them outright, wounded the sixt mortally, tooke the seventh prisoner, and brought him to the Fort. He braved[36] the *English*, as though they durst not kill a [10] *Pequet*. Some will have their courage to be thought invincible, when all is desperate. But it availed this Salvage nothing; they tied one of his legs to a post, and 20 men with a rope tied to the other, pulled him in pieces, Captain *Vnderhill* shooting a pistol through him, to dispatch him. The two Maids which were taken prisoners were redeemed by the *Dutch*.

Those 50 sent from the three plantations of *Connectacut* with Captain *Mason*, being joyned with Captain *Vnderhill* and his 20 men, (for the other 40 were not yet arrived with them) immediately went upon an expedition against the *Pequets*, after they had searched for them. The manner was this. The *English* with some *Mohigens* went to the *Naragonsets*, who were discontented that they came no sooner, saying they could arme and set forth two or three hundred at six houres warning, (which they did accordingly, for the assistance of the *English*) onely they desired the advice of the *Sagamore*, *Mydutonno*,[37] what way they should go to worke, and how they should fall on the *Pequets*: whose judgement, in all things, agreed with the *English*, as though they had consulted together. Then went they

---

[32] corps of guard (corps de garde)—a small body of soldiers stationed on guard or as sentinels

[33] paine (pain)—pain of a fine

[34] Captain John Mason (1586–1635), New England settler.

[35] expedition—promptness

[36] braved—defied, dared, challenged

[37] Miantonomo (ca. 1610–1643), chief of the Narragansetts.

to the *Nyanticke*, and [11] he set forth 200 more, but before they went, he swore
them after his maner upon their knees. As they marched they deliberated which
Fort of the *Pequets* they should assault, resolving upon the great Fort, and to be
there that night. Being on the way, and having a mile to march through woods
and Swamps, the *Nyanticke* hearts failed, for feare of the *Pequets*, and so they ran
away, as also did some of the *Narragansets*. Of five or 600 *Indians*, not above halfe
were left: and they had followed the rest had not Capttaine *Vnderhill* upbraided
them with cowardise, and promised them they should not fight or come within
shot of the Fort, but onely surround it afarre off. At breake of day the 70 *English*
gave the Fort a Volly of shot, whereat the *Salvages* within made an hideous and
pittifull cry, the shot without all question flying through the *Pallisadoes* (which
stood not very close) and killing or wounding some of them. Pitty had hindred
further hostile proceedings, had not the remembrance of the bloodshed, the cap-
tive Maid, and the cruell insolency of those *Pequets*, hardned the hearts of the
English, [and] stopped their eares unto their cries. Mercy marres all somtimes,
severe Iustice must now and then take place.

    [11] The long forbearance, and too much lenitie of the English toward the
Virginian Salvages, had like to have beene the destruction of the whole Plantation. These Barbarians (ever treacherous) abuse the goodnesse of those that con-
descend to their rudenesse and imperfections. The English went, resolutely up
to the dore of the Fort. What shall wee enter said Captaine Vnder-hill? What
come we for else? answered one Hedge, a young Northampton-shire gentleman:
who advancing before the rest, pluckt away some bushes and entred. A stout
Pequet encounters him, shootes his arrow (drawne to the head) into his right
arme, where it stuck. He slasht the Salvage betwixt the arme and shoulder, who
pressing towards the dore, was killed by the English. Immediatly Master Hedge
incountred another, who perceiving him upon him before he could deliver his
arrow, gave backe: but he struck up his heeles[38] and run him thorow; after him
hee killed two or three more. Then about halfe the English entred, fell on with
courage, and slew manie. But being straitned[39] for roome because of the Wigwams (which are the Salvage huts or cabins) they called for fire to burne them.
An English man stept into a Wig-wam and stooping for a fire-brand, an Indian
[12] was ready to knock out his braines. But he whipt out his sword and runne
him into the belly, that his bowels followed. Then were the Wigwams set on fire,
which so raged, that what therewith, what with the sword, in little more than an
houre, betwixt three and foure hundred of them were killed, and of the English
onely two, one of them by our owne Muskets, as is thought. For the Narragansets beset the Fort so close, that not one escaped. The whole worke ended, ere the
Sun was an houre high, the Conquerors retraited downe toward the Pinnace,[40]

---

38 struck up his heeles (heels)—caused him to fall
39 straitned (straitened)—enclosed within a limited area; confined
40 pinnace—a small, light vessel

but in their march were infested[41] by the rest of the Pequets: who scouting up and downe, from the swamps and thickets let flie their arrowes amaine,[42] which were answered by English bullets. The Indians that then assisted the English, waiting the fall of the Pequets, (as the dogge watcheth the shot of the fouler[43] to fetch the prey) still fetched them their heades, as any were slaine. At last the Narragansets perceiving powder and shot to faile, and fearing to fall into the hands of their enemies, betooke themselves to flight upon the sudden, and were as suddenly encompassed[44] by the Pequets: Feare defeateth great armies. If an apprehension of eminent[45] danger once possesse them, it is in [13] vaine to stay the runne awaies. No oratory can recall them, no command can order them againe. The onely sure way, is by all meanes that may be, promises, threats, perswasions, [et]c. to maintaine and keepe up courage, where yet it is. But these fearefull companions had one Anchor, whose cable was not broken. They sent speedily to the English, who came to their reskew: and after five Muskets discharged the Pequets fled. Thus freed from that feare, they vowed henceforth to cleave[46] closer to the English, and never to forsake them in time of need. The reason why the English wanted amunition was, because they had left that which they had for store with their drum at the place of their consultation: But found it in their returne. They now all went a ship-board and sayled to Seabrooke-Fort, where the English feasted the Narragansets three daies, and then sent them home in a pinnace.

Let mee now describe this military fortresse which naturall reason [and] experience hath taught them to erect, without mathematicall skill, or use of yron toole. They choose a piece of ground dry and of best advantage, forty or fifty foote square, (But this was at least 2 acres of ground.) here they pitch close together, as they can young [14] trees and halfe trees, as thicke as a mans thigh, or the calfe of his legge. Ten or twelve foote high they are above the ground, and within rammed three foote deepe, with undermining, the earth being cast up for their better shelter against the enemies dischargements. Betwixt these pallisadoes are divers loope-holes,[47] through which they let flie their winged messengers. The doore for the most part is entred side-waies, which they stop with boughes or bushes as need requireth. The space within is full of Wigwams, wherein their wives and children live with them. These huts or little houses are framed like our garden arbours, something more round, very strong and handsome, covered with close wrought mats, made by their women of flagges,[48] rushes, and hempen

---

41 infested—annoyed, molested, harassed
42 amaine (amain)—with full force, violently
43 fouler (fowler)—bird-hunter
44 encompassed—surrounded
45 eminent—imminent
46 cleave—adhere, cling, stick fast
47 loope-holes (loop holes)—the openings in the parapet of a fortification
48 flagges (flags)—a sort of reed or rush

threds, so defensive,[49] that neither raine, though never so sad and long, nor yet the winde, though never so strong can enter. The top through a square hole giveth passage to the smoke, which in rainy weather, is covered with a pluver.[50] This Fort was so crowded with these numerous dwellings, that the English wanted foote-roome to graple with their adversaries, and therefore set fire on all.

The Mohigens which sided with the English **[15]** in this action behaved themselves stoutly.[51] Which the other Pequets understanding, cut off all the Mohigens that remaine with them, (lest they should turne to the English) except seven: who flying to our Countrey-men related this newes, and that about an hundred Pequets were slaine or hurt, in the fight with the English at their returne from the Fort. Moreover that they had resolved to have sent an hundred choyce men out of their Fort as a party against the English, the very day after they were beaten out by them. But being now vanquished Sasacus[52] the Pequetan Captaine, with the remainder of this massacre was fled the Countrey.

It is not good to give breathing[53] to a beaten enemy, lest he returne armed if not with greater puissance,[54] yet with greater despight[55] and revenge. Too much security[56] or neglect in this kinde hath oft times ruined the Conquerours. The 200 English therefore, resolved on before, were now sent forth to chase the Barbarians and utterly roote them out. Whereupon Cap[tain]. *Vnderhill* with his 20 men returned and gave this account of those exploits of the New-Englanders, which here we have communicated to the old English world. This last partie invaded the Pequetan Countrie, **[16]** killed twenty three, saved the lives of two Sagamores for their use hereafter, as occasion shall serve, who have promised to doe great matters for the advancing of the English affaires. They pursued the remnant threescore miles beyond the Country (till within 36. miles of the Dutch plantations on *Hudsons* river) where they fought with them, killed fortie or fiftie besides those that they cut off in their retrait, and tooke prisoners 180, that came out of a Swampe and yeilded themselves upon promise of good quarter.[57] Some other small parties of them were since destroyed, and Captaine *Patrick* with 16. or 18. brought 80 Captives to the Bay of *Boston*. The newes of the flight of *Sassacus* their Sagamore, is also confirmed. He went with forty men to the Mowhacks, which are cruell bloodie Caniballs, and the most terrible to their neighbours of all these nations: but will scarce dare ever to carrie armes against the English,

---

[49] defensive—protective
[50] pluver—apparently, an object designed to ward off rain
[51] stoutly—valiantly, bravely
[52] Sassacus (1560–1637), Pequod chief.
[53] breathing—breathing room
[54] puissance—power, forces
[55] despight (despite)—anger, in response to ill-treatment
[56] security—confidence
[57] quarter—mercy, especially to an enemy

of whom they are sore afraid, not daring to encounter white men with their hot-mouth'd weapons, which spit nothing else but bullets and fire.

The terrour of victorie changeth even the affection of the allies of the van-quished, and the securing of our owne estates makes us neglect, yea [17] forsake, or turne against our confederates, and side with their enemies and ours, when wee despaire of better remedie. These cruell, but wily Mowhacks, in contempla-tion of the English, and to procure their friendship, entertaine the fugitive Pe-quets and their Captaine, by cutting off all their heads and hands, which they sent to the English, as a testimony of their love and service.

A day of thanksgiving was solemnly celebrated for this happie successe, the Pequetans now seeming nothing but a name, for not lesse than 700. are slaine or taken prisoners. Of the English are not slaine in all above 16. One occurrent *I* may not forget. The endeavours of private men are ever memorable in these be-ginnings: the meanest of the vulgar is not incapable of vertue, and consequent-ly neither of honour. Some actions of *Plebeians* have elsewhere beene taken for great atchievements. A pretty sturdy youth of new *Ipswich*, going forth, some-what rashly, to pursue the Salvages, shot off his Musket after them till all his powder and shot were spent; which they perceiving, re-assaulted him, thinking with their hatchets to have knocked him in the head. But he so bestirred him-selfe with the stock of his piece, and after with the barrell, when that [18] was broken, that hee brought two of their heads to the armie. His owne desert and the incouragement of others will not suffer him to bee namelesse. Hee is called *Francis Waine-wright*, and came over servant with one *Alexander Knight* that kept an Inne in *Chelmsford*.

I have done with this tragick scene, whose catastrophe ended in a triumph. And now give mee leave to speake something of the present state of things there. The transcribing[58] of all Colonies is chargeable,[59] fittest for Princes or states to undertake. Their first beginnings are full of casualty[60] and danger, and obnox-ious[61] to many miseries. They must bee well grounded, well followed, and man-naged with great stocks of money, by men of resolution, that will not bee daunted by ordinarie accidents. The *Bermuda's* and *Virginia* are come to perfection[62] from meane, or rather base beginnings, and almost by as weake meanes, beyond all expectation, and reason. But a few private men by uniting their stocks and desires have now raised new-England to that height, that never any plantation of Span-iards, Dutch, or any other arrived at in so small a time. Gaine is the load-stone[63]

---

[58] transcribing—copying; but here apparently "founding"
[59] chargeable—burdensome, costly
[60] casualty—uncertainty
[61] obnoxious—exposed, liable
[62] perfection—completion; possibly here "maturity"
[63] load-stone—magnet

of adventures: Fish and Furres, with Beaver wooll,[64] [19] were specious baites. But whiles men are all for their private profit, the publique good is neglected and languisheth. Woefull experience had too evidently instructed New Englands Colones in the precedents of Guiana, the Charibe Ilands, Virginia, and Novonia, or New-found-land, (now againe to bee planted[65] by Sir *David Kirke*,[66] though part of the old planters there yet remaine.) Wee are never wiser, than when wee are thus taught. The new Englanders therefore advanced the weale publique all they could, and so the private is taken care for.

Corne and Cattell are wonderfully encreased with them, and thereof they have enough, yea sometime to spare to new commers, besides spare roomes, or good houses to entertaine them in. Where they may make Christmas fires all winter, if they please for nothing. I speake not of the naturals of the Countrey, fish, fowle, [et]c. which are more than plentifull. They that arrived there this yeere out of divers parts of Old England say that they never saw [20] such a field of 400 acres of all sorts of English graine as they saw at Winter-towne there. Yet that ground is not comparable to other parts of New England, as Salem, Ipswich, Newberry, [et]c. In a word, they have built faire Townes of the lands owne materials, and faire Ships too, some where of are here to be seene on the Thames. They have overcome cold and hunger, are dispearsed securely in their Plantations sixty miles along the coast, and within the Land also along some small Creekes and Rivers, and are assured of their peace by killing the Barbarians, better than our English Virginians were by being killed by them.[67] For having once terrified them, by severe execution of just revenge, they shall never heare of more harme from them, except (perhaps) the killing of a man or two at his worke, upon advantage, which their Centinels, and Corps du guards may easily prevent. Nay, they shall have those bruites their servants, their slaves, either willingly or of necessity, and docible[68] enough, if not obsequious. The numbers of the [21] English amount to above thirty thousand, which (though none did augment them out of England) shall every day bee, doubtlesse, encreased, by a facultie that God hath given the British Ilanders to beget and bring forth more children, than any other nation of the world: I could justifie what *I* say from the mouthes of the Hollanders and adjoyning Provinces, where they confesse (though good breeders of themselves) that never woman bore two children, nor yet had so many by one man, till the English and Scotch frequented their warres and married with them. I could give a good reason hereof from nature, as a Philosopher (with modestie bee it spoken) but there is no neede. The aire of new England, and the Diet

---

[64] wooll (wool) — fur

[65] planted — colonized, settled

[66] Sir David Kirke (ca. 1597–1654), governor of Newfoundland from 1638 to 1651.

[67] The Jamestown Massacre of 1622. The Powhatans killed some four hundred colonists, about one-third of the English population in Virginia.

[68] docible — docile, teachable

equall, if not excelling that of old England: besides their honour of marriage, and carefull preventing and punishing of furtive congression[69] giveth them and us no small hope of their future puissance, and multitude of subjects. Herein, saith the Wiseman, consisteth the strength of a King,[70] and likewise of a nation, or Kingdome.

[22] But the desire of more gaine, the slavery of mankinde, was not the onely cause of our English endeavours for a plantation there. The propagation of Religion was that precious jewell, for which these Merchant venturers compassed both Sea and Land, and went into a farre Country to search and seat themselves. This, I am sure, they pretended,[71] and I hope intended. Onely this blessing from my heart I sincerely wish them, and shall ever beseech the Almightie to bestow upon them, devout Piety towards God, faithfull loyaltie towards their Soveraigne, fervent charity among themselves, and discretion and sobriety in themselves, according to the saying of that blessed Apostle, μὴ ὑπερφρονεῖν παρ' ὃ δεῖ φρονεῖν, ἀλλὰ φρονεῖν εἰς τὸ σωφρονεῖν *Rom[ans]*. 12.3.[72] Not to bee wise (in spirituall things) above what wee ought to bee wise; but to bee wise unto wise sobriety.

Doubtlesse there was no other way better to chastise the insolencie of these insulting homicides, than a sharpe warre pursued with dexterity and speed. *Virginia* our mother plantation, and for her precedent a rule, hath [23] taught us what to do in these difficulties; forewarned, forearmed. They were endangered by their friendship and peace, secured by their enmity and warre with the natives. From these experiments, shall the now inhabitants of those two Sister Lands, beat out unto themselves an Armour of proofe,[73] and lay a sure foundation to their future happinesse.

FINIS.

[24]　　　*Nihil obstare videtur quominus haec | Relatio typis mandetur.*[74]

Novemb[er]. ix. M.DC.xxxvii.

G. R. WECKHERLIN.

---

[69] congression — copulation

[70] "In the multitude of people is the king's honour: but in the want of people is the destruction of the prince" (Proverbs 14:28).

[71] pretended — claimed

[72] μὴ ὑπερφρονεῖν παρ' ὃ δεῖ φρονεῖν, ἀλλὰ φρονεῖν εἰς τὸ σωφρονεῖν — "Not to think *of himself* more highly than he ought to think; but to think soberly": Romans 12: 3.

[73] proofe (proof) — proven impentrability

[74] *Nihil obstare videtur quominus haec Relatio typis mandetur.* — Nothing appears to stand in the way of this account's being given to the press.

TEXTS

1. *Hereafter ensue the trewe encountre or . . . batayle lately don betwene. Engla[n]de and: Scotlande* (1513). Imprint: London, [R. Faques]. Facsimile edition reprinted under review of Mr. J. Smeeton, Printer, 1809. Copy from the Henry E. Huntington Library, Call #48047. A truncated digital reproduction is available on *Early English Books Online: Hereafter ensue the trewe encountre or . . . batayle lately don betwene. Engla[n]de and: Scotlande* (1513). Imprint: London, [R. Faques]. STC (2nd ed.) #11088.5. [2] p. *Early English Books, 1475–1640*: Reel #1986:09. Copy from the Cambridge University Library.

2. *The late expedicion in Scotlande made by the Kynges hyghnys armye, vnder the conduit of the ryght honorable the Erle of Hertforde, the yere of our Lorde God 1544* (1544). Imprint: Londini, [Reynolde Wolfe]. STC (2nd ed.) #22270. [32] p. *Early English Books, 1475–1640*: Reel #153:06. Copy from the British Library.

3. A. *[C]ertayn and tru good nues, fro[m] the syege of the isle Malta wyth the goodly vyctorie, wyche the Christenmen, by the fauour of God, have ther latlye obtayned, agaynst the Turks, before the forteres of Saint Elmo / translat owt of Frenche yn to Englysh* (1565). Imprint: Gaunt, [G. Manilius]. STC (2nd ed.) # 17213.5. [8] p. *Early English Books, 1475–1640*: Reel #1299:25. Copy from the Lambeth Palace Library.

   B. *Newes from Vienna the 5. day of August. 1566. of the strong towne and castell of Tula in Hungary xi. myles beyond the riuer Danubius, which was cruelly assaulted by the great Turke, but nowe by Gods mighty working relieued, the sayd Turks marueilouslye discomfited and ouerthrowen. Translated out of hye Almaine into English, and printed in Augspurge by Hans Zimmerman* (1566). Imprint: London, By John Awdeley, dwelling in litle Britaine streete without Aldersgate. STC (2nd ed.) #24716. [8] p. *Early English Books, 1475–1640*: Reel #1042:13. Copy from the British Library.

4. *A discourse of such things as are happened in the armie of my lordes the princes of Nauarre, and of Condey, since the moneth of September last. 1568* (1569). Imprint: London, By Henry Bynneman, for Lucas Haryson. STC (2nd ed.) #11269. [28] p. *Early English Books, 1475–1640*: Reel #241:09. Copy from the British Library.

5. George Gascoigne, *The spoyle of Antwerpe. Faithfully reported, by a true Eng-lishman, who was present at the same. Nouem. 1576. Seene and allowed* (1576). Imprint: London, by [J. Charlewood for] Richard Iones. STC (2nd ed.) # 11644. [52] p. *Early English Books, 1475–1640*: Reel #343:15. Copy from the Bodleian Library.

6. Thomas Churchyard, *A plaine or moste true report of a daungerous seruice stoute-ly attempted, and manfully brought to passe by English men, Scottes men, Wallons & other worthy soldiours, for the takying of Macklin on the sodaine, a strong citee in Flaunders: sette forthe at large with speciall pointes to bee noted: by Thomas Churchyard gentleman. 1580.* (1580). Imprint: London, By [Felix Kingston for] Ihon Perin, dwellyng in Paules Churchyarde, at the signe of the Angell. STC (2nd ed.) #5247. [32] p. *Early English Books, 1475–1640*: Reel #192:15. Copy from the Henry E. Huntington Library and Art Gallery.

7. A. M., *The True Reporte of the prosperous successe which God gave unto our Eng-lish Souldiours against the forraine bands of our Romaine enemies lately ariued, (but soone inough to theyr cost) in Ireland, in the yeare 1580. Gathered out of the letters of moste credit and circumstaunce, that haue beene sent ouer, and more at large set foorth them in the former printed copie. For a singuler comfort to all godly Christians, & true harted subiectes, and an exceeding encouragement to them to persist valiantly in their true religion and faithe towards God, their due obedi-ence and looue to their prince, and to repose their whole assured confidence in the strengthe of the Almightie, as most safe vnder the shield of his protection. Seene and allowed.* (1581). Imprint: London, [By J. Charlewood] for Edward White, dwelling at the little North doore of Paules Church, at the signe of the Gunne. STC (2nd ed.) #17124. [8] p. *Early English Books, 1475–1640*: Reel #1634:03. Copy from the Cambridge University Library.

8. *A discourse and true recitall of euerie particular of the victorie obtained by the French king, on Wednesday the fourth of March, being Ashwednesday Also of his good successe that he hath had since that time, in taking of certaine townes. Out of French into English. Seene and allowed.* (1590). Imprint: London, by Thomas Orwin, for Richard Oliffe, and are to be sold at his shop in Paules Church-yard, at the signe of the Crane. STC (2nd ed.) #13131. [14] p. *Early English Books, 1475–1640:* Reel #569:17. Copy from the Bodleian Library.

9. *The true reporte of the seruice in Britanie. Performed lately by the honorable knight Sir Iohn Norreys and other captaines and gentlemen souldiers before Guingand To-gether with the articles which the Prince D'ombes accorded to the defendants of the towne.* (1591). Imprint: London, Printed by Iohn VVolfe, and are to be sold at his shop right ouer against the great south-doore of Paules. STC (2nd ed.) #18655. [12] p. *Early English Books, 1475–1640*: Reel #326:10. Copy from the Henry E. Huntington Library and Art Gallery.

10. I. E., *A letter from a souldier of good place in Ireland, to his friend in London touching the notable victorie of her Maiesties forces there, against the Spaniards, and Irish rebels: and of the yeelding vp of Kynsale, and other places there held by the Spanyards.* (1602). Imprint: London, [by T. Creede?] for Symon Waterson. STC (2nd ed.) #7434. [2], 25, [1] p. *Early English Books, 1475–1640*: Reel #832:01. Copy from the British Library.

11. Anthony Nixon, *Svvethland and Poland vvarres. A souldiers returne out of Sweden, and his newes from the warres: or, Sweden and Poland vp in armes. And the entertainement of English souldiers there: with the fortunes and successe of those 1200. men that lately went thither.* (1610). Imprint: London, printed for Nathaniell Butter. STC (2nd ed.) #18596. [40] p. *Early English Books, 1475–1640*: Reel #2082:11. Copy from the Britwell Court Library.

12. *A iournall or daily register of all those warlike atchieuements which happened in the siege of Berghen-up-Zoome in the Low-countries betweene the armies of the Marquesse Spinola assaylants, and the Prince of Orange, defendants, of the said towne; together with the raising of the siege. In the end is added two letters, which discouer the errours fore-conceiued of the success of that siege, and the after-designes of the Spanish armies, if they had taken in Bergen: with some particular accidents of warre, which were occasions of mirth to the beholders. All faithfully translated out of the original Low-Dutch copie.* (1622). Imprint: London, Printed [by Eliot's Court Press?] for Nathaniel Butter, Bartholomew Downes, and Thomas Archer. STC (2nd ed.) #1898. [2]. 38 p. *Early English Books, 1475–1640*: Reel #1057:14. Copy from the British Library.

13. Hugh Peters, *Digitus Dei. Or, Good newes from Holland Sent to the wor. Iohn Treffry and Iohn Trefusis. Esquires: as allso to all that haue shot arrows agayst Babels brats, and wish well to Sion wheresouer.* (1631). Imprint: [Rotterdam], Printed by Abraham Neringh, printer in Rotterdam, by the ould Head. STC (2nd ed.) #19798.3. [14] p. *Early English Books, 1475–1640*: Reel #998:06. Copy from the Yale University Library.

14. Philip Vincent, *A true relation of the late battell fought in New England, between the English, and the salvages vvith the present state of things there.* (1637). Imprint: London, Printed by M[armaduke] P[arsons] for Nathanael Butter, and Iohn Bellamie. STC (2nd ed.) #24758. [6], 23, [3] p. *Early English Books, 1475–1640*: Reel #1013.03. Copy from the Henry E. Huntington Library and Art Gallery.